D0070303

TRADING IN OPTIONS ON FUTURES

JAMES T. COLBURN

NEW YORK INSTITUTE OF FINANCE

NEW YORK • TORONTO • SYDNEY • TOKYO • SINGAPORE

Library of Congress Cataloging-in-Publication Data

Colburn, James T.
    Trading in options on futures / James T. Colburn.
      p. cm.
    ISBN 0-13-638552-4
    1. Options (Finance). 2. Futures. I. Title.
    HG6024.A3C65 1990   89-49299
    332.64′5—dc20   CIP

© *1990 by NYIF Corp.*

All rights reserved. No part of this book may be reproduced in any form or by any means, without permission in writing from the publisher.

Printed in the United States of America

10   9   8

This publication is designed to provide accurate and authoritative information in regard to the subject matter covered. It is sold with the understanding that the publisher is not engaged in rendering legal, accounting, or other professional service. If legal advice or other expert assistance is required, the services of a competent professional person should be sought.
—*From the Declaration of Principles jointly adopted by a Committee of the American Bar Association and a Committee of Publishers and Associations*

ISBN 0-13-638552-4

ATTENTION: CORPORATIONS AND SCHOOLS

NYIF books are available at quantity discounts with bulk purchase for educational, business, or sales promotional use. For information, please write to: Prentice Hall Special Sales, 240 Frisch Court, Paramus, New Jersey 07652. Please supply: title of book, ISBN number, quantity, how the book will be used, date needed.

 NEW YORK INSTITUTE OF FINANCE
Paramus, NJ 07652

On the World Wide Web at http://www.phdirect.com

Contents

Preface

Two traders were bullish on the stock market. One translated the market opinion into a purchase of S&P 500 futures, the other into slightly out-of-the-money call options on S&P 500 futures. As the market moved lower, the futures trader immediately felt the heat and soon had to liquidate because the actual and potential losses were too great. The futures options trader, however, was secure in the knowledge that, no matter how low prices went, the position would lose no more than the premiums paid up front. As the market rallied, the futures trader—no longer confident of the market—did not establish new positions. But the options trader was able to participate in the upswing.

This true story illustrates just one of the many advantages that options have over futures—staying power. In extremely volatile markets, staying power has value.

Of the many other advantages to options trading, a key one is flexibility. Options strategies are as diverse as the traders who use them. Twenty successful traders will have as many different approaches to the market. For example, with an unemployment report due in a week, a trader feels the number will affect the direction of Treasury bond prices over the upcoming week. While he does not know the direction of the move, he is fairly certain that it will be sharp. If the trader is restricted to dealing only in futures contracts, this opinion could result in no position being taken until the unemployment number is released. With options, however, the trader can buy puts and calls (a strategy with limited risk) and thereby participate in a move *in either direction!*

Trading options on futures is different from trading any other instrument in that it is "three-tiered." The primary trading vehicle (the options contract) is a derivative instrument, whose underlying interest is another derivative contract (the futures contract), whose value in turn can depend on anything from stocks or bonds, to currencies, indexes, or interest rates. In addition, both contracts have to be handled as wasting assets. From this perspective, trading options on futures might be viewed as a three-dimensional chess game, with time limits set on two of the dimensions.

Yet it is not as complicated as it may sound. This book explains how to trade options on futures contracts for beginners and intermediates. (Advanced knowledge is learned only in the trading arena.) Given its audience, the book's format includes two features to facilitate learning:

First, throughout the text, each concept, term, and strategy is explained in simple language and then demonstrated in a clear example.

Second, it covers each dimension in isolation, and then puts them all together in a practical scenario.

- Part I (Chapters 1-3) explains options contracts and the trading strategies related to them. To simplify things for those just starting out, the underlying instrument in this part is not a futures contract, but rather common stock. Because equities are not "wasting assets" (unlike futures contracts), they simplify the explanations and illustrations of options strategies.

- In Part II (Chapters 4-8), the options trading and pricing principles explained in the first part are applied to futures contracts. For continuity and realism, an oil futures scenario is used in an ongoing set of cases and examples.

- Part III (Chapters 9-11) offers practical advice on portfolio analysis, making markets, and other considerations that are necessary before taking a position.

- The appendices include a series of implied volatility charts for various futures markets, a glossary, bibliography, and a brief primer on futures contracts (for those who are unfamiliar with these instruments).

A word of practical advice: Options strategies provide you with much greater flexibility in translating your market opinions into positions. But the complexity of a strategy does not guarantee profits. Profits accrue only to the trader whose market opinion is correct and whose options position suits that outlook. Begin your efforts by making sound judgments about market movement and then testing your skills with simple, easy-to-execute strategies.

This book, which is an outgrowth of a series of lectures given for the New York Mercantile Exchange and the New York Institute of Finance, provides you with the tools to take those first steps toward trading options on futures creatively and profitably.

You have my best wishes for success in this endeavor.

ACKNOWLEDGEMENTS

Although my name appears on the cover of this book, many helped with its development. Fred Dahl directed the project from beginning to end. His comments and suggestions on text and organization were greatly appreciated. He also was instrumental in putting together the first three chapters of the book and the appendix on futures contracts. Amalia Knoepffler, while at PaineWebber, provided an endless supply of volatility charts used in the appendix. Mary Davidowski, The Options Group, put together historical volatility charts and provided other relevant data. David Isbister developed the option evaluation package used throughout this book. Special thanks go to the people at The New York Mercantile Exchange (staff and members) and Man International Futures (my current employer) for their support. And, finally, very special thanks to the oil traders who have struggled through endless option seminars in order to make the crude oil option contract the most successful commodity option contract in the world.

JAMES T. COLBURN

PART I

OPTIONS CONTRACTS

CHAPTER 1

Learning the Language

Developing expertise in options is similar to learning a new language. Option terms draw from such diverse areas as the insurance business (writing, granting contracts), the Greek alphabet (deltas, gammas, thetas), the race track (in the money, out of the money), and the animal kingdom (butterflies, condors). In the beginning, the vocabulary can be overwhelming. Once the terms are understood, however, they are put together in various ways to convey more complex ideas or strategies.

Students studying a second language learn vocabulary. Later they begin to construct sentences, but still think in their native language. The options student and language student come of age when they start thinking in terms of the new language, bypassing the translating step. In this chapter, options terms and definitions are introduced to lay the foundation for more complex ideas and strategies in later chapters.

The approach is to progress from the simple to the complex, from the better known to the less known. So, although options are traded on a variety of underlying interests—indexes, currencies, Treasuries, and, of course, futures—we will begin with the first contracts, stock options.

For that reason, the introduction to options (Chapters 1-3) is in terms of equity contracts. While there are differences among the types of contracts, stock options are the most useful in explaining the rudiments, and the trading strategies remain fundamentally the same as for options on other underlying instruments.

Options are not securities in the true sense. Securities are issued by corporations, municipalities, or the U.S. Treasury. An option on an equity security, such as IBM stocks, is issued not by IBM, but rather by an individual known as a writer (or grantor). It may be "issued," or written, by you. An option is simply a contract entered into by two parties. The buyer of the contract is granted a privilege to buy or sell a security at a specific price. The seller (writer) of the contract assumes an obligation to accommodate the buyer should the buyer exercise his privilege. As the value of the underlying security can fluctuate sharply during the life of the contract, the buyer pays the seller a fee for granting the privilege. This fee is called the *premium.*

We can apply the logic of options to things other than securities. Suppose you owned a valuable oil painting, perhaps a Rembrandt valued at $1,000,000.00. You enter into a contract with another party, which allows that person to purchase the painting for $1,000,000.00 at any time during the next 12 months. Since the painting could be worth $1,100,000.00 within the year's time, you demand a fee of $10,000.00 for granting the option. If the value of the artwork does rise to $1,100,000.00 within the year, the owner of the contract will *exercise* the option and purchase it for $1,000,000.00. You will have lost the picture but would have received a total of $1,010,000.00, that is, the contract price plus the fee.

If on the other hand the market for fine art declines and your painting is worth only $900,000.00, the contract would not be exercised. You keep the $10,000.00 fee and still own the Rembrandt.

LISTED OPTIONS

Options on equity securities have been traded for many decades. Until 1973 the market was very informal. Someone who wished to purchase an option on General Motor stock would contact one of a handful of options dealers, which were generally small firms that specialized in the product. The options dealer would seek out another party willing to sell (write) the option. All of the terms of the contract, including the premium, would be negotiated and perhaps a transaction would occur.

A major change in the trading of equity options occurred in 1973. At that time the Chicago Board of Trade (CBT), which dealt in commodities, set up the subsidiary Chicago Board of Options Exchange (CBOE), and for the first time equity options began to trade on an exchange. This centralization of the market led to an increased interest in options. In time, other exchanges joined the CBOE and today equity options are also traded on the American Stock Exchange (ASE), Philadelphia Stock Exchange (PE), Pacific Stock Exchange (PSE), and New York Stock Exchange (NYSE).

The listing of equity options eliminated the uncertainties of the earlier markets. Before 1973 the parties to an option contract would have to agree on three important specifications:

1. The *exercise price* (also called the *strike price*): The buyer might want to have the contract exercised at $45.00 a share, the seller at $50.00 a share.
2. The *length of the contract:* The buyer might want the privilege to extend for one year, the seller only nine months.
3. The *premium:* The buyer might offer $400.00, and seller might hold out for $450.00.

With the listing of equity options, the need to negotiate two of these points was eliminated. The exercise price and the expiration date are now determined by the exchange on which the contract is traded. Only the premium is left for the parties to agree upon.

Another important development was the creation of a clearing house, the Options Clearing Corp. (OCC), which clears all listed options transactions. The clearing corporation sidestepped one of the major problems in trading securities. All Wall Street professionals are aware of the problems that stock and bond certificates present. They can be lost, stolen, or destroyed in a fire or flood. The processing of them is costly and time-consuming. In listed options trading, however, there are no physical securities to deliver or receive. The OCC simply records each transaction electronica.:y. For example, if a Goldman Sachs client purchases the options from a PaineWebber client, the clearing corporation credits the contract to Goldman Sachs and debits the account of PaineWebber. On the next business day after the trade, the amount of premium involved is debited to the buyer, Goldman Sachs, and credited to PaineWebber. The firms record the positions in the accounts of their clients.

None of these problems exists in options. The use of the OCC results in major savings of time and money for firms.

The rapid growth in the popularity of listed equity options led to the creation of other options products. Options contracts are now available on stock indexes, foreign currencies, and U.S. Treasury securities. These contracts are also cleared by the OCC, again eliminating the problems related to dealing in physical securities.

Types of Options

There are only two types of options—puts and calls.

Put. A put gives the holder the right to sell (or put) securities. The holder may *sell* a specific number of shares of a security at a fixed price for a given length of time. The buyer (owner) has purchased this right from a seller for a fee (the premium), which is paid in full when the transaction is settled.

Example: Buy 1 IBM July 110 put for a premium of 4½.

- *Buy:* The trader purchases the option contract.
- *1:* The number of contracts. Each contract generally represents 100 shares of stock.
- *IBM:* The underlying security is IBM.
- *July:* This is the month in which the option expires. (The determination of the exact day of the month is explained later in the chapter.)
- *110:* The exercise prices, or strike price, of the contract is $110.00. The holder may sell 100 shares of IBM to the writer for $110.00 per share. With respect to the strike price, another term to know is *aggregate exercise price (AEP)*, which is the amount of money paid

or received if the contract is exercised. It is determined by multiplying the number of shares in the contract by the exercise price. In this case, the aggregate exercise price is $11,000.00 (100 shares multiplied by the exercise price of $110.00 a share).

- *Put:* This contract allows the purchaser to sell (put) 100 shares of IBM stock at $110.00 a share anytime up to July.
- *Premium—4½:* Options premiums are expressed as dollars per share in the contract. Since most contracts are for 100 shares, the total premium is $450.00 (4½ times 100 shares). The buyer of the put option paid this amount to the seller.

By purchasing this contract, the owner now has the right to deliver 100 shares of IBM stock anytime up to July. If the holder exercises the option, he will be paid $11,000.00 for these shares ($110.00 a share).

Call. A *call* entitles the owner to *buy* securities. This type of contract gives the holder the right to buy (or *call*) a specified number of shares of a security at a fixed price for a given length of time. The buyer (owner) purchases this right from a seller, who agrees to accommodate him if the option is exercised. For this privilege the buyer pays a fee to the seller.

Example: Buy 1 GM Nov 80 call for a premium of 3¾.

- *Buy:* The trader purchases the contract.
- *1.* This is the number of contracts in the transaction. Again, one contract represents 100 shares.
- *GM:* The underlying security is General Motors common stock.
- *Nov:* The buyer can exercise the contract any time from the time of purchase until a given date in November.
- *80:* This is the exercise, or strike, price of the contract. The price per share that the owner would pay if he exercised the contract is $80.00. The aggregate exercise price is $8,000.00 ($80.00 times 100 shares).
- *Call:* This contract is a call, which gives the holder the right to buy (call) the GM shares.

- *Premium of 3¾:* The fee paid by the buyer to the seller is 3¾ per share, or $375.00 for the 100-share contract.

The owner of this call can exercise anytime up to next November. In so doing, he will purchase 100 shares of General Motor stock at $80.00 a share ($8,000.00).

Look at these two types of options from the points of view of both parties:

Example: 1 GE Feb 75 put—Premium 6

- The *buyer* of the put has the privilege of selling 100 shares of General Electric common stock at $75.00 a share. This privilege expires in February. The buyer pays a premium of $600.00 for this option.
- The *writer* has agreed to purchase 100 shares of General Electric stock at $75.00 a share from the holder of the option. For this the writer receives a premium of $600.00.

Example: 1 XRX Jun 45 call—Premium 2

- The *purchaser* of the call has the right to buy 100 shares of Xerox stock at $45.00 a share until June. He pays a fee of $200.00.
- The *writer* of this call agrees to deliver 100 shares of Xerox at $45.00 a share if the buyer exercises the call. The writer receives a premium of $200.00.

Selling Long and Short

When you sell a security, you sell either long or short. Selling *long* means that you own the security and will deliver it to the buyer. Selling *short* means that you do not own the security or do not intend to deliver it. In either of these cases, you have to borrow the stock or other type of security to make delivery.

Selling long or short in options is similar. Someone who purchases a put or a call three weeks ago and sells it today is selling long. He owns the option. If someone does not own the option and sells (or writes) one, he is selling short. If the option is exercised, the short seller has to make arrangements to live up to the contract. The short seller of an option if called the *writer*, which means the same as "short seller." Someone who writes an option does so in one of two ways: *covered* and *uncovered (naked)*.

- A *covered* writer does not own the underlying security but has access to it in some manner.
- An *uncovered* writer has nothing but an open contract.

Obviously, uncovered writing poses a greater risk than covered writing. In some cases the risk is unlimited.

THE OPTIONS EXCHANGES

The Specialist System

Trading of equity options on exchanges is similar to the trading of listed equity securities. The exchange provides a trading floor, and each option trades at a specified location on the floor. Although the methods of trading differ from one exchange to another, the markets are very similar.

For instance, the American Stock Exchange employs a specialist for each option. These specialists operate in the same manner as those in exchange-listed stocks in that they act as both principal and agent. As principal, they buy and sell option contracts for their firms' own accounts, thereby adding liquidity to the market. Specialists on the Amex also act as agent for clients, maintaining a book of buy and sell orders that are given to them by brokers. These orders are executed on the behalf of clients when market conditions allow, and also enable specialists to provide liquidity. For their efforts, specialists are paid a fee for acting as agents of the clients.

The CBOE employs a somewhat different system. The functions of principal and agent are performed by different people. The role of principal is filled by CBOE members known as *market makers,* who make bids and offers on specific option contracts for their own accounts only. They perform no agency function. *Order book officials* play the role of agent for clients, who place orders in their care. They are employees of the CBOE who maintain the "book" for orders. When they execute an order on behalf of a client, they report the transaction promptly. The order book official does not act as principal on any trades.

Contract Specifications

In addition to the exercise price and length of contract, other contract terms are fixed by the exchange on which the option is traded. These are the market hours, expiration time and dates, trading end, and settlement terms. (In all examples, assume Eastern Standard time; adjustments must be made for other time zones.)

- *Expiration:* Equity options expire at 11:59 P.M. on the Saturday following the third Friday of the expiration month. (This is usually, but not always, the third Saturday of the month.)
- *Trading end:* Options trading ends at 4 P.M. on the business day prior to expiration. This is generally a Friday unless a holiday falls on that day.
- *Market hours:* Trading hours are 9:30 A.M. to 4:10 P.M., except on the final day of trading of each month when trading ceases at 4 P.M.
- *Settlement terms:* Options contracts are settled on the next business day after the trade. On that day the buyer is credited with the option and debited the amount of premium. The seller is debited the option and credited the premium.

Example: In the month of April (see Figure 1-1), the third Friday of the month is April 21. Options expiring in April ("April" options) will expire on Saturday, April 22 at 11:59 P.M. Eastern time. This is the fourth Saturday of the month, but it is the Saturday following the third Friday. This will occur in any month in which the first of the month falls on a Saturday.

Trading in options will take place from 9:30 A.M. to 4:10 P.M. on each day of this month except Friday, April 21 (the last trading day for April options). All options will cease trading at 4 P.M. that day.

FIGURE 1-1

| | | | April | | | |
Sun.	Mon.	Tues.	Wed.	Thurs.	Fri.	Sat.
						1
2	3	4	5	6	7	8
9	10	11	12	13	14	15
16	**17**	**18**	19	20	**21**	**22**
23	24	25	26	27	28	29
30						

For any transaction taking place on the exchange floor on Monday, April 17, settlement occurs on Tuesday, April 18. On that day the Options Clearing Corp. debits the buyer the agreed-upon premium and credits the firm with the option contract purchased. The reverse entries are made for the account of the seller. Generally firms dealing in options maintain a balance at the OCC, out of which premiums are paid. If in this case the buying dealer had no such balance, the firm would be required to make payment of the premium on the business day following the transaction.

Figure 1-2 shows only a partial listing of the previous days' trading in equity options on the Chicago Board and on the American Stock Exchange. Figure 1-3 presents an entry in far left column for Bristol Meyers stock. It lists trading information on the three contracts trading on Bristol Meyers common stock:

The name of the underlying stock (Bris My) is listed in the column on the left. Beneath the name is the closing price for the underlying stock on the previous day (50⅛). The last transaction in Bristol Meyers shares was 50⅛. This price does not change, of course, from one option entry to another.

Next to the stock's name and closing price are the various strike prices available for Bristol Meyers options—45, 50, 55. These are the strike prices assigned by the exchange on which the option is traded. Strike prices are generally set at 5- or 10-point intervals. On low-priced stocks the interval is 2½ points. The design is to have a strike price that is close to the stock market price at all times. This rationale also results in the number of strike prices being greater for some stocks than for

FIGURE 1-2
Listed options quotations

LISTED OPTIONS QUOTATIONS

CHICAGO BOARD

Option & Strike NY Close Price	Calls - Last			Puts - Last		
	Oct	Nov	Dec	Oct	Nov	Dec

(Dense multi-column options quotation table for Chicago Board listings including Blkbst, BrisMy, Bruns, Chamln, CompSc, CypSem, Dow Ch, Entrgy, Ford, Fuqua, Gap, Gen El, G M, Hanson, Heinz, I T T, K mart, Litton, Loews, MayDS, Mc Don, Momsn, N C R, NorSo, Oracle, OutbdM, Pall, ParaCm, RalPur, SherW, SwAir, Syntex, Tektrn, Tekcrd, Telxon, Toys, USG, UCamp, Walmrt, Whitmn, and additional entries.)

Option & Strike NY Close Price — Calls Last / Puts Last

	Oct	Nov	Jan	Oct	Nov	Jan

(Includes Halbtn, Hitachi, Homfed, Homsh, I B M, In Min, In Pap, Itel, John J, Kerr M, L A C, L S I, LizCla, M C I, Macron, MdwAir, M M M, Momsn, NatEdu, PaineW, Pennz, Pepsi, Polar, Rockwl, St Jude, SeeCon, Sears, Squibb, SalleM, T J X, Teldyn, Tex In, Upjohn, etc.)

	Oct	Nov	Feb	Oct	Nov	Feb

(Includes Pegsus, PrecCs, Raythn, Reuter, Slumb, Shell, Skylin, South, Tribune, UAL, UST, U Tech, WarnCm, Wllms, Edw o, and Total call vol / Total put vol / Call open int / Put open int figures.)

r-Not Traded. s-No Option.

AMERICAN

Option & Strike NY Close Price	Calls - Last			Puts - Last		
	Oct	Nov	Dec	Oct	Nov	Dec

(Includes Alcan, Amax, AmBrnd, Aristc, Asarco, Blkbst, BenFer, Chase, ChemBk, ChemW, Chevrn, Circus, CenAg, CrosSv, Deere, Donely, Dover, EmrsEl, FrMcRP, G T E, GenRe, GlantF, Gillet, Hecla, Hercul, Kellog, and additional entries.)

FIGURE 1-3

CHICAGO BOARD

Option & Strike NY Close Price		Calls–Last			Puts–Last		
		Oct	Nov	Dec	Oct	Nov	Dec
Bris My	45	5⅜	r	6⅛	r	r	r
50⅛	50	1⅛	1¾	2¼	¾	1¹⁄₁₆	1¼
50⅛	55	³⁄₁₆	⁵⁄₁₆	½	r	r	r

others. If the stock undergoes a sharp rise or fall in price, the exchange will add a new strike price near the new level. While Bristol Meyers has only three strike prices, (45, 50, 55), in the far right-hand column of Figure 1-2, UAL (the parent of United Airlines) has 18 different strike prices, ranging from a low of 145 to a high of 310. UAL stock had been the subject of takeover activities and the stock rose sharply. As the prices rose, the CBOE added new strike prices to reflect the current market value.

Next are the closing prices for each of the three expiration months for Bristol Meyers calls. The exact month appears at the top of the page:

	Calls	
Oct	Nov	Dec
5⅜	r	6⅛
1⅛	1¾	2¼
³⁄₁₆	⁵⁄₁₆	½

The letter *r* indicates that there were no transactions in that option on the date reported.

The final three columns indicate the last price of each premium on the previous day for the puts on that stock.

	Puts	
Oct	Nov	Dec
r	r	r
¾	1¹⁄₁₆	1¼
r	r	r

Equity options trading is designed so that there is always an option available that expires in the current month. At the time of this listing, the current month is October. There is also always an option available for the following month, in this case November.

The third month listed will vary depending on the cycle to which that option is assigned. In the case of Bristol Meyers, the third month currently trading is December. Refer to Figure 1-2. At the top of the center column the currently trading months are October, November and January. At the top of the third column are October, November, and February. In both columns, the first two months are the same as for Bristol Meyers, but the third is different.

Class

A *class* of options includes all options of the same type (puts or calls) covering the same underlying security. For example, all Bristol Meyers calls constitute one class of options, all Bristol Meyers puts another class. So for each underlying security there are two classes of options—The put class and the call class.

Series

A *series* consists of all options in the same class having both the same strike price and the same expiration months. In the Bristol Meyers call class, there are nine different series. For each of the three strike prices (45, 50, 55), there are three different months (October, November, January). Each option in the class has either a different strike price and/or a different expiration month. Each one differs from the others in some manner. Thus, each of the nine constitutes a series of options.

THE RELATIONSHIP BETWEEN STRIKE AND STOCK PRICES

An option can be ''in the money,'' ''out of the money,'' or ''at the money.''

In the Money

An option is said to be *in the money* if the relationship between the strike price of the option and the market price of the underlying stock creates what is known as *intrinsic value,* that is, if exercising the option would result in a profit (disregarding premiums). A call is in the money if the market price of the stock is *higher* than the options strike price.

Example: Dow Chemical Oct 95 call
Note in Figure 1-2 that Dow Chemical stock closed at $101.00 a share. This call allows the holder to purchase the stock at $95.00 a share. The contract had an intrinsic value of 6 points a share (101 less 95). The option is 6 points ''in the money.'' The owner can buy the stock from the writer at 95 and sell it in the market for 101.

A put is in the money if the market price of the stock is *lower* than the strike price.

Example: IBM Jan 125 put
In the middle column of Figure 1-2, note that IBM stock closed at 116½ a share. Since this put allows the holder to sell IBM at 125 a share, the option has an intrinsic, or ''in-the-money,'' value of 8½ points a share (125 less 116½). The put holder can buy the stock at 116½ and sell it to the writer for 125.

Out of the Money

An option is *out of the money* if the relationship between the strike price and the market price of the underlying stock is such that there is no intrinsic value, that is, if exercising the option would result in a loss (disregarding premiums). A call is out of the money if the market price of the stock is *lower* than the strike price of the option.

Example: Dow Chemical Oct 110 call
According to Figure 1-2, Dow stock closed at 101 a share. This call permits the holder to buy stock at 110, 9 points above the current

price. There is no intrinsic value in this situation; the option is out of the money. If the holder exercises the contract, the result is a 9-point loss (110 strike price versus 101 market price).

A put is out of the money if the market price of the stock is *higher* than the options strike price.

Example: IBM Nov 115 put
This put allows the holder to sell IBM stock at $115.00 a share. The closing price of that stock last sold at 116½. If the owner were to exercise the option, a loss of 1½ points would result (116½ market price less 115 strike price). The option is 1½ points "out of the money."

In determining whether an option is in or out of the money, only the market price of the stock and the strike price of the option are considered, not the premium.

Example: The IBM Nov 115 put is out of the money because the stock is trading at 116½. Yet the premium for that option was 4⅜. Someone was willing to pay 4⅜ points for the privilege of selling the stock at $115.00 a share when the stock was $116.50 a share. So although this put is out of the money, it is not without value. The purchaser of this put expects that IBM stock will decline in value before the expiration in November, therefore enhancing the value of his option.

By the same reasoning, being in the money does not necessarily guarantee a profit.

Example: The Dow Chemical Oct 95 call is in the money since the stock price is 101. However, the premium for purchasing the option was 6¾. If the holder exercises the option, the stock would cost 101¾ (95 strike price plus 6¾-point premium). As long as the market price of the stock stays at 101, there is no profit to be made. When an option is in the money by the amount of its premium, it is said to be at *parity*.

It must be kept in mind, however, that the relationship between stock and strike prices is dynamic. One price does not stand still while the other changes. If an option goes deep into the money, its premium—

its market value—is likely to rise, in step with the contract's potential profitability. By the same token, options dropping deep out of the money will lose value and may even become "cheap enough" for speculative traders to buy up. (This ever changing relationship is explained in greater detail in Chapter 2.)

At the Money

An option is at the money when the market price of the stock and the options strike price are the same. The option is neither in nor out of the money

Example: In the far right-hand column of Figure 1-2, under American, note the Chase Oct 40 call. The closing price of Chase stock was 40, exactly the same as the strike price. This option is at the money.

ROLE OF THE OPTIONS CLEARING CORP. (OCC)

With the advent of listed options trading in 1973 the Options Clearing Corp. was established. At first only equity options were traded, and the OCC cleared all transactions. As other options products were introduced, the clearing function was assigned also to the OCC. They now handle, in addition to equity options, index, currency, and debt options.

A Typical Option Transaction

To describe the role of the Options Clearing Corp., a hypothetical transaction in an equity option will be traced through settlement.

A client of Merrill Lynch feels that the common stock of Loews Corp. is about to rise. To take advantage of that bright future, she decides to purchase a call on the stock and enters the following order:

Buy 1 Loews Dec 120 call at market

By placing a market order, she indicates that she will pay whatever premium the current market demands. (She could also have stated a maximum price.) The order is routed to the floor of the CBOE where the

Merrill representative takes it to the post where Loews options are traded. He will execute the clients orde

At about the same time a client of PaineWebber enters this order:

Sell 1 Loews Dec 120 call at market

The PaineWebber client is convinced that Loews stock will decline in price. Since he does not own this option, he is writing it, or selling it short. His strategy is to keep the premium if Loews stock does in fact decline. If the price drops to 105, the buyer of the call will not exercise and pay 120 a share.

The PaineWebber order is also sent to the floor of the CBOE. At the trading location the Merrill Lynch broker and the PaineWebber broker meet and agree to a trade for a premium of 5¼. ($525.00). Later that day the trade is matched, and on the following business day the records of the OCC reflect the following:

Loews Dec 120 Call	
Merrill Lynch + 1	PaineWebber − 1
Money Balance	
Merrill Lynch − $525.00	PaineWebber + $525.00

No physical delivery of a certificate is made. The OCC simply adjusts the total position in this option as the trades occur.

Both Merrill Lynch and PaineWebber send their clients a confirmation of the transaction and record the positions in their own accounts. If Merrill's clients had been long 942 Loews Dec 120 calls, the firm's position would read 943 (they are long one more call). If PaineWebber's clients had been short 628 Loews Dec 120 calls, the records would now show short 629. (They are now short one additional call.)

When buying or selling an equity option, option traders are not required to maintain their position until expiration. Buyers can sell if they so desire, and writers can repurchase if it is to their advantage. So what occurs next depends on the market action in Loews stock. Suppose the value rises and this call is now worth 8. The Merrill Lynch client might sell the contract and make 2¾ points above her cost of 5. If so, she would be selling "long" because she owns the option. On the other hand, if the Loews shares decline, the option premium might fall to 3. The PaineWebber client might repurchase the contract at that price and cover his short made at 5¼, for a profit of 2¼ points.

If, of course, Loews stock does not rise above 120 between the original trade date and the expiration in December, the option expires unexercised. The buyer, Merrill's client, loses the $525.00 premium. In this case, the writer, PaineWebber's client, was right, the stock declined, and he keeps the $525.00.

Exercising an Option

Suppose, however, that by expiration in December Loews stock has risen to $140.00 a share. The holder exercises and calls (purchases) the stock at the strike price of 120. On her behalf, Merrill Lynch sends an *exercise notice* to the Options Clearing Corp. (See Figure 1-4.) OCC, in turn, assigns the notice at random against one of the firms whose clients have written this call. In addition to PaineWebber, there might be two dozen other firms who are short Loews Dec 120 calls. The OCC randomly selects one of these firms and informs them that they must deliver 10ᴜ shares of Loews stock at $120.00 a share to Merrill Lynch. If the dealer selected is Kidder Peabody, that firm is instructed to deliver 100 Loews shares to Merrill. Kidder has five business days to make delivery (regular way settlement). The sequence of events is shown in Figure 1-4.

At Kidder, assume that many of the firm's clients had written the Loews Dec 120 call. Which of them should be exercised? Kidder Peabody may use one of two methods: Like the OCC, the firm might use the random selection method, or it can employ a first-in/first-out method. The Kidder client who first wrote this call gets exercised first, the second writer gets exercised next, and so forth.

Do all writers necessarily get exercise notices? If Loews stock stays above $120.00 a share until the December expiration, all writers will be exercised. But if the stock drops to $95.00, no holder of a 120 call will exercise and pay that price. The contract has no intrinsic value.

FIGURE 1-4
An options transaction and exercise

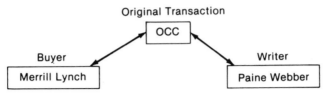

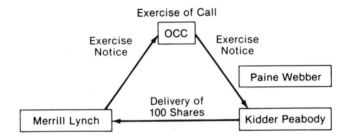

Opening and Closing Transactions

When an order is entered on an equity option, the order ticket must contain an item of information not required with orders for stocks and bonds. Any orders, whether for a sale or purchase, must be marked as either an *opening* or *closing transaction*.

- An *opening transaction* initiates or increases a position in the options contract.
- A *closing transaction* eliminates or reduces a position in the options.

Example: If an options trader feels that Syntex stock is about to rise in price, to profit from such a move, she might enter the following order:

Buy 1 Syntex Dec 45 call—Premium 3¼

If she has no preexisting position in Syntex calls, the order is marked "opening sale."

Another trader is of the opinion that Syntex stock will fall in price. He might attempt to profit by writing a call on the stock. If the stock declines, the call is not exercised, and he will profit by the amount of premium received. He enters the following order:

Sell 1 Syntex Dec 45 call—Premium 3¼

Because he has no existing position, the order is marked "opening sale."

Both the buy order and the sell order are opening transactions because they initiate positions. They would also be considered opening positions if the traders were increasing current positions. If the buyer already owns 5 Syntex Dec 45 calls and is buying an additional contract, the order is still "opening;" she is increasing her position. If the seller is short 6 Syn Dec 45 calls and writes another, it is still an opening transaction; he is increasing his short position from 6 to 7 short calls. These two parties have a transaction on this option at a premium of 3¼.

A few weeks later Syntex stock rises, and the options premium also rises to 5¼. The original purchaser decides to take her 2-point profit and enters the following order:

Sell 1 Syntex Dec 45 call—Premium 5¼

The order is marked as a "closing sale," because she is eliminating her previous position. The same would have been true had she been reducing a position.

Later Syntex stock declines in value, causing the option premium to decline to 1¼. The writer, who collected a 3¼-point premium, decides to repurchase it at the current price and cover his short at a profit of 2 points below his sale price. He enters the following order:

Buy 1 Syntex Dec 45 call—Premium 1¼

This order is marked as a "closing sale." By repurchasing the call, the writer is eliminating his short position, closing it out.

SUMMARY

The options contract is an interesting and exciting product that can be put to many uses and that is basically simple in concept. There are only two types of options: puts and calls:

- The holder of a put has the right to sell.
- The writer of a put agrees to buy if the holder elects to sell.
- The holder of a call has the right to buy.
- The writer of a call agrees to sell if the holder exercises the right to buy.

The buyer of an option pays a premium to the seller, the amount of which is determined by the forces of supply and demand. Once these few simple points are understood, the study of options becomes a simple matter. All that remains are the nearly limitless ways in which options can be employed.

Although a comprehensive glossary is included at the end of the book, it is worthwhile reviewing the brief list of terms that follow this chapter.

Appendix: Glossary

Aggregate Exercise Price (AEP)
>The total amount, in dollars, that would change hands if an equity option were exercised. To determine this amount, multiply the strike price by the number of shares in the contract.

At the Money
>When the strike price of an option and the market price of the underlying stock are the same, the option is said to be "at the money."

Buyer
>The purchaser of an options contract.

Call
>An equity option contract giving the holder the right to purchase the underlying security under specific terms and conditions.

Class
>All options of the same type (put or call) covering the same underlying security.

Closing Purchase
>A transaction in which a client buys an equity option that results in the elimination or reduction of a prior short position.

Closing Sale

A transaction in which a client sells an equity option that results in the elimination or reduction of a prior long position.

Covered Writer

The short seller of an equity options contract who has an offsetting position that enables him to complete the contract if it is exercised against him.

Exercise Price (Strike Price)

The dollar value per share at which the holder of an option is entitled to sell (put) or purchase (call) the shares of the underlying security in the options contract.

Expiration Month

The month in which an equity option ceases to be a valid contract.

Expiration Time

The date and time within the expiration month at which the option expires. Equity options expire at 11:59 P.M. EST on the Saturday following the third Friday of the stated month.

First-In/First-Out

A method that may be used by securities dealers to determine which of their clients will be assigned an exercise notice on a particular equity option. In this method the client who first wrote the option ("first-in") receives the first exercise notice ("first-out").

In the Money

Used to define an option that has an intrinsic value. A *call* is in the money if the market price of the stock is higher than the strike price of the option. A *put* is in the money if the market price of the stock is lower than the strike price of the option.

Long

Used to describe a position in which a client owns a security or option. Ownership is referred to as a "long position."

Market Maker

A member of the Chicago Board of Options Exchange who deals in specific options contract on the floor of that exchange. Market makers deal only as principal for their own accounts. They make no "as-agent" transactions.

Opening Purchase

A transaction in which an options trader buys an equity option that initiates a long position or that increases an existing long position.

Opening Sale

A transaction in which a trader sells an equity option that initiates a short position or increases an existing short position.

Option

A contract giving the holder the right to purchase (call) or sell (put) shares of an equity security under specific terms and conditions.

Options Clearing Corp. (OCC)

A clearing house established to handle the clearing and settlement of options contracts. The OCC performs this function for transactions in equity, index, currency, and debt options.

Order Book Official

An employee of the CBOE who maintains a book (listing) of orders to buy or sell equity options. He acts only as agent for the firms entering the orders, making no principal transactions.

Out of the Money

Used to define an equity option that has no intrinsic value. A *call* is out of the money if the market price of the underlying stock is lower than the strike price of the option. A *put* is out of the money if the market price of the stock is higher than the strike price of the option.

Premium

The fee paid by the purchaser of an option to the long seller or writer of the contract. The premium is stated as the number of dollars per share of stock represented by the contract.

Put

An equity options contract giving the holder the right to sell the underlying security under specific terms and conditions.

Quotation

The bid and asked (offer) prices of an options contract. The bid is the highest price buyers are willing to pay. The asked (offer) price is the lowest sellers are willing to accept.

Random Selection

A method used by the Options Clearing Corp., which may also be used by securities dealers, to determine which firm or which client will be assigned an exercise notice of an options contract. The party to be exercised is chosen at random.

Seller

The one who sells an equity options contract. The seller may be selling long or short.

Series

All options of the same class having both the same strike price and month of expiration.

Short Position

A position in which someone sells a security or an option he or she does not own or does not intend to deliver. A short position results from a short sale.

Short Sale

An order entered to sell a security or an option that the trader does not own or does not intend to deliver.

Specialist

A member of the American Stock Exchange who transacts business in equity options. Specialist acts as both principal (trading for their own accounts) and as agent (trading for other firms).

Strike Price

See *Exercise price*.

Uncovered Writer

The short seller of an equity option who does not have an offsetting position that will enable him to complete the contract if it is exercised.

Underlying Security

The common stock of the corporation that is the subject of an equity options contract.

Writer

The short seller of an equity options contract. The writer can be either covered or uncovered (naked).

CHAPTER 2

Options Markets

PREMIUMS

In options trading the only contractual term that is determined in the open market is the premium, and premiums vary greatly. There are three major influences on the value of an option.

1. The market value of the underlying instrument.
2. Duration, or the time of the option to expiration.
3. The volatility of the underlying instrument.

Market Value of the Underlying Instrument

The price of the underlying instrument allows us to measure the intrinsic value of the option. If the contract is in the money, that fact should be reflected in the premium.

Example: The following *call* options are trading on the CBOE:

Bank America	Dec 35	(market price 37)
Mead Corp.	Jan 40	(market price 42)
Philip Morris	Dec 170	(market price 172)

Each call is in the money by two points. That is, the market price of the stock is two points higher than the strike price. Therefore, intrinsically, each option is worth two points.

At the same time, however, the actual premiums are:

Bank America	Dec 35 —premium 3
Mead Corp.	Jan 40 —premium 4
Philip Morris	Dec 170—premium 9

Two points of the premium are attributable to intrinsic value and are determined by simple arithmetic. The balance is the result of the other two factors, but predominantly duration.

Duration, or Time to Expiration

The duration of an option can be easily measured, and the related time value easily calculated:

Example: The three options in the previous example are being quoted in October. In the case of the Bank America call and the Philip Morris call, approximately two months are left until expiration (December). The Mead Corp. call has about three months of life until its expiration in January. The amount of premium above the intrinsic value is the time value of the option. Much can happen to the value of a stock or other type of underlying instrument over a period of several months. The additional premium is "buying time." The purchaser of these calls has two or three months for the stock to rise and make their positions profitable. The components of these options' premiums are therefore intrinsic value and time value. If there is no intrinsic value, the entire premium reflects time value.

		Intrinsic Value	Time Value		Total Premium
Bank America	Dec 35	2	+1	=	3
Mead Corp.	Jan 40	2	+2	=	4
Philip Morris	Dec 170	2	+7	=	9

But this does not provide a total explanation. The Bank America and Philip Morris calls have two months left to expiration. Yet the time component of the premium for the Bank America contract is 1 point, but it is 7 points for the Philip Morris call. Also the Mead Corp. call, with one month longer duration than the Philip Morris call, shows only 2 points in time value, against 7 for Philip Morris. To explain these differences we must look at the third factor in price determination, volatility.

Volatility of the Underlying Instrument

The *volatility* (that is, the tendency to fluctuate sharply in price) of the underlying instrument contributes to variations in premiums among otherwise similar contracts. Assigning an accurate percentage of premium to volatility is difficult, if not impossible.

Example: Although the Bank America and Philip Morris calls have the same amount of time left to expiration and the same intrinsic value, they do not command the same premium. Of the two stocks, however, Philip Morris is far more volatile, more subject to wide fluctuations in price. Bank America stock has a more narrow trading range. Market participants therefore believe that it is just as likely for Philip Morris stock to rise 7 points in price in two months as it is for Bank America stock to rise 1 point in the same time.

Volatility also explains the difference between the Philip Morris and Mead Corp. premiums. Although the Mead call has one additional month until expiration, the stock has been trading in a narrow price range. The market senses that the contract might make up the 2 points of time value in this option over a three-month period, and that Philip Morris is capable of making up 7 points of time value in only two months.

Volatility varies greatly with different securities. It is easy to understand that stocks such as Teledyne, IBM, Squibb, or Procter & Gamble will generally have a wider price trading range than such stocks as American Electric Power, Detroit Edison, or Columbia Gas. But this is only the first step in measuring volatility.

Time and volatility are dynamically linked. Two stocks might both move up 10 points. If one makes this move in two months and the other in two years, there is a great difference in the premium value of the related options. If one runner completes a mile in five minutes and another in fifteen minutes, the distances covered are the same but not the time taken. Options values are similar.

OPTIONS DERIVATIVES

The relationships among the three factors just discussed can be measured to a degree, giving rise to what are known as *options derivatives, which are used to measure the reactions of premium to various changes. There are four options derivatives:*

1. *Delta:* The extent of change in premium that may be expected, given a change in the price of the underlying instrument.
2. *Gamma:* The extent of change in the delta that may be expected, given a rise or fall in the price of the underlying instrument.
3. *Theta:* The progressive loss of value of an options contract as expiration nears.
4. *Vega:* The extent of change that may be expected in the premium, given a change in the volatility of the underlying instrument.

Note: These derivatives are tools used by the options trader in implementing strategies, not for forecasting prices of the underlying instrument.

Example: The change in an option's premium varies to some degree with fluctuations in the value of the underlying security. In equity options, each series must be analyzed separately. Even options on the same security will be subject to varying changes. Consider the following put options:

Xerox Jan 70 put
Xerox Jan 60 put
Market price of Xerox stock—66

Although both options are based on the same security, their intrinsic values are different. The Jan 70 put has an intrinsic value of 4 points while the Jan 60 put is 6 points out of the money. If Xerox stock were to decline to $65.00 a share, the premiums of both puts should reflect that decline. The 70 put is now 5 points in the money, and its premium may be expected to increase in value by all or a good portion of that 1 point of intrinsic value. But the Jan 60 put is still out of the money by 5 points. That option may experience an increase in premium but only minimally. It still has 5 points to go to start showing intrinsic value (strike price of $60.00 and stock price at $65.00). The *delta* for the in-the-money put is greater than that of the out-of-the-money contract.

Another factor is the passage of time. As each day passes, the two options come nearer to expiration. Just prior to expiration, time runs out and the only value the option has is its intrinsic value. If no such value exists, the option becomes worthless. *Theta* decreases as expiration nears.

Delta

Delta represents the expected change in value of an option premium when a change occurs in the market value of the underlying instruments. Delta is expressed as a percentage of the change in the value of the security. For instance, if option has a delta of 25 percent, a one-point change in the value of the stock should result in a ¼-point change in the option's premium. The delta could be 0 percent if the option is deep out of the money, as in the case of the Xerox 60 put; changes in the price of Xerox have negligible effect on the option's price. It could be as high as 100 percent if the option is deep in the money; in this case, for every change in the value of the stock, the option's premium should increase or decrease by the same amount.

Delta is typically not constant. In general, if an option moves out of the money and in to the money, delta increases, that is, the premium reacts more to price changes in the underlying instrument. If a contract moves from in the money to out of the money, the delta decreases: the premium reacts progressively less to underlying price movement. How much delta changes is an option derivative known as "gamma."

Gamma

Gamma, which is expressed as a percentage, measures the expected change in delta as the price of the underlying security rises or falls. As delta changes continually, the gamma predicts the degree of delta change for each series of options.

Example: An option has a delta of 40 percent and a gamma of 5 percent. This indicates that a 1-point change in the value of the underlying security results in an increase in delta of 5 percent. If the underlying security rises by one point, delta would increase to 55 percent (50 percent delta plus 5 percent gamma). Subsequent price changes in the stock should be accompanied by a move in the premium of 55 percent of the change in stock price.

But what about the time factor? As options expire, they eventually lose all but the intrinsic value. How can we measure the wasting away of value caused by the passing of time?

Theta

Theta, expressed in terms of cents per day, measures the loss of value in a premium as each day passes, and expiration nears. As a rule, options lose value over time, which is why they are regarded as *wasting assets.* The amount of time until expiration is a major determinant of theta.

Vega

Volatility is a most important factor. Generally, the premium for contracts on an underlying instrument that moves in a narrow trading range is not as great as for those based on securities that are subject to wide price fluctuations.

Vega, which is expressed in cents, measures the expected change in premium that would accompany a change in the volatility of the underlying security. The vega is added to the premium in proportion to the change in underlying volatility. A high vega reflects high sensitivity to change in the underlying volatility.

Example: If the underlying volatility factor is 30 percent and the vega is .15, the premium should increase .15 for each point of increase in underlying volatility. If the premium is 3.00 and underlying volatility increases to 31 percent, the option's premium should increase by .15 to 3.15.

POSITION LIMITS

Because options are created by a writer, not by an issuing entity, there is no limit to the number of options that may be traded in the marketplace. It is conceivable that a corporation with 10,000,000 shares outstanding could have calls written covering 15,000,000 shares. If all the calls were exercised, there would not be enough stock for all deliveries. Chaos could result. It is also possible that option trading could be used to distort the market price of the underlying financial interest.

Example: If a group of investors were to buy 25,000 calls on XYZ stock and exercise them, this would require the delivery of 2,500,000 shares of XYZ (25,000 contracts times 100 shares per contract). If these calls were exercised simultaneously, many of the call writers would no doubt be uncovered and would have to purchase the stock in the market. This large influx of buy orders would lead to a major rise in the price of XYZ shares. As the price rose, those who exercised the calls might be able to sell the shares at an artificially inflated price.

To prevent such a situation, the regulators have set *position limits,* that is, limits on the number of options positions that an individual or a group may hold. No person or group acting in concert may have a position exceeding 8,000 options covering the same security on the same side of the market. More specifically:

- A *person* is any entity. An individual is a person, but so is a corporation, a partnership, a trust, or any other type of legal entity.
- A *group acting in concert* is any group of persons who trade in union or whose investment decisions are made by the same advisor.
- The phrase *on the same side of the market* refers to the *upside* and the *downside*.

Example: A person who thinks the market is about to rise could simultaneously go long calls and short puts. (See Figure 2-1).

FIGURE 2-1
Upside and downside strategies

Upside	Downside
Long calls	Long puts
Short puts	Short calls

If the stock rises, the long call increases in value and the short put expires unexercised, allowing the writer to retain the premium.

If, on the other hand, the client expects the market to decline, he or she could go long puts and short calls (see Figure 2-1). A market decline adds value to the long put and might make the call worthless, with the writer retaining the premiums.

The 8,000 option position limit applies to each side of the market separately, that is, the client could have a maximum position on each side. (A security cannot go up and down at the same time).

Example: The following is an acceptable position under this regulation:

General Electric Options	
Long 4,000 calls	Long 2,000 puts
Short 3,000 puts	Short 3,000 calls

Although the total position is 12,000 options, neither side exceeds 8,000 contracts. The upside total is 7,000, the downside total 5,000.

A position that would be in violation of the limit is:

Long 5,000 calls	Long 1,000 puts
Short 5,000 puts	Short 1,000 calls

Again the total position is 12,000 contracts, but 10,000 of them are on the "same side of the market."

Position limits are not "violated" if they are exceeded by events beyond the control of the holders.

Example: When a corporation splits its stock, an adjustment is made in the terms of an options contract. ABC splits its stock 2 for 1, and the position of 1 ABC Jun 90 call is adjusted to 2 ABC Jun 45 calls. The number of contracts is doubled, and the strike price is halved to reflect the split.

If an investor owns 5,000 ABC Jun 90 calls prior to the split, after the split she owns 10,000 ABC Jun 45 calls. This exceeds the position limit of 8,000 contracts, but it is not a violation. The investor did not create the position in excess of 8,000 contracts; it arose by an event over which she had no control. It would be a permissable position.

The limit of 8,000 contracts on each side is the maximum limit for the most actively traded stocks. The limit for options on less actively traded stocks declines to 5,500 contracts for some issues and 3,000 contracts on the least active ones.

EXERCISE LIMITS

There is a way for unscrupulous market participants to sidestep the position limit—by keeping their holdings under the position limits, but buying and quickly exercising large blocks of contracts.

Example: Someone could buy 8,000 calls on Monday and exercise them on Tuesday morning. Tuesday afternoon he or she buys 8,000 more and exercises them on Wednesday morning. By following this program each day, an unscrupulous trader might well accomplish his purpose. At no time were position limits exceeded.

But this program *would* violate another regulation, which prohibits any person or group acting in concert from exercising more than 8,000 contracts covering the same security over any five consecutive business days. In our example, exercising the 8,000 contracts on Tuesday brought the trader to the five-day limit.

Like position limits, the exercise limit of 8,000 contracts is for options on more active stocks. It drops to 5,500 or 3,000 on issues with lower trading volumes.

Position and exercise limits have been changed several times since listed trading of equity options began in 1973. The initial limit was 1,000 contracts, and the limit has been raised as the volume of trading in the product has increased. Traders should be aware of position and exercise limits for the types of options they are trading.

COVERED OPTIONS

An options contract is considered *covered* if the writer owns the underlying instrument or has another offsetting options position. Without one of these conditions, the writer is exposed to the risk of having to fulfill the contractual obligations at an unfavorable price. The call writer might have to purchase the underlying instrument at a price that is higher than the strike price; the put might have to buy the instrument from the holder at a price that creates a loss. When they face such a risk, writers are said to be *uncovered* (or *naked*).

Covered Calls

Call writers are considered to be covered if they have any of the following positions:

- A long position in the underlying instrument
- An escrow-receipt from a bank
- A security that is convertible into sufficient shares of the underlying security

- A warrant exercisable for sufficient shares of the underlying security
- A long position in a call on the same security that has the same r a lower strike price and that expires at the same time or later than the option being written

   Example: An individual trader wishes to write the following call:

   1 MMM Nov 75 call

   He is a covered writer on any one of the following conditions:

- He owns 100 shares of MMM stock. If MMM rises to $95.00 a share and he is called at 75, he has the stock to deliver.
- He provides an escrow receipt from a bank. The trader can furnish his broker with a receipt from Citibank, which states that the bank is holding 100 shares of MMM stock in his account and will deliver it on demand. If MMM rises to 95 and he is called at 75, the broker requests the shares from Citibank and makes delivery.
- He owns MMM convertible bonds or convertible preferred stock, which is exchangeable for 100 shares of MMM stock. If the trader is called at 75, the broker converts the bonds or preferred into common stock and delivers them against the exercised call.
- He owns warrants to purchase 100 shares of MMM stock. If the call is exercised against him, he exercises the warrants and delivers the MMM stock. (*Note:* Most companies do not issue convertible securities or warrants, but those that do provide a means of covering a call.)
- He is long (owns) 1 MMM Jan 70 call. If the stock rises to 95 and he is called at 75, he exercises the call and buys the stock at 70. In this example, he shows a 5-point profit. To be covered, the call he writes must expire before the call he buys. In this example, he writes a November call but owns a January call; he is covered. Had he written a November and was long an October call, the position would be uncovered.

   Anytime an option is covered, the broker is not at risk. Although the option writer is said to be covered, the rules are designed to protect the broker. So it might also be said that the broker is covered.

Covered Put

There is only one way for put writers to be covered: They must own a put on the same underlying instrument with the same or a later expiration month and the same higher strike price than the option being written.

Example: A trader wishes to write the following put:

1 Monsanto July 115 put

At the time she writes this put, the trader is long (owns)

Monsanto Aug 120 put

She is covered. If Monsanto stock declines to $90.00 a share and she is put at 115, she exercises her long put and sells at 120:

Buys (is put) at 115
Sells (puts) at 120

A 5-point profit results.

Again there is no risk to the broker carrying this client's account. This observation is important with respect to margin requirements (explained in greater detail later in the chapter):

- A covered writer is not required to deposit margin.
- An uncovered writer must deposit margin.

MARKET PARTICIPANTS

Options are used by all types of investors—individuals, institutions, traders, and broker-dealers. Many of these participants, however, can be grouped in the category of hedgers. Such options are often used by brokerage houses, banks, and other institutions whose capital is invested in large equity portfolios to curb the risk of an across-the-board market decline, and even of drops in individual stock prices. Other participants, such as technical analysts, employ options strategies to implement their speculative theories.

Hedging

Example: A large brokerage firm, such as Bear Stearns, has a client who wishes to sell 1,000,000 shares of Apple Computer at $45.00 a share. The firm determines that it can place 800,000 shares with other clients at a profit, but can find no buyer for the remaining 200,000 shares. Not wishing to lose the order, Bear Stearns purchases the 200,000 shares for its own account and with its own capital.

To make the profit on sale of the 1,000,000 shares, Bear Stearns had to buy 200,000 shares at a cost of $45.00 a share. Any substantial decline in price could eliminate the profit and even convert it to a substantial loss.

Equity options provide a solution. (Refer to Figure 2-1.) To protect against losses in the event of a protracted downside move, Bear Stearns' traders could go long puts, by purchasing 2,000 Apple Jan 45 puts at a premium of perhaps 3. Should the stock decline, they can exercise the puts, sell the stock at 45, and have no loss on the position.

But the put premium would present a substantial cost. The 2,000 put contracts, at $300.00 each, add up to a cost of $600,000.00. While the expense might not entirely offset the profit, it certainly reduces it greatly.

The alternative of selling calls short might be preferable.

Now Bear Stearns receives $600,000.00 of premium, or $3.00 a share. If Apple declines, they could sell the 200,000 shares as low as 42 and incur no loss. The risk is that, if Apple declines below 42, a loss on the position would occur.

If Apple rises in price to 48, the calls are exercised, and they deliver the stock at $45.00 a share. Since this was their cost, no loss results and the $600,000.00 premium received is added to the total profit.

When faced with a choice of paying a premium to purchase options or receiving one to write options, most professionals would prefer to write.

The same technique can be used on the other side of the market.

Example: A client wishes to purchase 500,000 shares of Goodrich stock at 55. The broker handling the order can find only 400,000 shares available in the market. To expedite the trade, the broker sells the client the additional shares short. The trade is profitable, but it leaves the firm in a very vulnerable position. If Goodrich stock rises above 55, the short position becomes a loss that theoretically can be unlimited.

In a rising market, either buying calls or writing puts is recommended. (Refer to Figure 2-1.) To protect the short position, the firm can purchase 1,000 Goodrich Feb 55 calls at a premium of perhaps 2. If the stock rises, they can exercise the calls to cover the short but would lose the $200,000.00 premium cost.

The broker can also choose to write 1,000 Goodrich Feb 55 puts for a 3-point premium. These can cover the short as high as 58 and the 3-point premium protects against the loss. If Goodrich goes down, the puts are exercised, and the short is covered at no loss. The premium received represents additional profit.

Speculation

Technical analysts often employ options to implement a theory.

Example: A market technician feels that IBM, now trading at 108 a share, has a support level at 104. At that level he expects buyers to appear in great enough numbers that the stock will decline no further. He might implement his theory by entering an order to buy 1,000 shares of IBM at 104. If the stock does decline to that level, he purchases the stock at a cost of 104. If IBM continues to decline, he shows an immediate loss. If the stock never reaches 104, he has nothing other than an unexecuted limit order.

The analyst could use options to produce better results. He writes 10 uncovered IBM Jan 105 puts for a premium of 4. He receives a $4,000.00 premium, $400.00 for each contract. If, as he expects, the price declines to 104, he is put and purchases 1,000 shares at 105. But his actual cost is only 101—the strike price of 105 less the 4-point premium received. If IBM continues to decline, he suffers no loss until it falls below 101.

If his theory proves to be wrong and IBM does not decline to 104, he retains the $4,000.00 premium.

A similar strategy can be used to implement a short sale.

Example: If a technician feels that Digital Equipment stock, currently at $90.00 a share, had a resistance level at 96, she might enter an order to sell short 1,000 shares at 96. If the order is executed, any rise above 96 represents a loss. If the stock never reaches 96, she does nothing.

An alternative options strategy is to write 10 uncovered Digital Jan 95 calls for a premium of 6½. If the stock reaches 96, she is called and sells short at 95. But she has 6½ points in premium to protect her against a continued rise in price. If Digital never rises above 95, she does not buy the stock but has $6,500.00 of premium.

Note: All options strategies entail some degree of risk. This risk is compounded by the fact that options are a wasting asset. With each passing day, they lose some of their time value. Writing naked options creates a greater-than-usual risk. The strategy should not be employed by anyone who is unable to assume such a risk. Individual investors should limit their activity to more conservative buying techniques. For some, even options buying and covered writing are not appropriate.

OPTIONS MARGIN

Margin is the minimum amount that must be deposited when making transactions (purchases and short sales) in securities. Most market investors are familiar with the minimum margin (''Reg T'') requirement for stocks, which for years has been 50 percent. A client purchasing $20,000.00 worth of General Motors stock has to deposit a minimum of $10,000.00, 50 percent of the total cost.

Margin requirements are established by the Federal Reserve. The Federal Reserve regulation that governs brokers in these matters is Regulation T. A similar rule, Regulation U, governs customers of banks dealing in securities.

Initial Requirements

The federal margin requirements for trading equity options are different from those for equity transactions, but they cover the same areas of buying and selling short. As in equities, margin is not required for selling options long, since the client closes out a position and receives payment of the premium. Margin is required, however, for three types of transactions:

1. Buying
2. Writing (shorting) covered
3. Writing (shorting) uncovered

Buying Options. Options have no loan value. The client must pay in full even if the option is in the money by a substantial amount. This reflects the fact that options inevitably expire. Consequently, when equity options are purchased, the margin required is 100 percent of the total premium. No partial payment is permitted under Federal Reserve regulations.

Example: Buy 10 Baytheon Feb 75 calls—premium 10

The margin required for this position is $10,000.00. A premium of 10 indicates $1,000.00 for each of the 10 contracts purchased.

Example: Buy 20 VAL Feb 280 puts—Premium 13

The margin required is $1,300.00 for each contract for a total of $26,000.00 for the 20 options.

The 100 percent requirement covers all equity options purchases, including puts, calls, straddles, and combinations.

Example:

Buy 5 Avon Dec 35 puts—Premium 3

Buy 5 Avon Dec 35 calls—Premium 3½

This position is a *long straddle:* A put and a call are bought on the same security, both with the same expiration month and the same strike price. The premium for the puts and the calls must be paid for in full.

Put premium of 3 or	$ 300.00 per contract
	× 5 contracts
Margin on put	$1,500.00
Call premium of 3½ or	$ 350.00 per contract
	× 5 contracts
Margin on call	$1,750.00
Total margin required	$3,250.00

Example:

Buy 7 Monsanto Jan 110 Puts—Premium 2

Buy 7 Monsanto Jan 115 Calls—Premium 13

This position is a long *combination:* the strike prices are different, 110 for the put and 115 for the call. The total margin required for this position is $10,500.00.

Put premium of 2 or	$ 200.00 per contract
	× 7 contracts
	$ 1,400.00
Call premium of 13 or	$ 1,300.00 per contract
	× 7 contracts
	$ 9,100.00
Total margin required	$10,500.00

Writing (Shorting) Covered. A covered writer of a put or a call has an offsetting position that enables him to complete the contract if it is exercised.

- A *covered call writer* either owns the underlying instrument, has an exchangeable position, or is long a call on the same security.
- A *covered put writer* is long a put on the same security. If the short put is exercised against him, the long put can in turn be exercised.

Because covered writers do not create any risk for the broker handling the account (the offsetting position provides protection), no margin deposit is required of the covered option writer.

Example: A client owns 100 shares of Polaroid and later enters the following order:

Sell 1 PRD May 45 call—Premium 2½

If the call is exercised against her, she can deliver the 100 shares of stock that she owns. No additional risk is created. In fact she receives a $250.00 premium.

Writing (Shorting) Uncovered. Uncovered writers have no offsetting position to protect themselves or their brokers. If the option is exercised against them, they have to buy or sell in response to the exercise. To protect the brokers, a minimum margin is required to write uncovered equity options. The margin requirement for writing uncovered equity options is:

20 percent of the market value of the underlying stock
Plus the premium received
Less the out-of-the-money amount (if any)

Example:

Write 1 uncovered Telephone Jul 50 call—premium 3

If the market price of Telephone is 48:

20 percent of the market value of $4,800.00 ($48.00 a share)	$ 960.00
Plus the premium received (3)	+ 300.00
	$1,260.00

The next step is to determine whether the option is in the money or out of the money. If it is in the money, the margin figuration is complete; the requirement is $1,260.00. If it is out of the money, the out-of-the-money amount must be subtracted from the $1,260.00.

This call is $200.00 (2 points) out of the money. The option allows the holder to buy (call) at 50, and the price of the stock is 48. The final step is therefore:

20 percent of the market value of $4,800.00 ($48.00 a share)	$ 960.00
Plus the premium received (3)	+ 300.00
	$1,260.00
Less the out-of-the-money amount (2)	− 200.00
Margin requirement	$1,060.00

Example: Suppose the contract in the preceding example is a put.

Write 1 uncovered Telephone Jul 50 put—premium 5½

Again, the market price of Telephone is 48:

20 percent of the market value of $4,800.00 ($48.00 a share)	$ 960.00
Plus The premium received (5½)	+ 550.00
Margin requirement	$1,510.00

This option is in the money. The right to sell (put) at 50 is intrinsically worth $200.00, since the market price is 48. No further calculation is necessary. The margin required to write the uncovered put is $1,510.00.

Minimum Requirement

If an option is deep out of the money, the margin required might be a very small or even a negative amount.

Example: Write 1 XYZ Jul 30 call—Premium ½

If the XYZ market price is 26:

20 percent of market value of $2,600.00	$520.00
Plus premium received (½)	+ 50.00
	$570.00
Less out-of-the-money amount (4)	−$400.00
Margin required	$170.00

This amount, $170.00, does not provide enough protection. So there is a minimum margin requirement for writing uncovered equity options, which is:

10 percent of the market value of the underlying stock
Plus the premium received

The minimum requirement is the greater of this or the "regular" calculation. Applying this calculation to writing the XYZ call:

10 percent of the market value of the stock ($2,600.00)	$260.00
Plus the premium received (½)	+ 50.00
Minimum margin requirement	$310.00

In this case, the $310.00 minimum is greater than the $170.00 arrived at using the regular method, and the greater amount ($310.00) is required.

These are the margin requirements of the Federal Reserve. Individual brokerage firms are free to set higher requirements. Indeed, many firms increased their so-called "house" rules following the severe market decline of October 1987.

Maintenance Requirements

Margin requirements are recalculated each day. If a change in the market value of the stock or the premium create a higher requirement, the writer receives a *call* for the additional amount. If he or she does not respond promptly, the position is closed out.

TAXES

Capital Gains and Losses

The tax aspects of trading in options are similar to trading in the underlying securities themselves. A purchase or sale results in a capital gain or a capital loss.

Example:

June 13, 19XO: Buy 1 ABC Nov 40 call—Premium 3
August 20, 19XO: Sell 1 ABC Nov 40 call—Premium 6

The trader has a $300.00 capital gain. The option is purchased at 3 ($300.00) and sold at 6 ($600.00).

Example:

December 11, 19XO: Write (sell) 1 DJR Feb 60 put—Premium 9
Jan 20, 19X1:   Buy 1 DJR Feb 60 put—Premium 11

This trader shows a $200.00 loss. She sells (writes) the put for a premium of 9 ($900.00) but repurchases it at a premium of 11 ($1,100.00).

The Effects of Expiration

The difference between options and their underlying instruments is that options expire. Someone who purchases 100 shares of Ford Motor stock may hold them for as long as the company continues to do business. Someone who buys 1 Ford Oct 60 call may hold it only until October when it ceases to exist.

At expiration of an option, one of two events may occur: It may be exercised or remain unexercised. If the contract has intrinsic value, it is exercised. If there is no value, it expires. Each situation creates a different tax result.

Unexercised. If an option expires unexercised, the premium becomes a loss to the buyer and a gain to the seller.

Example: Trader A purchases the following option, which is written by trader B:

1 ABC Jan 85 call—Premium 4½

At expiration in January, ABC is trading at 82. Trader A does not exercise, and the call is allowed to expire. The result is a loss of $450.00 (the premium) to the buyer (A) and a $450.00 gain to the writer (B). The reasoning is that, when the option expires, it is worthless. What trader A bought at 4½, he "sells" at zero. What trader B sold at 4½, she "buys back" at zero.

Exercised Calls. Refer to the same call as in the preceding example.

Example: At expiration of the ABC call, the underlying stock is trading at $93.00 a share. Now the 85 call is exercised. To determine the tax effects, add the premium to the strike price. This sum becomes the purchase price of the stock for the one who exercises the option and the sale price for the writer. On the exercise date:

Strike price	85
Premium	4½
	89½

The original buyer of the option shows a purchase of 100 shares of ABC stock at 89½ per share on that day. When he later sells the stock, the sale price will determine the gain or loss. No tax liability accrues when the holder exercises the call. Only the "cost" of the stock is determined at that time.

By the same reasoning the trader who writes the call sells 100 shares of ABC stock at 89½ on the exercise date. To determine her tax liability, her purchase cost must be known. If she had purchased the shares many years ago at 67, she would have a 22½-point capital gain. Had her purchase price been $100.00 a share, she would record a loss of 10½ points.

Exercised Puts. Puts are the opposite of calls. Put holders purchase the right to sell an underlying instrument at a fixed price, for which they pay premiums. If they exercise the put, the sale price is determined by subtracting the premium from the strike price.

Example: Trader A purchases and trader B writes the following option:

1 XYZ Aug 90 put—Premium 3

At expiration, XYZ stock is trading at $82.00 a share, and trader A exercises the put at 90. To determine his sale price for tax purposes, the following calculation is made:

Put strike price (90)	$9,000.00
Minus premium (3)	− 300.00
Sale price	$8,700.00

Although he receives 90 when he delivers the stock, he paid 3 points for the privilege of doing so. So the price is 87. His tax situation is ascertained by comparing this sale price to the purchase price of the shares delivered.

The price of 87 also becomes the purchase price of the shares for the writer who was exercised. On the exercise date, she purchases 100 shares of ABC at $87.00 a share.

While she pays $90.00 when the put is exercised, she received a 3-point premium for writing the option. Her net cost is $87.00. When she sells the stock, her profit or loss is based on the sale price versus the net cost of 87. It may result in a gain or a loss.

Having learned the language of options and having familiarized with how options markets work, the next step is to learn the rudiments of options strategies. The next chapter explains the basic approaches, again with equity options, in preparation for treatment in greater detail in Chapter 5.

CHAPTER 3

Options Strategies

In Chapter 2, the use of puts and calls to protect a position or to implement a strategy was explained. In anticipation of an upside price move, both hedgers and speculators can buy (long) calls or write (short) puts. Before an expected downside move, they can buy (long) puts or write (short) calls. They can engage in any of these strategies either covered or uncovered (naked).

Options strategies, however, take on many other forms, of which the basic ones are explained in this chapter. These are:

- Long straddles.
- Short straddles.
- Combinations.
- Short uncovered straddles.
- Covered call writing.
- Variable ratio writing.
- Spreads.

Finally, before getting into options on futures in the next section, other types of options are described.

STRADDLES

A *straddle* consists of a put and a call on the same underlying security, with the same strike price and the same expiration month. All the terms of the two options involved in a straddle are the same except that they are different types of options: one put and one call. Straddles may be long or short.

Long Straddle

In a long straddle, the two options are bought.

Example: A trader believes that Hitachi stock, currently at 110, will experience a wide price fluctuation in the coming months, but he does not know if the movement will be up or down. He might consider a long straddle:

Buy 1 Hitachi Jan 110 call—Premium 7

Buy 1 Hitachi Jan 110 put—Premium 5

As in all instances of buying options, the trader's maximum risk is the premium paid, but in this case there are two premiums, $700.00 (7) for the call and $500.00 (5) for the put. While possible, it is not highly probable that the entire 12 points of premium will be lost. For this to occur, the stock would have to be exactly 110 at expiration in January. In such a case, both the put and the call are of no value, and the trader loses the entire $1,200.00 premium. But if the stock is at, say, 116 at expiration, the 110 call is intrinsically worth 6 points ($600.00). This reduces the loss from $1,200.00 to $600.00—still a loss but not a total one.

To break even on this position at expiration in January, Hitachi stock must be above or below the 110 strike price by 12 points. (Trading expenses, such as commissions, are not included in these examples.) At expiration in January, Hitachi stock is $122.00 a share. The trader exercises his call (buys) at 110 and sells at the current price of 122. The result is a 12-point profit equal to the total cost of the two premiums. On the downside, Hitachi stock could be trading at 98 at expiration in

January. The trader buys 100 shares at 98 and exercises his 110 put (sells). This gives him a 12-point profit, again equal to the total premium cost.

Any price above 122 or below 98 results in a profit, which could be unlimited in the case of the call. Figure 3-1 displays the possible risks and rewards of this long straddle.

FIGURE 3-1

Risks and rewards of the long straddle

Buy 1 Hitachi Jan 110 call—Premium 7

Buy 1 Hitachi Jan 110 put—Premium 5

Price of Stock at Expiration	Potential Risk and Reward
Above 122	Profit Potential Unlimited*
122	Breakeven
Between 110 and 122	Loss of up to 11⅞ Points
Strike 110 Price	Loss of Entire Premium
Between 98-110	Loss of Up to 11⅞ points
98	Breakeven
Below 98	Profit Potential of 98 points*

*The long call allows the possibility of unlimited profit.

The long call has the potential for theoretically unlimited profit; there is no ceiling on a price rise. The long put can result in a profit of up to 98 points (if for some reason the stock becomes worthless). The trader could acquire it at no cost and sell (put) it at 110. Since the straddle cost 12 points, the profit would be 98 points (110 less 12).

Note: The owner of a straddle is not required to hold the options until expiration. He might sell one or both prior to that time, but our example presumes that he held both positions to the end.

Short Straddle

In a short straddle, both options are written.

Example: An individual trader believes American Brands, currently at 75, will experience minor price movement over the coming months. She might consider a short straddle:

Sell (write) 1 American Brands Dec 75 call—Premium 5

Sell (write) 1 American Brands Dec 75 put—Premium 4

Having written a call, she faces a maximum loss that is unlimited, assuming the call is uncovered. Her maximum profit potential is the total of $900.00 premium received for writing the options (call premiums of 5, put premium of 4).

If American Brands stock is at 75 upon expiration in December, neither the put nor the call is exercised and she retains the $900.00 premium.

She retains some of the $900.00 as long as the stock is no more than 9 points above or 9 points below the strike price at expiration. See Figure 3-2.

FIGURE 3-2

The risks and rewards of the short straddle

Sell (write) 1 American Brands Dec 75 call—Premium 5

Sell (write) 1 American Brands Dec 75 call—Premium 4

Prices of Stock at Expiration	Potential Profit or Loss
Above 84	Loss potential unlimited
84	Breakeven
Between 75 and 84	Gain of up to 8⅞ points
Strike price 75	Gain of Entire Premium
Between 66 and 75	Gain of up to 8⅞ Points
66	Breakeven
Below 66	Loss potential of 66 points

Assuming that the call writer is uncovered, an exercise forces her to buy the stock in the open market to deliver it to the holder. This opens the door to an unlimited potential loss. If the stock becomes worthless, the put is exercised against her, obliging her to pay the strike price of $75.00 a share. She would lose this amount less the 9-point premium received.

COMBINATIONS

A *combination*, which is similar to a straddle, consists of a put and a call on the same security, with either different strike prices and/or different expiration months.

Long Combinations

In a *long combination*, the options are purchased.

Example: A trader purchases the following options contracts:

> 1 IBM Jan 115 put—Premium 3
>
> 1 IBM Jan 120 call—Premium 3¾

The underlying security (IBM) and the expiration month (January) are the same, the strike prices differ. The trader has the right to sell (put) at 115 and the right to buy (call) at 120.

To determine the breakeven points and risk-reward potential, first add the two premiums:

Put premium	3
Call premium	3¾
Total	6¾

Then add the total to the call strike price and subtract it from the put strike price:

> Call: 120 strike + 6¾ = 126¾ breakeven point
>
> Put: 115 strike − 6¾ = 108¼ breakeven point

If at expiration the underlying stock is at 126¾, the 120 call has an intrinsic value of 6¾ points, equivalent to the total premiums paid. If the stock is at 108¼ at expiration the 115 put is intrinsically worth 6¾ points, equal again to the total of the premiums.

Underlying prices outside this range result in profit. Any price above 126¾ makes an unlimited profit possible. Any price below 108¼ results in a profit of up to 108¼ points. Should the stock be worthless, the owner of the put can acquire it at no cost and put (sell) it at 115. From the sale proceeds subtract the 6¾ points paid in premiums for up to 108¼ points in potential profit.

There is in this combination the greater chance that the buyer can lose all of the premium at expiration. In the long straddle of the preceding example, the trader has a total loss only if the stock is trading exactly at the strike price upon expiration. (In the straddle, the strike prices are the same for both the put and the call.) In this combination, however, the strike prices are different (the call strike is 120, the put strike is 115). If at expiration the underlying stock is trading between those two prices, neither option has any value and the total premium is lost.

For example, if at expiration IBM stock is trading at $118.00 a share, neither the right to sell at 115 (the put) nor the right to buy at 120 (the call) has any value. They are both out of the money, and the $675.00 in premium is lost. See Figure 3-3 for the possible risks and rewards. In any event, the buyer of this combination can lose no more than the premiums paid for the contracts.

FIGURE 3-3
Risks and rewards of the long combination

Long 1 IBM Jan 115 put—Premium 3

Long 1 IBM Jan 120 call—Premium 3¾

Price of Stock at Expiration:	Potential Risk and Reward:
Above 126¾	Potential Profit Unlimited
Between 120 and 126¾	Potential Loss of 6⅝ Points
Between 115 and 120	Loss of Entire Premium (6¾ Points)
Between 108¼ and 115	Potential Loss of 6⅝ Points
Below 108¼	Potential Profit of 108¼ Points

Note: The example assumes that the buyer holds both options until expiration, which is not always the case. He might sell either option at any time if, in his judgment, doing so is appropriate.

Short Uncovered Straddle

In a *short straddle*, the trader sells the two calls short. If the combination is uncovered, risk increases.

Example:

Short 1 IBM Jan 115 put—Premium 3

Short 1 IBM Jan 120 call—Premium 3¾

Because the call is uncovered, the maximum potential loss to the writer is unlimited. The potential profit to the writer is the 6¾ points worth of premium received. This maximum profit occurs when at expiration the stock is trading between 115 and 120, because within this range neither option has any value.

Figure 3-4 shows the potential for this short straddle which is simply the opposite of the long straddle. The potential loss for the long position becomes the potential profit for the short position, and so on. The two positions are mirror images of each other. They contain the same components, but they are reversed.

FIGURE 3-4

Risks and rewards of the short straddle

Short 1 IBM Jan 115 put—Premium 3

Short 1 IBM Jan 120 call—Premium 3¾

Price of Stock at Expiration	Potential Risk and Reward
Above 126¾	Potential Loss Unlimited
Between 120 and 126¾	Potential Gain of 6⅝ Points
Between 115 and 120	Profit of Entire Premiums (6¾ points)
Between 108¼ and 115	Potential Gain of 6⅝ Points
Below 108¼	Potential Loss of 108¼ Points

Note: In the last two examples, both the put and the call were assumed to be uncovered. This is not always the case. If the writer of the IBM straddle (or combination) owns 100 shares of IBM stock, the potential is limited. He or she has the stock to deliver and is not required to purchase it in the open market. In this case, the loss potential depends on the price paid for the stock. It is possible that the writer would even have a profit.

Long Stock—Short Straddle

Professional options traders frequently attempt to create positions that earn substantial premiums with less than total risk. Their aim is to keep all or a portion of the premiums received while reducing their risk if the strategy proves faulty. Such strategies can be implemented in anticipation of an upward or downward movement in prices and are therefore classified as ''bullish'' or ''bearish.''

In anticipation of a rising market, a trader may create a bullish position in which he is long the underlying instrument and short the options.

Example: A trader feels that the stock of Monsanto Chemical is about to rise and executes the following transactions:

Long: Buy 100 shares Monsanto stock @ 120

Short: Sell 1 Monsanto Feb 120 call—Premium 6

Sell 1 Monsanto Feb 120 put—Premium 8

He is now long 100 shares of Monsanto stock and short a Monsanto Feb 120 straddle. He has also received total premiums of 14 points ($1,400.00).

If he is correct and Monsanto stock rises to 130, the 120 call that he wrote will be exercised against him. He will have to deliver 100 shares of Monsanto at $120.00 a share. But since he is long the stock purchased at the same price, no loss results. His reward is the retention of the $1,400.00 in premiums received to write the straddle.

Suppose he is wrong and Monsanto drops to $115.00 a share. Now the put that he wrote is exercised against him and he is required to purchase 100 shares of Monsanto at 120. He now owns 200 shares, the 100 originally purchased and the 100 that were put to him at the same price. His total position is long 200 shares Monsanto Chemical @ $120.00.

With the stock trading at 115, he has a paper loss on the stock of

$1,000.00 ($5.00 a share on 200 shares), but he still has the $1,400.00 of premium received for a gain of $400.00. This type of position is not without risk. If Monsanto drops below $113.00 a share, he loses money. He has only 14 points protecting him on the 200 shares purchased at 120. That is 7 points for each 100. His breakeven point is $113.00 a share.

Covered Call Writing

A covered call writer is in a position to make delivery of the underlying security if the option is exercised. Investors often use this method to increase income and protect an existing position.

Example: An investor purchases 100 shares of Polaroid common stock at $42.00 a share. She then writes the following call:

1 Polaroid Dec 45 call—Premium 3

Since she owns the Polaroid stock, this call is covered. Her position is:

Long: 100 shares Polaroid at $42.00 a share

Short: 1 Polaroid Dec 45 call (covered)

The $300.00 premium received provides protection for her long position in the stock. She can lose 3 points in the stock price and still be even, because the loss is offset by the premium received.

Per-share cost of stock	$42.00
Call premium received	− 3.00
Breakeven price on stock	$39.00

If the stock rises above 45 before expiration in December, she is called, but her sale price is 48:

Strike price of call	$45.00
Call premium received	+ 3.00
Sale price if called	$48.00

Having paid only $42.00 a share, she shows a profit of $6.00 a share. She cannot make any greater profit than the 6 points. If the stock rises to 60, she is called at 45 and in effect sells at 48. The rest of the gain belongs to the holder who exercised the call.

If the stock does not rise above 45 prior to expiration, the call expires unexercised and the investor retains the $300.00 premium. She may decide to write another call and earn an additional premium, further reducing her risk and increasing her income.

Many institutional investors write covered calls against their stock positions. This practice brings in substantial income. The only added risk is that they may not participate in all the profits if the stock price rises sharply.

Variable Ratio Writing

If an options trader was bearish, expecting a stock to decline, he might employ *variable ratio writing*. In this strategy the trader writes more calls than he has covered. The writing earns a substantial amount in premiums, which protects a long position and possibly adds to return by earning income.

Example: A trader takes the following positions:

> Buy: 100 shares Polaroid at 42
> Write: 3 Polaroid Dec 45 calls—Premium 3

The position is now:

> Long: 100 shares Polaroid at 42
>
> Short: 3 Polaroid Dec 45 calls (1 covered, 2 uncovered)
>
> Total premium received $900.00 ($300.00 per call)

If the stock declines, the $900.00 premium received protects him on the 100 shares purchased at $42.00. He breaks even if forced to sell the shares at 33.

Per-share cost of stock	$42.00
Total premium received	− 9.00
Breakeven point on stock	$33.00

If the stock does not rise above 45 a share by expiration in December, the calls are not exercised and the stock retains the premium of $900.00. It is also possible that he would have a profit in the 100-share long position.

If at expiration Polaroid stock is at 44, he sells the 100 shares purchased at 42 for a 2-point profit. Add to this the $900.00 received in premium, and he has a profit of $1,100.00 on these transactions.

The risk on this position, however, is unlimited. If the trader is wrong and Polaroid rises above $45.00 a share, he is exercised on the 3 calls, requiring delivery of 300 shares at that price. He is long only 100 shares and is forced to buy the additional 200 shares in the open market. Since the price he would have to pay cannot be determined, the potential loss is unlimited.

What is his upside breakeven point? If the trader is called at $45.00, he delivers the 100 shares purchased at 42, giving him a $300.00 profit. He then has to purchase 200 shares in the market to deliver at 45. His protection is the total of the $300.00 profit and the $900.00 premium:

Profit on 100 shares	$ 300.00
Premium received	+ 900.00
Total protection	$1,200.00

This $1,200.00 is applied as protection on the repurchase of 200 shares. So for each 100 shares he has $600.00 to lose. His breakeven point, should Polaroid stock rise in price, is $51.00 a share.

Call strike price	$45.00
Points of protection per 100 shares	+ 6
Breakeven price	$51.00

If he has to purchase 200 shares of Polaroid at $51.00 and deliver them against the call at 45, he loses 6 points ($600.00) on each 100 shares. This total loss of $1,200.00 is offset by the $900.00 premium received and the $300.00 profit on the 100 shares he was long.

Any rise above $51.00 represents a loss of $200.00 for each point. The maximum loss potential cannot be measured.

FIGURE 3-5

The risks and rewards of the variable ratio writing strategy

		Unlimited loss potential	
Breakeven	51		
Strike price	45	Profit range	
Breakeven	33		
		Loss	

See Figure 3-5, between the price levels of 33 and 51, the trader shows some profit. Above or below these levels, his loss can be sizable.

SPREADS

In a *spread,* the trader buys (long) one series in a class of options and writes (shorts) another series in the same class. Spreads can involve the use of options with different expiration months, with different strike prices, or with both terms different. The trader, who may be either bullish or bearish, employs the spread to make a profit while reducing the risk of loss.

Call Spreads

The following example is a call spread bullish, using different expiration months. These are referred to as *time spreads* or *horizontal spreads.*

Example: Consider the following hypothetical class of options.

	Calls			
		Feb	*Mar*	*May*
XYZ	50	2	4	6
51	55	½	2	3
51	60	¼	½	¾
51	65	r	r	r

All of the XYZ calls represent a class of options, and each option within the class is a series. There are 12 series in the XYZ call class.

In a spread, the trader purchases one series and sells another in the same class:

Bullish Call Time Spread

The bullish call time spread is put on before an expected upswing.

Example:

> Write: 1 XYZ Mar 50 call—Premium 4
>
> Buy: 1 XYZ May 50 call—Premium 6

The trader is anticipating a rise in value in XYZ stock but chooses not to purchase just a call. If she buys the May call and does nothing else, she is risking the full $600.00 premium if she is wrong. By shorting the March call, she receives $400.00 in premium, reducing her risk to $200.00. All spreads result in either *credits* or *debits*. Since the trader pays $600.00 and receives only $400.00, she has a $200.00 debit.

The profit potential rests in the fact that, if XYZ rises, the value of the May option that she owns rises faster than that of the March option that she is short. At the time the spread is initiated, the difference in premium is 2 points (4 versus 6). If that difference widens to more than 2 points, she has a profit.

Example: XYZ rises in value by 3 points. The premium on the March option also increases 3 points from 4 to 7. But the May option, due to the longer time until expiration, rises 5 points, from 6 to 11. Our client now closes out her spread. The May option, purchased at 6, is sold at 11 for a 5-point profit. The March option, sold at 4, is repurchased at 7 for a 3-point loss. The net profit is 2 points.

	Mar 45 Call		*May 45 call*
Purchased	7	Purchased	− 6
Sold	−4	Sold	11
Loss	3	Gain	5
	Net Gain = 2 points		

The original spread in the premium is 2 points (4 versus 6), and it widens to 4 points (7 versus 11). The 2-point profit belongs to the trader.

Bearish Call Time Spread

The bearish call time spread is put on before an anticipated drop in price.

Example: Suppose the trader is bearish on XYZ stock, expecting the stock to drop sharply in price. She might create the following spread:

Buy: 1 XYZ Mar 50 call—Premium 4

Write: 1 XYZ May 50 call—Premium 6

This results in a $200.00 credit (received $600.00 premium versus $400.00 paid). In this case, she wants the spread to narrow, which will allow her to retain all or part of the $200.00 credit.

XYZ stock declines sharply in price to $40.00 a share. Neither the call she purchased nor the one she wrote has any value and expires unexercised. The premium for both options is 0, and the spread narrows to 0. The trader keeps the $200.00.

If the stock rises, she is protected by the March call that she had purchased. If she is called at 50, she exercises her own 50 call to make delivery. The danger is that her long call expires in March. The call that she sold short runs until May, but at least she is protected until the March expiration.

When a call spread uses different months, the option with the longer time until expiration has the greater premium value: It is still alive when the shorter contract expires.

Bullish Call Money Spread

Spreads can be created using the same expiration month but different strike prices. These are called *money spreads* or *vertical spreads*. In the case of call spreads, the contract with the lower strike price has the greater premium value. A bullish call money spread is created before an expected upward move in prices.

Example: If a trader is bullish on XYZ, he might:

Buy: 1 XYZ May 50 call—Premium 6

Write: 1 XYZ May 55 call—Premium 3

This results in a debit of 3 points (6-point premium received versus 3-point premium paid). If the stock rises, the May 50 strike should increase in premium at a greater rate than the May 55 because it is intrinsically worth 5 points more. If the spread in premiums widens beyond the original debit of 3, the trader profits on the spread.

Note: The maximum difference in value of these options at expiration is 5 points. This occurs if the stock is at 55. The May 50 is worth 5 points while the May 55 is without intrinsic value.

Bearish Call Money Spread

A bearish call money spread is put on in expectation of a downswing.

Example: A bearish trade takes a position that is contrary to that of the preceding example:

Write: 1 XYZ May 50 call—Premium 6

Buy: 1 XYZ May 55 call—Premium 3

This results in a $300.00 credit ($600.00 premium received versus $300.00 premium paid). If XYZ declines and both options become worthless, the trader keeps the $300.00 credit. If he is wrong and the stock rises to 75, the most he can lose is $200.00. He is called at 50 but delivers by exercising his 55 call. The resulting $500.00 loss is partially offset by the $300.00 credit he received when he "put on" the spread.

FIGURE 3-6
Summary of call spread positions

Time Spreads (different expiration months):
   Bullish: Buy longer month, short (write) nearer month—result, debit
   Bearish: Buy nearer month, short (writes) longer month—result, credit
Money Spreads (different strike prices):
   Bullish: Buy lower strike price, short (write) higher strike price—result, debit
   Bearish: Buy higher strike price, short (write) lower strike price—result, credit

Spreads can also be created using both different expiration months and different strike prices. These are known as *diagonal spreads*.

Put spreads

Spreads can be created using puts for the opposite effect of call spreads. As bullish call spreads (vertical or horizontal) result in a debit, bullish put spreads create a credit. Bearish put spreads create a debit, whereas bearish call spreads result in a credit.

If a put option gives the holder the right to sell the underlying shares, then the higher the strike, the more attractive the option. When put options carry the same strike prices, the contract with the longer time to expiration is the more valuable.

Bullish Put Time Spread

A bullish put time spread is put on in anticipation of an upside movement.

Example: Refer to the following chart:

		Puts		
		Nov.	*Dec.*	*Feb.*
ABC	45	¼	½	¾
49	50	2	3	5
49	55	6	7	9

A trader enters the following options orders:

<blockquote>

Buy: 1 ABC Dec 50 put—Premium 3

Write: 1 ABC Feb 50 put—Premium 5

</blockquote>

This spread produces a $200.00 credit. The trader buys at 3 ($300.00) and sells as 5 ($500.00). Each option gives the holder the right to sell (put) at $50.00 a share. If the stock does in fact rise in price to $70.00, neither option has any value and both expire unexercised.

If the trader is wrong and the stock drops to $40.00 a share, both puts are exercised. He must purchase stock at $50.00 from the buyer of the Feb 50 put that he wrote. But he owns a Dec 50 put, which allows him to sell the stock at $50.00; no loss results.

His protection is not total, however, since his put expires two months earlier (December) than the one he wrote (February). For the remaining 2 months, his risk is 48 points. He might have to purchase stock at 50 when it is worthless. This 50-point loss is reduced only by the 2-point credit received for the spread.

Bearish Put Time Spread

A bearish put time spread is created before an expected downswing.

Example: A trader is bearish on ABC stock and puts on the following spread:

<blockquote>

Buy: 1 ABC Feb 50 put—Premium 5

Write: 1 ABC Dec 50 put—Premium 3

</blockquote>

This spread results in a $200.00 debit: He pays a premium of $500.00 and receives one of $300.00. If the stock declines, both puts should increase in value because they give the right to sell the stock at $50.00 a share. Since the trader owns the put with the longer time to run, that option's premium should show a greater increase in value.

ABC stock declines to $45.00 a share. The Dec put, which he wrote, might now trade at a premium of 7½, but the Feb put might increase in value to 11½. The trader could now close out the spread with the following transactions:

Buy: 1 ABC Dec 50 put—Premium 7½

Sell: 1 ABC Feb 50 put—Premium 11½

The original spread of 2 points (3 versus 5) has widened to 4 points (7½ versus 11½). He shows a profit of 2 points:

Dec 50 Put		Feb 50 Put	
Purchased	7½	Purchased	5
Sold (Wrote)	3	Sold	11½
Loss	4½	Profit	6½
	Net gain = 2 points		

Note: In these simplest of forms, spreads are constructed to produce either a debit or a credit.

- In the case of a debit, the trader wants that debit to widen.
- In the case of a credit, the trader wants the credit to narrow.

FIGURE 3-7

Summary of put spread positions

Time Spreads (different expiration months):
Bullish: Buy nearer month, short (write) longer month—Result, credit
Bearish: Buy longer month, short (write) nearer month—Result, debit.

OTHER OPTIONS PRODUCTS

Options contracts are available on products other than equity securities. Exchange trading is conducted in options on stock indexes, currencies, U.S. Treasury securities, and, of course, on futures.

Index Options

Index options differ from equity options in that they do not represent a specific number of shares of an equity security. The value of the contract is determined by the use of a multiplier. For example, if the multiplier is stated as 100 and a given index had a 325 dollar value, the total value of the contract would be $32,500.00 ($325.00 × 100).

A very actively traded index option is based on the Standard & Poor's 100 stock index. Each day a value is placed on the index depending on the performance of the 100 common stocks included in this index.

Options are exercised based on this price, just as the value of an equity option is founded on the market value of the underlying stock.

Another distinction between index and equity option is how settlement is made in the event of exercise. Index options settle in cash.

Example: If you own 1 Exxon Jun 45 call, the stock is trading at $50.00 a share, and you exercise the call, you receive 100 shares of Exxon stock. You pay $45.00 a share, the strike price of your option. But suppose you owned 1 S&P Nov 325 call. If the index is valued at 328, your call is in the money. You may purchase at 325, and the value is 328. If you exercise the call, you receive $300.00 cash from whoever is assigned your exercise notice. The exercise value of the contract is $32,500.00 ($325.00 × 100), and the market value is $32,800.00 (328 × 100).

In Figure 3-8, note that on the trading day in the listing all of the most actively traded options on the Chicago Board were based on the S & P 100 stock index. This is not unusual. Interest in index options is exceedingly high,

FIGURE 3-8
A sample of index options listing

MOST ACTIVE OPTIONS
CHICAGO BOARD

		Sales	*Last*		*Chg.*	*NY Close*
			CALLS			
SP100	Oct 325	19028	6	+	1	327.16
SP100	Oct 330	14873	3⅛	+	⅝	327.16
SP100	Oct 320	11638	10	+	1⅝	327.16
SP100	Oct 335	8962	1 7/16	+	⅜	327.16
SP100	Dec 320	6339	14⅜	−	¾	327.16
			PUTS			
SP100	Oct 320	14459	1⅜	−	11/16	327.16
SP100	Oct 325	12140	2⅝	−	1¼	327.16
SP100	Dec 320	6809	4⅞	−	1⅛	327.16
SP100	Oct 315	6261	¾	−	⅜	327.16
SP100	Oct 330	4697	5	−	1⅝	327.16

Example: On this day the index value was 327.16, $32,716.00 (327.16 × 100). If a holder of an Oct 325 call exercises her option, she receives a settlement of $216.00. This represents the difference between her aggregate exercise value of $32,500.00 (325 × 100) and the closing value of $32,716.00. If a client exercised an Oct 330 put, he receives $284.00. He sells (puts) the index at $33,000.00 (330 × 100) when the current value is $32,716.00.

Uses of Index Options

Although the settlement of index options differs from equity options, the uses of each product are very similar. If you expect the price of General Motors stock to rise, you might buy GM calls or write GM puts. Suppose, however, your market opinion is more broadbased. You feel the market in general will rise, but you do not wish to be tied to one security. You could purchase SP100 Index calls or write SP100 Index puts. Now your contract encompasses the performance of the 100 stocks in the index, not just one security.

While index options can be used to speculate, they are more often used by professional investors to protect positions or to participate in the market at a reduced cost.

Example: A pension fund manager has a portfolio of common stocks worth many millions of dollars. His research tells him that the market is about to suffer a decline. It might not be economical or sensible to liquidate his portfolio because he does not expect the decline to be long lived.

So he buys index puts or writes index calls. If the general market declines, the profits from the options positions offset any temporary drop in the value of the portfolio.

Or perhaps a money manager sees a forthcoming rise in the market. At this time her funds are fully invested but she would like to participate in the rally. At a fraction of the cost of buying stocks, she can purchase calls on an index. Or at no cost, she can write puts on an index. If the anticipated rise occurs, she profits from either type of contract.

Currency Options

Options on foreign currencies have traded on exchanges since 1982. As of 1989, option contracts were available on the

- Australian dollar,
- British pound,
- Canadian dollar,
- West German mark,
- French franc,
- Japanese yen, and
- Swiss franc.

Although the size of these contracts vary, they are generally based on a specific number of units of the underlying foreign currency. For example, on the Philadelphia Exchange the British pound option represents 31,250 pounds, and the Japanese yen contract is for 6,250,000 yen. The contracts are quoted in cents per underlying unit.

Currency option are used to speculate as well as to protect positions, particularly those involving exchange note risk.

Options on Treasury Securities

Options on U.S. Treasury securities trade on the American Stock Exchange and the Chicago Board, which offer contracts on 13-week Treasury bills, 5-year Treasury notes, and longer-term Treasury bonds. In all cases, the contract represents a specific face value amount of the underlying instrument:

- Each bill option is for $1,000,000.00 face value of bill.
- Each note and bond contract is for $100,000.00 of face value.

Treasury options are for the most part traded by professional investors to protect large position in debt securities or to participate in market at low cost.

Regardless of the underlying instrument, the language of option contracts and their related trading strategies remain fundamentally the same. In the next part of the book, we apply these strategies to options on futures.

PART II

OPTIONS ON FUTURES

CHAPTER 4

Applying Options to Futures Trading

Trading options on futures is similar to trading options on other underlying interests. In this chapter, options basics are applied to the futures markets.

PUTS AND CALLS ON FUTURES

Buyers of futures options pay premium to sellers for the right to buy (go long) futures (call) or for the right to sell (go short) futures (put). A put gives the buyer the right to sell futures contracts at a fixed price (strike or exercise price) for a specific period of time (expiration period). A call gives the buyer the right to buy futures contracts at a fixed price for a specific period of time. Writers, or grantors, sell rights to option buyers for a premium.

Example: Trader A buys a December Swiss franc $.6800 call from trader B for a $500.00 premium. Trader A has the right to buy December Swiss franc futures at $.6800 at any time from now until the expiration date. Trader B is obligated to sell Swiss franc futures to A at $.6800 if A decides to exercise the right to buy at $.6800.

Options sellers have obligations to buy futures (put writers) or to sell futures (call writers) if the option buyer decides to exercise.

Figure 4-1 illustrates the differences between future option buyers and sellers.

FIGURE 4-1

Differences between option buyers and sellers

Buyer/Holder, Long Options	Seller/Writer/Grantor, Short Options
Pays premium	Receives premium
Has rights	Has obligations
Features risk limited to premium	Features unlimited risk
Features unlimited profits	Features profits limited to premium
Requires no margin	Requires margin

A powerful feature of buy option strategies is that risk is limited to the premium regardless of where futures trade. If trader A pays $740.00 for the right to buy gold at $480.00 per ounce, the most trader A can lose is $740.00. This means that speculators can take positions in futures markets with a known quantifiable risk using buy option strategies. Hedgers can protect themselves against an adverse price movement yet still participate in a favorable price movement using buy option strategies because the maximum cost of hedge is known when the option is bought. Because of the limited-risk feature of buy option strategies, no margin is required.

Potential profits of buy option strategies are virtually unlimited. A long $.6800 live cattle call will show increasing profits if prices continue to rise. A long $2.00 corn put will show increasing profits if prices continue to fall. Long put profits are limited in the sense that commodity prices cannot fall below zero. More important, though, the unlimited profit potential of buy option strategies means tremendous leverage to the speculator and unlimited price protection for the hedger. From a hedging perspective, buy option strategies are similar to purchasing insurance. A premium is paid for price protection above (call) or below (put) a certain level (strike price). Sell option strategies are analogous to the insurance company writing insurance contracts. A premium is received in exchange for providing price protection. In the case of futures options, a price level is being insured.

For option sellers, reward is limited to the premium they receive in return for the obligation to take the other side of the futures contract. The most an option seller can earn is the premium because the premium is the most an option buyer can lose. An option seller, however, has unlimited risk.

Example: If trader A sells $19.00 crude oil call and prices move sharply higher, trader A will continue to accrue losses. With crude oil trading much higher than $19.00, it is likely that buyers of the $19.00 call option will exercise (the option buyer is now long a crude oil futures contract marked at $19.00). The option seller must assume a short position at $19.00.

Because of the risk potential of short option positions, margin must be placed with the exchange as a good faith deposit.

LONG AND SHORT FUTURES OPTIONS POSITIONS

By introducing puts and calls, and buying and selling, a trader has greatly increased ways to take market positions (Figure 4-2). A trader who understands puts and calls can now establish bullish market positions by buying futures, buying calls, or selling puts. Or a trader can establish bearish positions by selling futures, selling calls, or buying puts. Remember that being long or short the market is different from being long or short options.

FIGURE 4-2
Ways of taking market positions

Long the Market (Bullish)	Short the Market (Bearish)
Buy futures	Sell futures
Buy calls	Sell calls
Sell puts	Buy puts

A buy call strategy gives the holder the right to buy futures; the strategy profits if prices go up. A sell put strategy gives someone else the right to go short futures; this strategy also profits if prices go up.

Conversely, selling calls gives someone else the right to go long; therefore, selling calls profits when prices decline. Buying puts gives the holder the right to sell futures; buying puts profits when prices decline.

Puts can be confusing to the beginning option student because they go against a trader's nature: *buying* puts will show a profit when prices go *down*, and *selling* puts will show a profit when prices go *up*.

Adding options to a hedging or trading program increases flexibility and complicates the decision-making process. The optimal option strategy is the one that most reflects the hedger's market opinion and ability to assume risk. Futures option strategies and when to use them are discussed in the next chapter. For now, it is important to recognize which of the simple buy and sell option strategies earn profits when prices go up or down.

OPTIONS VERSUS FUTURES

Perhaps the chief difference between options and futures contracts is that options permit traders to participate in futures markets without actually having to deal in the underlying commodity or financial interest itself. When a trader buys a futures contract, he in effect owns the commodity. If exercised, the futures contract obliges the holder to take delivery of the commodity or instrument. If a futures options contract is exercised, the holder takes delivery of the futures contract, not the commodity. The options contract holder becomes a futures contract holder.

In addition, option contracts are what their name connotes—optional. They may be left to expire. Not so with futures, which must be offset or sold off. Otherwise, "the pork bellies are coming." With options, therefore, the trader's risk is limited to the amount of the premium.

Example: Trader A buys a gold futures contract for $460.00 per ounce. Trader B pays $1,500.00 for a $460.00 call option. What is the difference? Trader A has effectively bought and owns 100 ounces of gold at $460.00 per ounce regardless of where futures trade. Profits and losses accrue to A's position depending on where the gold futures contract is sold. At $470.00, a profit of $10.00 per ounce is realized. At $400.00, a loss of $60.00 per ounce is realized. Option positions are different. Trader B has the right to buy 100 ounces of $460.00 per ounce and will do so only if prices go up. The most trader B is at risk for is $1,500.00, regardless of where futures trade.

Trading futures is similar to options in that both are bought and sold, quantities and contract months must be designated, and each has a price associated with it. Contract months in options not only designate the underlying futures contract, but also determine the expiration date. Option expiration dates are usually in the preceding month to the underlying futures month, depending on the particular option. (Contact the appropriate futures exchange for specific expiration dates. See the Appendix to this chapter.)

Option traders need to articulate two more modifiers than are required in futures trading: strike prices and whether the option is a put or a call.

Example: A futures trader could buy 10 December silver futures, where an options trader could buy 10 December silver $8.00 calls.

A comparison of options and futures is shown in Figure 4-3.

FIGURE 4-3
Characteristics of options versus futures

Options	*Futures*
Long/short	Long/short
Quantity	Quantity
Month/expiration	Month
Premium	Price
Strike price	
Put/call	

With many strike prices and two kinds of options (puts and calls), the decision-making process as to what is the best trade can get complicated. As the novice option trader becomes more proficient, the confusion arising from having so many choices gives way to added flexibility and opportunity to profit or hedge efficiently. No longer is the trader just bullish or bearish. Option strategies allow varying degrees of bullishness or bearishness, and for specific periods of time.

GETTING OUT OF FUTURES OPTION POSITIONS

There are three ways to get out of option positions:

- Let them expire worthless
- Offset
- Exercise

Most often, options are *offset*. To offset an option means to trade it back to the market.

Example: Trader A has sold 10 December T-bond 80 puts. To offset, trader A must buy back 10 December T-bond 80 puts. (The difference in premiums paid and received determines the trade's profit or loss.) If trader A tried to offset a long 10 December T-bond 80 put position by buying 10 December T-bond 80 calls, A would have two separate positions: long 10 December calls and long 10 December puts. To offset, the quantity, month, strike price, and option type must be the same.

An option buyer has the right to *exercise* at any time, which means converting the option into a futures position.[1]

Example: Trader B is long 10 December S&P 310.00 puts and decides to exercise. Trader B notifies the exchange. The exchange notifies traders who are short the same option usually on a random basis

---

[1]Options that can be exercised at any time prior to expiration are called American options. Options that can only be exercised at expiration are called European options. All options on futures contracts traded in the United States are American options.

(depending on the exchange). The next morning trader B is short 10 December S&P futures contracts at $310.00. The long side of the futures position is assumed by one or more traders who were short the same option the previous day.

Most of the time, an option is worth more by trading it back to the market. However, as the expiration day approaches and/or as an option becomes deep in the money, exercising may be the most profitable method of disposing of the option. (Exercising behavior is discussed in more detail in Chapter 10.) Once the option is exercised, the futures position is assumed, and the option no longer exists.

An option can *expire worthless.*

Example: If trader A buys $.0700 sugar calls and the futures price is $.0650 at expiration, why exercise the option and buy sugar futures at $.0700? Trader A can let the option expire worthless and buy sugar futures at $.0650. On the following day, the option is no longer valid, and trader A loses the entire premium on the option.

FUTURES OPTION PRICING FACTORS

What gives an option value? In addition to the three factors discussed in Chapter 2 (the underlying price relative to strike price, volatility, and time to expiration), there is a fourth factor in options on futures: interest rates.

Futures Price Relative to Strike Price

We know that, as strike prices increase, call premiums decrease and put premiums increase.

Example: Figure 4-4 lists settlement premiums for D mark options. The market charges more money to buy the right to go long D marks at $.5500 than it does for the right to buy them at $.5900. The market also charges more money to buy the right to go short at $.5900 than it does for the right to sell at $.5500.

Usually, as futures prices go up (down), call premiums increase (decrease) and put premiums decrease (increase).[2] Option traders like to know more precisely how much an option premium will change due to a change in the underlying futures. Option premiums can be broken down into intrinsic or exercise value plus time or extrinsic value:

Option premium = intrinsic value (exercise value)
+ time value (extrinsic value)

FIGURE 4-4
West German Deutsche Mark
Settlement Prices, September 9, 1987

	December Options	
Strike Price	Calls	Puts
$.54	2.41	.43
.55	1.71	.72
.56	1.14	1.13
.57	.73	1.70
.58	.46	2.42
.59	.27	3.21
Futures settlement = $.5601		

Example: Refer to Figure 4-4. December D mark futures on September 9 settled trading at $.5601. The $.5500 call settled at $.0171. This premium has $.0101 of exercise value because the futures price is exactly $.0101 above the call's strike price. (A trader could buy the call, sell the future, exercise the option, and realize a value of $.0101.) Exercise value is also called intrinsic value. However, the $.0101 intrinsic value, determined by the futures price relative to the strike price, does not explain the entire premium of $.0171. The additional $.0070, the time value, is determined mostly by time left to expiration and volatility.

Figure 4-5 summarizes option classifications, which are important because in-, at- and out-of-the-money option premiums behave differently to moves in futures prices. The $.5500 call in this example is in

[2]This is not always true because changes in time or in volatility will sometimes overwhelm the effect of a move in futures prices. See Chapter 4.

the money. The $.5500 put, having no immediate intrinsic value, is out of the money. An option with a strike price equal to the futures price is at the money. Traders will refer to the $.5600 call and put in this example as at the money even though the futures price is $.5601, a tick away from the strike price.

In our D mark example with futures at .5601, a call option with a strike price of, say, $.5000 would trade for at least $.0601, its intrinsic value. To pay $.0601 or $7,512.50 ($.0601 × 125,000)[1] for an option begins to lose a basic feature of a buy option strategy: the risk is limited to the premium. The risk is still limited to the premium, but the cash payout is so high that the risk of the trade becomes similar to purchasing a futures contract. In fact, deep-in-the-money options will trade virtually tick for tick with the underlying futures contract. That is, when futures prices move by 25 ticks to $.5626, the option's premium moves by 25 ticks ($.0025) to .0626, a one-for-one relationship.

FIGURE 4-5
West German Deutsche Mark Settlement Premiums, September 9, 1987, December Options, In-, At-, and Out-of-the-Money Options

Strike Price	Settlement Premiums	Intrinsic Value	Time Value	In, Out, At
		Calls		
$.54	$.0241	$.0201	$.0040	in
.55	.0171	.0101	.0070	in
.56	.0114	.0001	.0113	at
.57	.0073	0	.0073	out
.58	.0046	0	.0046	out
.59	.0027	0	.0027	out
		Puts		
$.54	.0043	0	.0043	out
.55	.0072	0	.0072	out
.56	.0113	0	.0113	at
.57	.0170	.0099	.0071	in
.58	.0242	.0199	.0043	in
.59	.0321	.0299	.0022	in

Futures settlement = $.5601

[1]One deutschemark contract contains 125,000 D marks.

At-the-money options are about half as responsive to moves in futures prices. If futures increase by $.0020, an at-the-money call will increase by about $.0010. At-the-money options are the most uncertain as to whether they will expire in the money. Out-of-the-money options become less responsive to moves in futures. Deep out-of-the-money options may not respond at all to a move in futures prices. An option trading at .0001 or one tick may still trade at one tick even after futures prices have changed.

The responsiveness or sensitivity of option premiums to moves in futures prices is the option's *delta.* Using deltas (the changes in an option's premium due to changes in the underlying futures price), a trader can convert option positions into futures equivalents to determine overall risk of market moves.

Example: A trader who is long 100 at-the-money calls with a delta of .5 knows that the position is equivalent to being long 50 futures (100 × .5).

Option deltas are examined in more detail in Chapters 5 and 6.

Volatility

Recall that the intrinsic, or exercise, value in an option's premium is determined by the futures price relative to the strike price. What's left over or the time value is determined mostly by expected market volatility, time left to expiration.

Example: In Figure 4-6, the time value for each option in Figure 4-5 is graphed against the corresponding strike price. Notice that the maximum amount of time value occurs with the at the money option. This will always be the case. The line labeled B in Figure 4-6 illustrates the graph of time value for our D mark example. We will refer to lines A and C later.

Time value appears to trace out a probability distribution across strike prices. In fact, the at-the-money option happens to be the option with the most uncertainty as to whether it will expire in or out of the money. The market prices the at-the-money option as if it has roughly a 50-50 chance of expiring in the money. Actually, the market usually

FIGURE 4-6

West German D mark (settlement prices, September 9, 1987, December options)

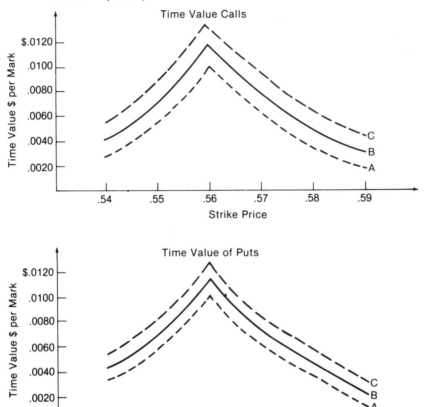

prices commodity options slightly weighted toward an increase in prices. For example, at $19.00 per barrel, crude oil future prices are more likely to reach $38.00 than $0.00 per barrel. Deep in-the-money options have a high probability that they will expire in the money. These options have very little time value attached to them relative to the at-the-money option. Deep out-of-the money options have a high probability that they will expire out of the money. These options also have very little time value attached compared with the at-the-money option.

But what determines the absolute level of time value premium? Two factors, time left to expiration and expected market volatility, are the major determinants of the amount of time value of an option.

Volatility

Volatility is simply how much prices are moving up and down, or how much prices are expected to move up and down. If the market expects high volatility, premiums will be high. If the market expects low volatility, premiums will be low. During highly volatile markets, the limited-risk feature of buy option strategies is in high demand. Traders are willing to pay up in order to take bullish positions (buy calls) or bearish positions (buy puts). Hedgers are willing to pay more for price insurance because the probability of an "accident" is high. Option sellers require higher premiums when market volatility increases. The effect of an increase in volatility is illustrated in Figure 4-6. Time value along curve C indicates premiums with higher volatility, while time value along curve A indicates lower volatility.

Markets trading quietly, without violent swings in prices, will cause option premiums to contract. Now the demand for buy option strategies is low, and the supply of traders selling options is high. Premium levels come down.

Sometimes, even though the market is moving quietly sideways, option premiums may be increasing. For example, ahead of scheduled OPEC meetings or merchandise trade reports, oil and currency markets, respectively, might trade quietly sideways as traders wait for the outcome of the event before taking positions. However, option premiums normally become more expensive before the scheduled event as hedgers and speculators take positions via buy option strategies. A hedger who is long crude oil in the cash market might have the opinion that prices will trade sharply higher or sharply lower depending on the outcome of the OPEC meeting. The trader could buy put options to cover against a fall in prices and still participate in a market rally because the hedging cost is limited to the premium paid out. Appreciation in the cash crude position will eventually more than offset the cost of the hedge. In this type of market, when scheduled OPEC meetings occur or the G-7 nations meet, option premiums can increase in value without any visible increase in price volatility.

Premiums may move from B to C in Figure 4-6 as the market charges a higher price for the limited risk feature of buy option strategies. Changes in expected market volatility can sometimes over-whelm moves in the underlying futures. However, if a trader purchases puts during a very volatile period, the puts may actually decline in value even while prices are declining. (Even though put options normally increase in value when underlying prices decline). This would happen if expected market volatility declines substantially. The contraction in the put's premium due to a decline in volatility more than offsets the increase in the premium due to a decline in price. Option traders who have seen value disappear, while calling the market correctly, are probably feeling the effects of changing market expectations of future volatility. In Figure 4-6, premiums are moving from C to A.

A seller of calls can lose money even if prices drop. Increases in volatility increase option premiums and can sometimes overwhelm the futures price effect. An extreme example of this occurred on Black Monday when the Dow Jones Average dropped more than 500 points. Some call premiums exploded even though prices dropped because market volatility increased at such a rapid rate.

Option traders track standard deviation measures of volatility, which are discussed in Chapter 6. These measures help them to deter-mine when options are relatively expensive and when they are relatively cheap and help lead to an optimal strategy. That is, they help traders determine whether options are trading along curves A, B, or C in our example. For now, the more volatility in the marketplace, or the more volatility expected, the higher option premiums will be.

Time to Expiration

The more time an option has until expiration, the more value it has, because more time means the option has a higher chance to expire in the money. The market charges for this value.

Time decay, or the loss of option value as the option nears expira-tion, accelerates as the option gets closer and closer to expiration. Figure 4-7 illustrates time decay of option premiums for an in-, at-, and out-of-the-money option. Notice that the rate of decay is not constant throughout the life of the option. Time decay is most drastic for the at-the-money call during the last two weeks of the option's life. The

FIGURE 4-7

Time decay of option premiums for an in-, at-, and
out-of-the-money option

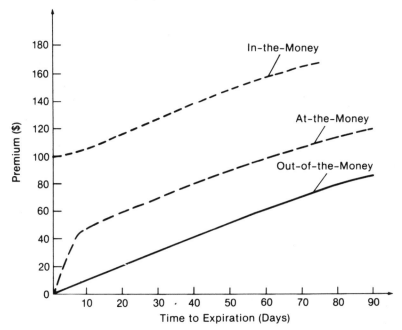

at-the-money option has the most time value and the most value to lose.
Out- and in-the-money options lose time value at a more constant rate.
These options, of course, have less time value to lose.

Time works against long option positions. A trader who buys calls
expecting prices to move higher has a time limitation. Each day that
option will lose value (everything else being equal) as expiration day
nears. Time works in favor of short option positions as options become
cheaper to buy back while time ticks away. We will examine time decay
in more detail in Chapter 7.

Interest Rates

Isolating the effect of interest rates on futures option premiums is
difficult, and often impossible, to accomplish. A change in interest rates
influences the net present value calculation of an option premium, the

cost of carrying or the cost of buying and storing a commodity, and even the actual price of the commodity. The interest rate effect on an option premium is most important in relationship to arbitrage strategies and will be discussed in Chapter 7. Most of the interest rate effect will already be incorporated in the futures price through the cost of carry. For this reason, interest rates are much more important when pricing options on cash instruments.

In this chapter, the fundamentals of option pricing have been related to futures contracts. In Chapter 5, the same is done for basic option trading strategies.

Appendix: Where to Call for Further Information on Option Contracts

NEW YORK MERCANTILE EXCHANGE	212-938-2879
Crude Oil, Heating Oil	
COFFEE, SUGAR, COCOA EXCHANGE	212-938-2845
Coffee, Sugar, Cocoa	
COMMODITY EXCHANGE	212-938-7921
Gold, Silver, Copper, Aluminum	
NEW YORK COTTON EXCHANGE	212-938-2702
Cotton, Orange Juice, Dollar Index, Five-Year Treasury Note	
NEW YORK FUTURES EXCHANGE	212-656-6072
CRB Index, NYSE Composite Index	
CHICAGO BOARD OF TRADE	312-435-3500
Corn, Wheat, Soybean, Soybean Oil, Soybean Meal, Treasury Bonds, Treasury Notes, Municipal Bonds, Silver	

CHICAGO MERCANTILE EXCHANGE   312-930-3500
    Swiss Franc, Deutsche Mark, British
    Pound, Canadian Dollar, Australian
    Dollar, Treasury Bill, Eurodollar,
    S&P 500 Index,
    Random Length Lumber,
    Live Cattle, Feeder Cattle, Live Hog,
    Pork Belly

MINNEAPOLIS GRAIN EXCHANGE   612-338-6212
    Wheat

KANSAS CITY BOARD OF TRADE   816-753-7500
    Wheat

CHAPTER 5

Futures Options Strategies

A major benefit in adding options to a hedging or trading program is increased flexibility. Option strategies allow hedgers to fine-tune price risk. With options, traders not only think in terms of bullishness and bearishness, but also in terms of intensity of market moves, time frames, and expected market volatility. There is no question that options complicate decision making when determining the optimal hedging or trading strategy. However, for the trader who is fully conversant in option strategies, market opinions are much more easily articulated as option positions.

While the number of option strategies available to traders is infinite, this chapter describes the fundamental option strategies—the simple buy call, sell call, buy put, and sell put strategies—in the context of futures trading. Next, futures option volatility and spread trades are examined. At the close of the chapter, synthetic options are discussed.[1] Each trade is dissected using profit/loss diagrams for various futures prices. Key parameters (such as maximum profit, maximum risk, and

[1]The format used borrows heavily from ''Strategies at a Glance,'' a New York Mercantile Exchange publication.

breakeven prices) are indicated for each strategy. Option premiums in our energy futures example were estimated using the Black[2] option pricing model with the following assumptions:

- Crude oil futures are at $16.00 per barrel when the trade is established.
- Volatility is 35 percent (see Chapter 7 for a discussion of volatility).
- The risk-free interest rate is 6%.
- Each option expires in 90 days.

In Chapter 7 we will introduce the concept of implied volatility that will help to sort out the many potential strategies.

LONG CALL

Recall that a long call strategy gives the holder the right to buy the futures contract at a specified price over a given period. It anticipates a rise in prices.

Example: The following long call position gives the holder the right to buy crude oil futures at $16.00 from now until 90 days from now. The buyer pays $1.09 per barrel (or $1,090.00 per contract) for this right.

Long call

Position	Premium	Dollar Premium	Delta
Buy 1 $16.00 call	$1.09	$1,090.00	+.53

Maximum Risk:	$1.09 per barrel or $1,090.00 per contract
Maximum Profit:	Unlimited on the upside
Breakeven Futures Price:	$17.09
Current Price:	$16.00

[2]See F.M. Black, "The Pricing of Commodity Contracts," *Journal of Financial Economics, January, March 1976.*

The profit/loss profile for this trade is illustrated in Figure 5-1. Along the vertical axis is the trade's profit or loss in dollars. The horizontal axis shows different futures price scenarios. The solid line traces out profit/loss levels if the trade is held to expiration while the dashed line indicates the value of the trade with 90 days until expiration. For example, if the call is purchased today and prices move up to $17.00 today, a profit can be realized by trading out of the option (dashed line). However, if prices are at $17.00 at expiration, a loss of $.09 is realized (solid line).

Let us focus on the expiration line (solid), keeping in mind that most options are traded back to the market rather than held to expiration. The option was bought with 90 days left and it is now expiration day. If futures prices are at $16.00 at expiration, the option expires worthless: The right to buy futures at $16.00, (with zero time value) has no advantage over buying futures at $16.00. However, a $1,090.00 premium was paid 90 days ago. This trade shows a loss of $1,090.00 if

FIGURE 5-1
Long call

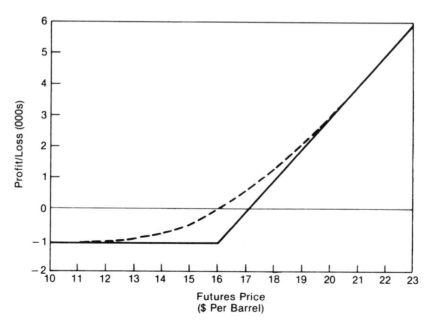

futures are at $16.00 on expiration day. If futures are trading at $19.00 on expiration day, this trade earns profits of $1,910: $19.00 − $16.00 = $3.00 − $1.09 = $1.91 × 1,000 barrels = $1,910.00.

If prices trade down to $14.00 on expiration day, the trade loses $1,090.00: the $16.00 call expires worthless; thus none of the $1,090.00 premium is recovered. Note that if prices continue to rally, profits continue to increase. Note also that as prices decline, losses reach a maximum of $1,090.00. This position has a breakeven price of $17.09, which is the premium paid plus the strike price. If held to expiration, prices must rally above $17.09 for this strategy to profit.

A trader can determine market exposure by examining option deltas. (Recall that the delta is a measure of the change in option premium due to a change in futures price.) In this example, the option's delta is + .53. A long call strategy is a bullish position. Bullish positions have positive deltas and bearish positions have negative deltas. A delta of + .53 means that if futures increase by $.10 today, the option will increase by about $.05. Trader A knows that buying ten $16.00 call options is similar (but not equal) to being long 5.3 futures contracts. Deltas are sometimes referred to as hedging ratios because a delta's reciprocal tells the hedger how many options are needed to cover a cash position fully. (Deltas and how they are calculated are discussed in more detail in Chapter 8.)

Why would a trader buy an at-the-money call? The market opinion is bullish. Call options earn profits when prices rally. But a bullish market opinion should not blindly lead a trader to a buy call strategy. The cost of the premium is an important consideration. Are options expensive or cheap? Is $1.09 per barrel too expensive to pay for a 90-day $16.00 crude oil call? If OPEC is meeting tomorrow to discuss production quotas, $1.09 may be considered cheap.

The only real way to determine if options are cheap or expensive is with 20-20 hindsight. However, a more systematic way to determine relative value is discussed in Chapter 7.

Time works against buy option strategies. In this example the entire premium is time value. The premium slowly erodes at first and then at a more rapid rate as the expiration day approaches. A decrease in volatility also works against this position. If the market is at $1.09 per barrel for a 90-day $16.00 call because the market expects volatile prices, the buyer of the call is at risk if the market reassesses expected volatility. For example, the $1.09 per barrel premium may be a good price before an OPEC meeting, but after the meeting, $1.09 may be too high as the market adjusts to a lower level of expected volatility.

The market does not give anything away for free. Even though risk is limited to $1,090.00 in this example, the trade is exposed to time ticking away and declining volatility expectations. The buyer of the call feels that the value of knowing the maximum risk ($1,090.00, in this example) more than compensates for the risk that prices may trade sideways or lower, and that volatility expectations may decline in the next 90 days.

Hedging with Long Calls

A hedger with a short cash position could buy calls to protect against a rise in prices, yet still be able to participate in lower *costs* of product if prices decline.

Example: A refiner with a desire to place a ceiling on a purchase price of crude oil could buy the $16.00 calls. The most the refiner pays is $17.09 per barrel ($16.00 strike + $1.09 premium) regardless of how high prices trade. If prices decline the refiner pays lower cash prices plus the $1.09 premium. A hedger who is bearish the market and also short the cash market may still buy calls to cover the risk of having an incorrect market opinion. Buy call strategies offer hedgers unlimited protection when prices rally, once the premium is covered.

SHORT CALL

The other side of a long call position is a short call, which is created with the expectation of declining prices.

Example: In the following position, a trader has received $.70 per barrel or $700.00 in return to sell the obligation to futures at $17.00 per barrel at any time within the next 90 days, should the call buyer exercise.

Short call

Position	Premium	Dollar Premium	Delta
Sell 1 $17 call	$.70	$700.00	− .40

Maximum Risk:	Unlimited on the upside
Maximum Profit:	$.70 per barrel or $700.00 per contract
Breakeven Futures Price:	$17.70
Current Price:	$16.00

The profit/loss diagram of this trade is illustrated in Figure 5-2. Prices are currently at $16.00. If, at expiration, prices are still at $16.00, the trader earns the entire $700.00 because the holder of a $17.00 call will not exercise and buy futures at $17.00 when prices are at $16.00, so the option expires worthless. In fact, if prices trade at $17.00 or below at expiration, the trader earns $700.00. (There are times when out-of-the-money options will be exercised. See Chapter 10 for a discussion on getting "pinned.") The horizontal solid line in Figure 5-2 at $17.00 and below indicates that no matter how low prices go, a short call only earns, at most, the premium. If prices rally to $20.00, at expiration, this trade loses $2.30 per barrel or $2,300.00. The call option is exercised; the short call position is converted into a short futures position at $17.00. With prices now at $20.00, the trader is losing $3.00 per barrel. Subtracting the $.70 premium received yields a loss of $2.30 per barrel or $2,300.00. Short option strategies have limited profit potential with unlimited risk. The breakeven price at expiration is $17.70, $17.00 strike plus $.70 premium.

A short call strategy is a neutral to bearish strategy. Maximum profits are earned in this example if prices remain below $17.00. The delta for this trade is − .40, meaning that a $.10 increase in futures price will cause this trade to lose $.04. Selling 10 of these options would indicate a futures equivalent position of − 4.0, or being short 4 futures.

Traders selling calls expect prices to move sideways to down. They would do the same to take advantage of a decline in volatility expectations.

Time works in favor of short option strategies. As the option moves closer to expiration, time value disappears at an increasing rate.

FIGURE 5-2
Short call

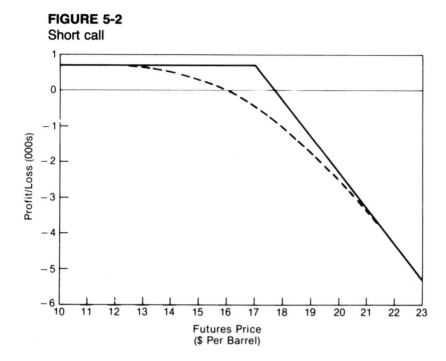

Futures Price
($ Per Barrel)

Time decay is helping the short option trade. Declining volatility also works in favor of short option positions. If the market lowers its expectation of future volatility, option premiums will contract.

Selling options has unlimited risk, and limited profits. But traders will assume the risk if they are slightly bearish the market and or feel that option premiums are high.

Hedging with Short Calls

Since a short call is a bearish position, hedgers with long cash positions could get price protection using short calls. Much hedging is inventory hedging, meaning that a portfolio of stocks, bonds, corn, soybeans, gold, silver, crude oil, and so on is hedged by selling futures. Selling futures profits as prices decline, offsetting the decline in inventory value. Selling calls will be a better hedge during times of sideways to slightly lower prices.

Example: An oil producer could sell $17.00 crude oil calls for $.70 per barrel against future production. Selling calls against a long cash position or a long futures position is considered a *covered call;* selling options without such positions is regarded as *naked.* If prices increase by $1.00 to $17.00 at expiration, the producer sells oil at $17.70, a $17.00 market price plus the $.70 premium. If prices decline, the producer sells oil at the cash price plus the $.70 premium. The short call acts as a hedge against lower prices but only to the extent of the premium received. If prices drop below $.70 in this example, the short call no longer protects a further decline.

COVERED CALL

Future call options may be covered by a long cash position, a long futures position, or a short call position. Covered call strategies anticipate an upside movement in prices.

Example: A trader buys a futures contract at $16.00 and sells a $17.00 call for $.70.

Covered call

Position	Premium	Dollar Premium	Delta
Buy 1 $16.00 futures	N/A	N/A	+1.00
Sell 1 $17.00 call	$.70	$700.00	−.40
Net credit	$.70	$700.00	N/A
Net delta	N/A	N/A	+.60

Maximum Risk:	Unlimited on downside
Maximum Profit:	$1.70 per barrel or $1,700.00 per covered call
Breakeven Futures Price:	$15.30
Current Price:	$16.00

The profit/loss diagram is illustrated in Figure 5-3. If prices rally to $17.00 at expiration, the trader earns $1.00 from the futures side and the entire $.70 premium for a total of $1.70. If prices rally further to $20.00

FIGURE 5-3
Covered call

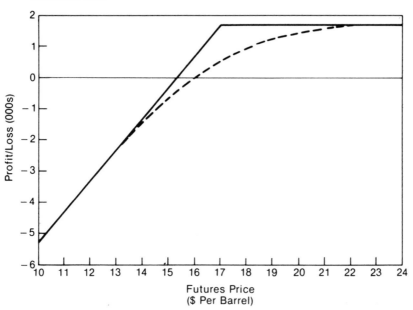

at expiration, the trader earns $4.00 from the futures position, but loses $2.30 from the option trade ($20.00 − $17.00 − $.70 = $2.30) for a net profit of $1.70. No matter how high futures trade, further gains on the futures side are offset by losses on the option trade, and the net profit is $1.70. If prices trade lower to $14.00 at expiration, losses accrue. At $14.00, the futures side loses $2.00 and the options trade earns $.70 for a net loss of $1.30. The option premium offers some downside protection to the long futures position, but risk is unlimited if prices move lower. The breakeven point is $15.30 or $.70 below current prices.

A trader might execute a covered call to take advantage of high premiums. The market opinion would be neutral to slightly bullish. If futures prices move sideways, the entire premium is earned. If prices move higher, profit increase to some maximum level. The risk is if prices move sharply lower.

The combined delta of this trade is +.60. If prices increase by $.30, this position's value will increase by about $.18. A long futures position has a delta of +1.00. A $.30 move up in price shows an equal

$.30 profit on the futures position. The $17.00 call has a delta of − .40. If prices move up by $.30, the call should lose about $.12 (.30 × .40). The total trade earns $.30 from the futures minus $.12 from the call for a net increase of $.18. Deltas are always changing with changes in prices, volatility, and time, but they are useful for indicating sensitivity of a position to a move in market prices.

Because a covered call involves selling options, the passing of time works in favor of a covered call. A covered call writer benefits from a decline in volatility.

CALL RATIO WRITE

This strategy takes advantage of high-option premiums by selling multiple call options for each long futures position.

Example: Two $18.00 calls are sold against a long futures contract. Maximum profits occur if prices rally to $18.00 at expiration. Risk is unlimited if prices rally or decline sharply.

Call ratio write

Position	Premium	Dollar Premium	Delta
Buy 1 futures	$16.00	N/A	+1.00
Sell 2 $18.00 calls	$.43	$430.00	− .28
Net credit	$.86	$860.00	N/A
Net delta	N/A	N/A	+.44

Maximum Profit:	$2.86 per barrel or $2,860.00
Maximum Risk:	Unlimited on upside and downside
Breakeven Futures Prices:	$20.86 and $15.14
Current Price:	$16.00

See Figure 5-4. If prices are at $18.00 on expiration day, the $18.00 calls expire worthless and the trade earns $.43 or $430.00 per option ($860.00 total).

FIGURE 5-4
Call ratio write

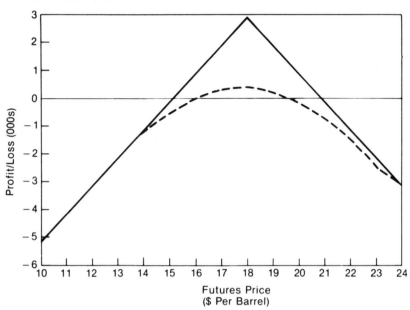

Futures Price
($ Per Barrel)

Profits also are earned on the long futures contract established at $16.00. However, since two call options were sold, further price strength cuts into profits. At $20.00, the $18.00 call loses $2.00 ($20.00 − $18.00) minus $.43 or $1.57 per barrel. Two $18.00 calls lose $3.14. The futures contract earns $4.00, so all the trade still profits. Further increases in prices will eventually turn the trade into a loser because one futures contract is offsetting only one short call. The other short call is exposed. The breakeven price on the upside is $20.86: the futures profits by $4.86 (20.86 − $16.00); the two options lose a total of $4.86 ($2.86 loss per option × 2 options − $.86 premium received). This trade has taken in a total of $.86 or $86.00 of premium (2 × $430.00). The long futures contract has $.86 of downside protection. The breakeven point on the downside is $15.14: $16.00 − $.86.

This trade takes advantage of the fact that the futures contract with a delta of + 1.00 can cover multiple options with deltas of less than 1. The deltas of the $18 calls are − .28 each, or − .56 for two. The delta for the entire position is + .44, a slightly bullish strategy. Because of the potential risk of multiple short option positions, ratio writes need to be monitored very closely. In Chapter 9 on portfolio analysis, some pitfalls of selling many options with low-delta exposure are discussed.

Short option positions benefit from declining expectations of market volatility as well as from the passage of time.

LONG PUT

Long put positions are created in anticipation of a downside price movement.

Example: The following position gives the buyer the right to sell futures at $16.00 for 90 days. The buyers pay $1.09 per barrel or $1,090.00 for the right.

Long put

Position	Premium	Dollar Premium	Delta
Buy 1 $16.00 put	$1.09	$1,090.00	− .47

Maximum Risk:	$1.09 per barrel or $1,090.00 per contract
Maximum Profit:	Unlimited on the downside
Breakeven Futures Price:	$14.91
Current Price:	$16.00

Figure 5-5 illustrates a long put strategy. If prices are still $16.00 on expiration day, the trade loses the entire $1,090.00 premium. The $16.00 put expires worthless. If prices rally to $20.00 by expiration, the put expires worthless. All the $1,090.00 premium is lost, but no more. Losses are limited to the premium regardless how high prices go.

Prices trading at $14.00 at expiration indicate a profit of $.91 per barrel. The trader can exercise the $16.00 put and buy futures at $14.00, thus, earning $2.00 per barrel. Subtracting the premium paid out yields a $.91 profit. The breakeven price at expiration, $14.91, is calculated by subtracting the premium from the strike price.

Long put strategies are bearish positions. This particular option

FIGURE 5-5
Long put

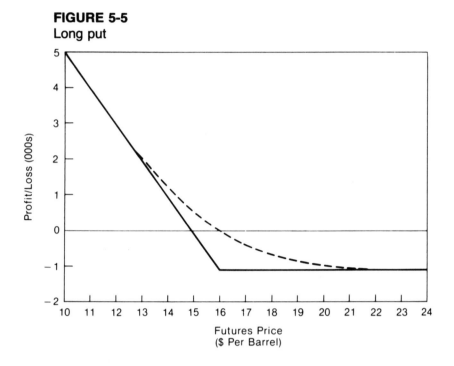

has a delta of $-.47$. If prices decline by $.20, the position will earn roughly $.09. A long put trade is exposed to the passage of time and to declining expectations of market volatility. As expiration nears, the option's time value rapidly disappears. If the market expects the market to trade quietly, option premiums will contract. The put buyer has swapped unlimited price risk for time and volatility risk.

Hedging with Long Puts

A hedger who is long inventory or who expects to be long the cash market can buy puts to protect against a decline in prices. Long puts earn unlimited profits as prices continue to decline. (Put profits are actually limited because prices can't trade below zero.) Long puts offer unlimited protection against declines in inventory value. If prices rally, the hedger can still participate because eventually, the appreciation in inventory more than offsets the fixed cost (premium) of the hedge. Long put strategies offer downside protection and upside participation to hedgers.

The risk, of course, is that the hedger pays so much for the put option that a significant move in prices is required to receive the benefits. The put premium in this example is $1.09 per barrel. Would an oil producer pay $1.09 for 90 days of price protection? If prices are highly volatile, he might. If the outlook were for sideways to slightly higher or lower price movement, he probably would not. Volatility opinions are important when trading options. The optimal strategy for the hedger will depend on market opinion and volatility opinion, as well as the ability to assume price risk. (In Chapter 7, some tools are discussed that will help determine which strategy is optimal.)

SHORT PUT

Short put positions anticipate upside price movements.

Example: The put seller with the following position receives $640.00 in return for the obligation to buy futures at $15.00 within 90 days should the put buyer decide to exercise. Because the put seller may have to assume a long futures position, short puts profit when prices rally.

Short put

Position	Premium	Dollar Premium	Delta
Sell 1 $15.00 put	$.64	$640.00	+ .32

Maximum Risk:	Unlimited on the downside
Maximum Return:	$.64 per barrel or $640.00 per contract
Breakeven Futures Price:	$14.36
Current Price:	$16.00

Refer to Figure 5-6. If prices settle at $15.00 at expiration day, the $15.00 put expires worthless and the put seller profits the entire premium, or $640.00. Regardless of how high prices trade, this position

FIGURE 5-6
Short put

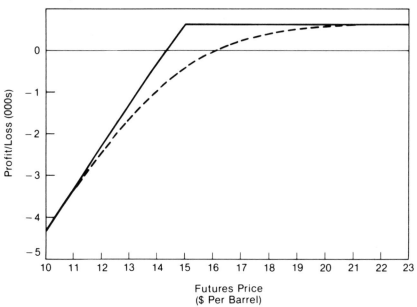

Futures Price
($ Per Barrel)

has a maximum profit of $640.00. If the market moves lower, this position has unlimited exposure. If prices settle at $13.00 at expiration, a loss of $1.36 per barrel ($15.00 strike − 13.00 futures − $.64 premium) is realized. The breakeven point is $4.36 ($15.00 strike − $.64 premium).

This position has a delta of + .32. Short puts earn profits as prices rally. A trader would sell a put because of neutral to slightly higher price expectations, and because premiums are thought to be rich.

Time works in favor of short option positions. Time decay reduces option premiums slowly at first but increases as expiration day nears. Decreasing volatility also favors short-option trades. If the market ⌐xpects little price volatility, option premiums will contract.

Hedging with Short Puts

Writing puts gives some protection if prices increase. Such strategies work well for hedgers who are short the cash market. These might include corporate money managers who know they must purchase stocks or bonds three months from now, or an airline company that needs to lock in future fuel requirements, or an importer that might require foreign exchange in the next quarter. All these hedgers have exposure to an increase in prices.

Example: In the preceding example, a hedger can reduce cash purchases by the amount of the premium, or $.64. However, upside protection is limited to the premium received. If prices decline, the hedger pays the strike price minus the premium. There is no participation in buying cheaper oil if prices drop sharply.

A hedger would sell puts only to protect a short cash exposure only if premiums are high and future market volatility is expected to be low. Otherwise, a buy call strategy or a buy futures strategy is more appropriate for the long hedger.

COVERED PUT

Puts sold against a short cash position or against a short futures position are covered. This is a bearish position.

Example: In the following position, one futures contract is sold at $16.00, and a $15.00 put is written for $.64. The position makes money if prices go down.

Covered put

Position	Premium	Dollar Premium	Delta
Sell 1 futures at $16.00	N/A	N/A	−1.00
Sell 1 $15.00 put	$.64	$640.00	+.32
Net credit	$.64	$640.00	N/A
Net delta	N/A	N/A	−.68

Maximum Risk:	Unlimited on the upside
Maximum Profit:	$1.64 per barrel or $1,640.00
Breakeven Futures Price:	$16.64
Current Price:	$16.00

FIGURE 5-7
Covered put

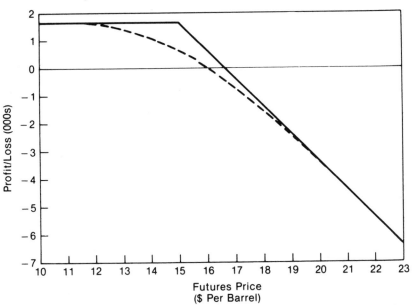

Futures Price
($ Per Barrel)

Refer to Figure 5-7. At expiration, a $15.00 futures price indicates profits of $1.64. The futures side earns $1.00 ($16.00 − $15.00). The option expires worthless for a profit of $.64. If prices decline to $13.00, the futures profits by $3.00, but the option loses $1.36 ($15.00 strike − $13.00 futures − $.64 premium). The net profit is $1.64 no matter how low futures go because profits from the short futures contract offset losses on the short put. If prices rally, risk is unlimited. Losses accrue on the short futures contract with a maximum of only $.64 protection from the short put. If, for example, prices are at $19.00 at expiration, the futures contract loses $3.00 ($19.00 − $16.00), and the put profits $.64 for a net loss of $2.36. The breakeven point in this example is $16.64 ($16.00 futures plus $.64 premium).

The entire trade exhibits a delta of − .64, indicating a bearish position. A short put by itself is bullish (note the + .32 delta), but when combined with a short futures, the trade is bearish. Time works in favor of this position (or any short option trade), as does declining market volatility.

VOLATILITY TRADES

Some option strategies are market neutral in the sense that the position can earn profits if prices move sharply in either direction. A trader might have the opinion that prices are likely to move in either direction due to some scheduled economic release. The trader could buy puts and calls with the expectation that a violent move in prices will earn profits on one side, more than offsetting losses on the other side. For example, if Treasury bond prices rally due to the release of an employment report, the profits accruing to the long call position could more than offset the losses in the long put position. These option strategies are classified as long volatility trades because profits are earned when prices move sharply in either direction.

Conversely, other option strategies are market neutral because maximum profits are earned when prices remain at current levels. A trader with the opinion that prices will move relatively sideways and that option premiums are expensive can sell puts and calls. If prices do move sideways, and time value ticks away, the trader could buy back the options at lower prices. These strategies are classified as short volatility trades because they profit when price movement and expected price movement is slight.

Long Straddles

One way to take advantage of an expected violent market move in either direction is to buy straddles. Recall that a long straddle is a long put and a long call with the same strike price.

Example: In the following position, a trader pays $2.18 per barrel or $2,180.00 for a $16.00 put and a $16.00 call.

Long straddle

Position	Premium	Dollar Premium	Delta
Buy 1 $16.00 call	$1.09	$1,090.00	+ .53
Buy 1 $16.00 put	$1.09	$1,090.00	− .47
Net debit	$2.18	$2,180.00	N/A
Net delta	N/A	N/A	+ .06

Maximum Risk:	$2.18 per barrel or $2,180.00
Maximum Profit:	Unlimited in either direction
Breakeven Futures Prices:	$18.18 and $13.82
Current Price:	$16.00

Refer to Figure 5-8. The ideal situation is for prices to break sharply away from $16.00. The worst situation would be for prices to sit around $16.00. Maximum risk is limited to $2,180.00 and occurs if prices are at $16.00 at expiration.

Time works against long option strategies, and certainly against long straddles. For this reason, long straddles are usually not held to expiration. A decline in expected volatility will also work against long straddles. A currency trader who is long Japanese yen straddles ahead of a merchandise trade report might show significant losses if the actual number is not a surprise to the market. The release of the number could reduce the expected volatility in the marketplace, thus putting downward pressure on premiums and straddles.

FIGURE 5-8
Long straddle

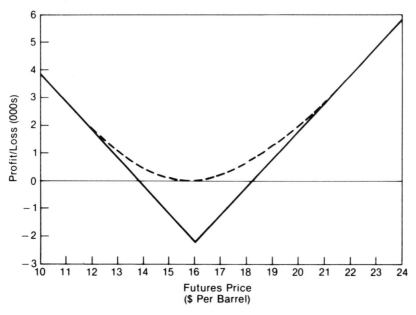

Futures Price
($ Per Barrel)

Notice that the delta of this trade is +.06, a relatively neutral market position. However, if prices rally, the delta value will get more and more positive. If prices decline, the delta value will become more and more negative. This phenomenon is referred to as *long gamma*. (Gamma is discussed in more detail in Chapter 8.)

Short Straddle

One way to take advantage of expensive option premiums and markets that are expected to trade quietly is to sell straddles, that is, sell puts and calls with the same strike prices (the opposite of the long straddle).

Example: A $16.00 call and a $16.00 put are sold for a total premium of $2.18 per barrel or $2,180.00.

Short straddle

Position	Premium	Dollar Premium	Delta
Sell 1 $16.00 call	$1.09	$1,090.00	− .53
Sell 1 $16.00 put	$1.09	$1,090.00	+ .47
Net credit	$2.18	$2,180.00	N/A
Net delta	N/A	N/A	− .60

Maximum Risk:	Unlimited in either direction
Maximum Profit:	$2.18 per barrel or $2,180.00
Breakeven Futures Prices:	$18.18 and $13.82
Current Price:	$16.00

Refer to Figure 5-9. The maximum profit that can be earned in this trade is $2,180.00. This occurs if prices are $16.00 at expiration. Losses are unlimited if prices move sharply away from $16.00.

The position's delta is − .06, relatively neutral. If prices rally, this position's delta will become more and more negative. If prices decline, the position's delta becomes more and more positive. The weakness of using only delta as a measure of market exposure is illustrated in a short straddle. In this example, selling 100 straddles would indicate a delta

FIGURE 5-9
Short straddle

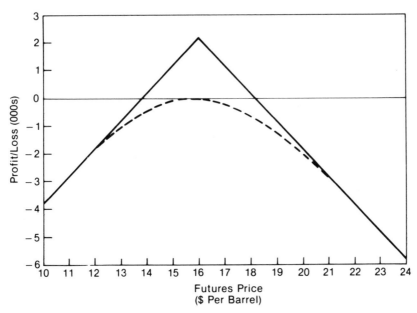

position of −6 (100 × .06) or short an equivalent 6 futures. However, the actual exposure can become 100 futures equivalents if prices move sharply in either direction. (More is said on this gamma effect in Chapter 8.)

The passage of time works in favor of short straddles, as does a decline in expected market volatility.

Long Strangle

Another way to take advantage of an increase in volatility is to buy strangles, which can be established at a significantly lower cost than a long straddle. A *long strangle* consists of buying a put and a call with different strike prices.

Example: A trader pays a total of $1.34 for a $17.00 call and a $15.00 put.

Long strangle

Position	Premium	Dollar Premium	Delta
Buy 1 $17.00 call	$.70	$700.00	+.40
Buy 1 $15.00 put	$.64	$640.00	−.32
Net debit	$1.34	$1,340.00	N/A
Net delta	N/A	N/A	+.08

Maximum Risk:	$1.34 per barrel or $1,340.00
Maximum Profit:	Unlimited in either direction
Breakeven Futures Prices:	$18.34 and $13.66
Current Price:	$16.00

Refer to Figure 5-10. At expiration, breakeven points are at $18.34 ($7.00 strike plus $1.34) and $13.66 ($15.00 strike minus $1.34.)

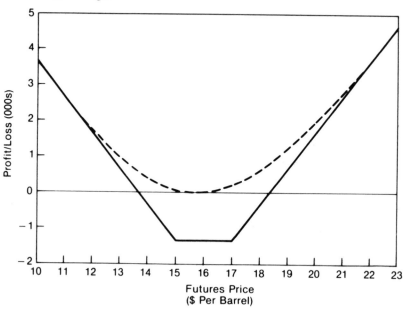

FIGURE 5-10
Long strangle

Maximum risk is $1.34, while profits are unlimited. Both options expire worthless if prices are between $15.00 and $17.00 at expiration. The long strangle holder would like to see prices break out in either direction, that is, an increase in volatility. This position's delta is +.08, a relatively neutral position. Time works against long strangles, as does a decline in volatility.

Short Strangle

A short strangle consists of selling a put and a call with different strike prices. The trade is established with a market opinion that price volatility will decline and that premiums are currently high.

Example: Refer to the following position:

Short strangle

Position	Premium	Dollar Premium	Delta
Sell 1 $17.00 call	$.70	$700.00	− .40
Sell 1 $15.00 put	$.64	$640.00	+ .32
Net credit	$1.34	$1,340.00	N/A
Net delta	N/A	N/A	− .08

Maximum Risk:	Unlimited in either direction
Maximum Profit:	$1.34 per barrel or $1,340.00
Breakeven Futures Prices:	$18.34 and $13.66
Current Price:	$16.00

Figure 5-11 illustrates this short straddle trade. The position profits the entire $1.34 premium at expiration if prices remain within $17.00 and $15.00. Within these prices both options expire worthless. Profits are limited to $1.34, while risk is unlimited if prices break out in either direction. Time works in favor of short option trades, as does a decline in volatility.

FIGURE 5-11
Short strangle

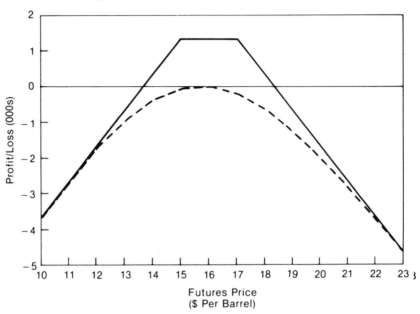

OPTION SPREADS

Sometimes a trader likes the idea of the limited risk feature of buy option strategies but doesn't want to pay for the entire premium. Another trader might like the idea of selling options and receiving the premium but doesn't want to face unlimited risk. These traders could establish one of many option spreads.

Bull Call Spread

A *bull call spread* is buying a call with a lower strike price and selling a call with a higher strike price. The maximum risk of such a spread is the premium paid out.

Example: A trader is bullish the market, desires a limited risk trade, but doesn't want to pay out much premium. With futures at $16.00, this trader could buy a $16.00 call for $1.09 per barrel and at the same time sell a $17.00 call for $.70. The total net outlay is $.39 per barrel or $390.00 per contract, much less than if the trader had only purchased the $16.00 call.

Bull call spread

Position	Premium	Dollar Premium	Delta
Buy 1 $16.00 call	$1.09	$1,090.00	+.53
Sell 1 $17.00 call	$.70	$700.00	−.40
Net debit	$.39	$390.00	N/A
Net delta	N/A	N/A	+.13

Maximum Risk:	$.39 per barrel or $390.00
Maximum Profit:	$.61 per barrel or $610.00
Breakeven Futures Price:	$16.39
Current Price:	$16.00

Examine the profit/loss profile of this bull call spread in (Figure 5-12). At expiration, assume that future prices are at $16.00 per barrel.

FIGURE 5-12
Bull call spread

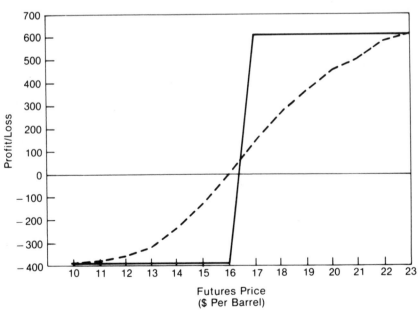

Both the $16.00 call and the $17.00 call expire worthless. Losses are equal to the entire $390.00 originally paid. If prices traded down to $15.00, both options would still expire worthless, and losses would still be $390.00.

At expiration, if prices rally to $17.00, this position profits $.61 per barrel or $610 per contract. The $17.00 call expires worthless, the $16.00 call is now worth +$1.00 or $1,000.00 per contract, and the position cost $390.00 to establish. If prices rally further to $20.00, this position still profits only by $610.00. The short $17.00 call is worth −$3.00, or $3,000.00 per contract; the long $16.00 call is worth +$4,000.00. After the original cost of $390.00 is subtracted, maximum profits are limited to $610.00. This is the trade-off: a bull call spread requires less cash outlay than does a long call strategy, but profits are limited to the difference in strike prices and the premium paid.

The net delta of this trade is +.13. This is a mildly bullish position, less buliish than the long call by itself. Selling the $17.00 call subtracts deltas from the net position.

A bull call spread allows a trader to establish a long market position with limited risk and low cost. Time and volatility effects are lessened on the spread position because one option is bought and one is sold. However, prices need to move higher to realize profits. Sideways movement of prices works against this trade.

Bear Put Spread

Analogous to the bull call spread is the *bear put spread*, which involves buying a put with a higher strike price and selling a put with a lower strike price. This type of spread has a maximum risk limited to the net cost of establishing the spread and a maximum profit equal to the difference in strike prices minus the cost of establishing the trade.

Example: A trader is interested in establishing a bearish position at low cost and low risk. This trader could buy a $15.00 put for $640.00 and sell a $14.00 put for $320.00, a net debit of $320.00.

Bear put spread

Position	Premium	Dollar Premium	Delta
Buy 1 $15.00 put	$.64	$640.00	−.32
Sell 1 $14.00 put	$.32	$320.00	+.20
Net debit	$.32	$320.00	N/A
Net delta	N/A	N/A	−.12

Maximum Risk:	$.32 per barrel or $320.00
Maximum Profit:	$.68 per barrel or $680.00
Breakeven Futures Price:	$14.68
Current Price:	$16.00

Refer to Figure 5-13. If prices are trading at $15.00 and above, both options expire worthless. The trade loses a maximum $320.00. If

FIGURE 5-13
Bear put spread

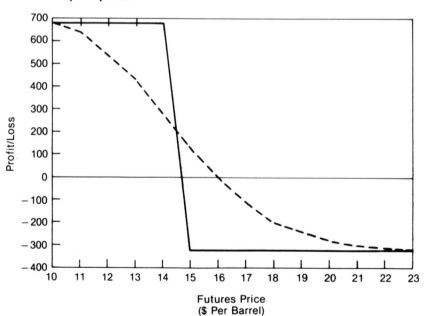

Futures Price
($ Per Barrel)

prices decline to $13.00 the trade profits; the $15.00 put is worth $2.00 per barrel or +$2,000.00 and the short $14.00 put loses $1,000.00. Subtracting the initial cost of the trade, $320.00, yields a maximum profit of $680.00.

The delta of this trade is − .12, a mildly bearish position. The long $15.00 put by itself exhibits a delta of − .32, but the short $14.00 put, a bullish position, increases the overall delta to − .12. The passage of time will erode the value of this trade, but the time effect is less when compared to the long put strategy. Time works against the long $15.00 put but in favor of the short $14.00 put. Since premium is paid out, the passage of time has an overall negative effect on this position. Prices do need to trade lower for this trade to profit; sideways to higher price movement works against this position.

Bear Call Spread

Bear call spreads consist of selling calls with lower strike prices and buying calls with higher strike prices. A trader would establish a bear call spread to take advantage of premiums being very high: selling options in return for high premiums. Other calls with higher strikes are bought to reduce the risk of holding short options. Or the trader's market opinion may be neutral to only slightly bearish, depending on what options are bought and sold. A bear call spread could earn maximum profits when prices exhibit sideways movement. These spreads have profits limited to the amount of premium received. Maximum risk is limited to the difference in strike prices minus the premium received.

Example: A trader sells a $17.00 call for $.70 per barrel or $700.00 per contract and buys an $18.00 call for $.43 or $430.00 per contract. The trader receives a $270.00 net credit.

Bear call spread

Position	Premium	Dollar Premium	Delta
Sell 1 $17.00 call	$.70	$700.00	− .40
Buy 1 $18.00 call	$.43	$430.00	+ .28
Net credit	$.27	$270.00	N/A
Net delta	N/A	N/A	− .12

Maximum Risk:	$.73 per barrel or $730.00
Maximum Profit:	$.27 per barrel or $270.00
Brekeven Futures Price:	$17.27
Current Price:	$16.00

Refer to Figure 5-14. If prices stay at or below $17.00, both options expire worthless and the trader profits the entire $270.00. If prices move above $18.00 at expiration the trade loses $730.00, but no more. For example, at $20.00 the short $17.00 call is worth $-$3,000.00. The $18.00 call is worth $+$2,000.00 for a loss of $1,000.00. Add to this the $270.00 net credit received when the trade was established for a total loss of $730.00.

The delta of this position is $-.12$, a slightly bearish position. However, a weakness in using only delta is illustrated. Our example of a bear put spread also had a delta of $-.12$. With prices at $16.00, the bear put spread required a drop in prices to $14.68 at expiration to breakeven

FIGURE 5-14
Bear call spread

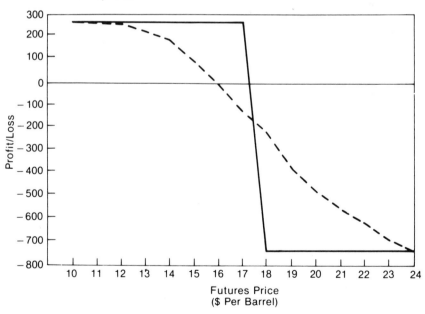

($15.00 strike − .32 net debit). Profits require a further drop in price. The bear call spread, however, would earn maximum profits if prices remain at $16.00 until expiration. Delta is a dynamic concept which only tells a small part of the risk story.

Time works in favor of this position. The net premium is a credit; as time passes, both options lose value. Since the short option has more value to lose, time passing helps to reduce its value more than on the long option.

Bull Put Spread

A trader with a neutral to slightly bullish market outlook might establish bull put spreads. A bull put spread consists of selling a put with a high strike price and buying a put with a low strike price. The trader may feel that option premiums are relatively high, but does not want to take on the unlimited risk of being naked short options.

Example: A trader sells a $16.00 put for $1.09 per barrel or $1,090.00 and buys a $15.00 put $.64 per barrel or $640.00. The trader receives $450.00, a net credit.

Bull put spread

Position	Premium	Dollar Premium	Delta
Buy 1 $15.00 put	$.64	$640.00	− .32
Sell 1 $16.00 put	$1.09	$1,090.00	+ .47
Net credit	$.45	$450.00	N/A
Net delta	N/A	N/A	+ .15

Maximum Risk:	$.55 per barrel or $550.00
Maximum Profit:	$.45 per barrel or $450.00
Breakeven Futures Price:	$15.55
Current Price:	$16.00

Refer to Figure 5-15. If prices drop to $15.00 at expiration, the $15.00 put expires worthless, but the short $16.00 put loses $1,000.00. The net loss is only $550.00 because the trader received $450.00 to

FIGURE 5-15
Bull put spread

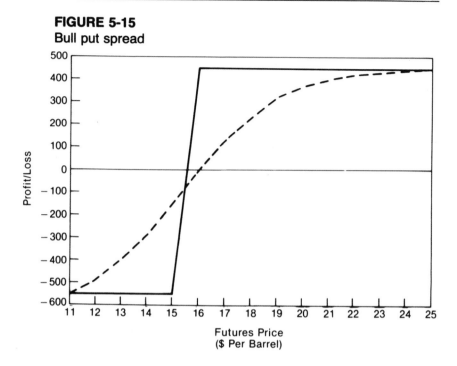

Futures Price
($ Per Barrel)

establish this trade. If prices drop farther, the maximum loss is $550.00. At $16.00, the trade profits by $450.00. Both options expire worthless, and the trader keeps the $450.00 net credit. Maximum profits of a bull put spread are equal to the net credit while maximum losses are equal to the difference in strike prices minus the net credit.

The net delta of this trade is + .15, or a slightly bullish position. Prices in this example, however, need only to remain at $16.00 for maximum profits. The passage of time works in favor of this position because the higher-priced option is sold. There is more short option premium than long option premium.

Long Butterfly

A *long butterfly* contains two short options at a middle strike price, one long option at a lower strike, and one long option at a higher strike. Options are either all calls or all puts. Strike prices are equidistant from each other. This trade may be seen as a combination of a bull call (put) spread and a bear call (put) spread.

Butterflies are usually only traded by locals because of their low transaction costs. Many traders leg into butterflies, always trying to establish the trade at a net credit.

Example: Two $16.00 calls are sold for $1,090.00 each, one $15.00 call is bought for $1,620.00 and a $17.00 call is bought for $700.00. The net payout is only $140.00, which is also the maximum risk.

Long butterfly

Position	Premium	Dollar Premium	Delta
Buy 1 $15.00 call	$1.62	$1,620.00	+ .68
Sell 2 $16.00 call	$1.09	$1,090.00	− .53
Buy 1 $17.00 call	$ .70	$ 700.00	+ .40
Net debit	$ .14	$ 140.00	N/A
Net delta	N/A	N/A	+ .02

Maximum Risk:	$.14 per barrel or $140.00
Maximum Profit:	$.86 points or $860.00
Breakeven Futures Prices:	$15.14 and $16.86
Current Price:	$16.00

Refer to Figure 5-16. Losses accrue if prices trade away from the middle strike at expiration. For instance, at $18.00, the $15.00 call is worth $3.00 per barrel or $3,000.00, the $16.00 call is losing $2.00 per barrel or $4,000.00 for two contracts, and the $17.00 call is worth $1.00 per barrel or $1,000.00 for a total net of zero. At $18.00, this trade loses only $140.00 the initial cost of the trade. At $14.00, all options expire worthless, and $140.00 is the net loss. Maximum profits occur when prices are at $16.00 at expiration. The $16.00 and $17.00 calls expire worthless. The long $15.00 call earns $6,000.00 per barrel or $1,000.00. After subtracting the cost of the trade, the maximum net gain

FIGURE 5-16
Long butterfly

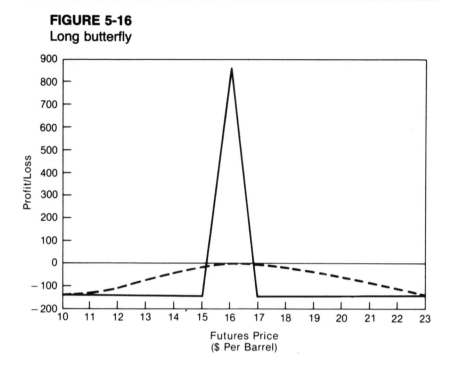

Futures Price
($ Per Barrel)

is $860.00. The position delta is +.02, indicating a market neutral position.

Long Condor

A *long condor* is similar to a long butterfly except that the two short options have different strike prices. Condors are mainly traded by locals because of their low transaction costs. Usually traders won't approach the market looking to put on a condor, but after active trading, may actually end up with a series of condors or butterflies.

Example: One $16.00 call and one $17.00 call are sold while a $15.00 call and an $18.00 call are bought.

Long condor

Position	Premium	Dollar Premium	Delta
Buy 1 $15.00 call	$1.62	$1,620.00	+ .68
Sell 1 $16.00 call	$1.09	$1,090.00	− .53
Sell 1 $17.00 call	$ .70	$ 700.00	− .40
Buy 1 $18,00 call	$ .43	$ 430.00	+ .28
Net debit	$ .26	$ 260.00	N/A
Net delta	N/A	N/A	+ .03

Maximum Risk:	$.26 per barrel or $260.00
Maximum Profit:	$.74 per barrel or $740.00
Breakeven Futures Prices:	$15.26 and $17.74
Current Price:	$16.00

Refer to Figure 5-17. Maximum risks are limited to the net premium paid, or $260.00. Maximum profits are realized when prices are

FIGURE 5-17
Long condor

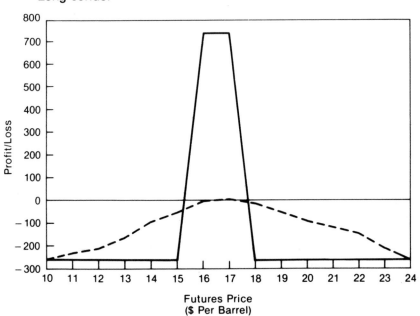

Futures Price
($ Per Barrel)

between the two middle strike prices, $16.00 and $17.00. For example, if futures are trading at $16.00 at expiration, the $16.00, $17.00, and $18.00 calls expire worthless. The long $15.00 call is worth $1,000.00. After subtracting the cost of the trade, $260.00, a profit of $740.00 is realized.

Calendar Spreads

Time, calendar, or *horizontal spreads* are put on to take advantage of the rapid decay in a nearby option relative to an option with longer time to expiration. For example, a December $5,400.00 Swiss franc call could be sold against a long March $54.00 call. The idea is that the rapid time decay of the December option will more than offset the slower time decay in the March option.

Trading calendar spreads in commodity options is complicated by constantly changing spread values among the different months traded. For example, new crop futures versus old crop futures for soybeans, wheat, or corn can exhibit highly volatile spread values. Crude oil intermonth spreads are constantly changing, and these volatile spread values can overwhelm the time effect of options. (Calendar spreads are examined in more detail in Chapter 9 on portfolio analysis.)

OTHER SPREADS

Call Ratio Backspread

A *call ratio backspread,* involves selling fewer calls at a low strike price and buying more calls at a high strike price. Some traders like to leg into these spreads and try to put them on for a net credit. If prices drop, the trader makes at least the net credit. Legging into spreads, however, can be very risky.

Example: Three $16.00 calls are sold and five $17.00 calls are bought. A total of $3,270.00 is taken in for selling three calls and $3,500.00 is paid out to buy the five calls, for a net payout of $230.00.

Call ratio backspread

Position	Premium	Dollar Premium	Delta
Sell 3 $16.00 calls	$1.09	$1,090.00	−.53
Buy 5 $17.00 calls	$ .70	$ 700.00	+.40
Net debit	N/A	$ 230.00	N/A
Net delta	N/A	N/A	+.41

Maximum Risk:	$3,230.00
Maximum Profit:	Unlimited on the upside
Breakeven Futures Price:	$18.62
Current Price:	$16.00

Refer to Figure 5-18. Profit potential for this trade is unlimited when prices rally sharply. Although the breakeven futures price is $18.62 at expiration, this trade (as are most option trades) will be removed well in advance. Prices need not move up to $18.62 to show

FIGURE 5-18
Call ratio backspread

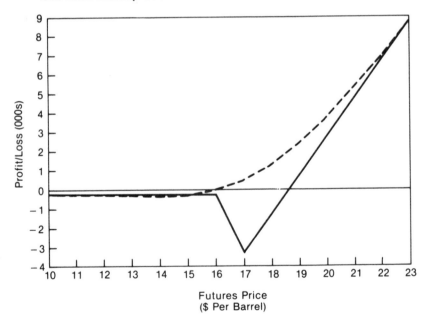

Futures Price
($ Per Barrel)

profits. It is constructive, however, to see where profits and losses accrue at various futures prices at expiration. At $19.00, the five long $17.00 calls are worth $2.00 per barrel for a total of $10,000.00. The three short $16.00 calls show a loss of $3.00 per barrel or a total of $9,000.00. The trade cost $230.00 for a net profit of $770.00. Consider prices at $18.62 at expiration. The short calls lose $262.00 per barrel or $7,860.00 on three contracts. The long $17.00 calls earn $1.62 per barrel or $8,100.00 on five contracts. The trade cost $230.00 for a net profit of $10.00. The worst situation or maximum loss of this trade is if prices settle at $17.00 at expiration. The short calls lose $1.00 or $3,000.00; the long calls expire worthless for a net maximum loss of $3,230.00. Losses are limited to $230.00 regardless of how low prices drop.

The position delta is calculated by summing the individual option deltas: $(-.53 \times 3) + (+.40 \times 5) = +.40$. This is a bullish position. By selling three calls premium is received which subsidizes the purchase of five calls.

Put Ratio Backspread

A *put ratio backspread* involves selling fewer puts at a high strike price and buying more puts at a low strike price.

Example: Three $15.00 puts are bought and one $16.00 put is sold, for a net debit of $830.00.

Put ratio backspread

Position	Premium	Dollar Premium	Delta
Sell 1 $16.00 put	$1.09	$1,090.00	+ .47
Buy 3 $15.00 put	$ .64	$ 640.00	− .32
Net debit	N/A	$ 830.00	N/A
Net delta	N/A	N/A	− .49

Maximum Risk:	$1.83 dollars per barrel or $1,830.00
Maximum Profit:	Unlimited on the downside
Breakeven Futures Price:	$14.08
Current Price:	$16.00

Refer to Figure 5-19. This position earns profits if prices decline. Risk is limited. If prices rally to $18.00 at expiration, the long $15.00 puts expire worthless, and the short $16.00 puts expire worthless. Total losses are $830.00, the net premium paid regardless how high prices go. Maximum losses occur when prices are at $15.00 at expiration. The long $15.00 puts expire worthless, but the short $16.00 put is worth −$1,000.00. Add to this the cost of the trade, $830.00 yields a maximum loss of $1,830.00. At $12.00, the short put loses $4.00 per barrel or $4,000.00, the three long puts earn $3.00 per barrel or $9,000.00. The net profit is $4,170.00 after including the $830.00 cost of the trade. The breakeven futures price at expiration is $14.08.

This is a bearish trade. Note that net delta is −.49, similar to buying an at-the-money put. However, an at-the-money put in this example costs $1,090.00, compared with an $830.00 payout for the put backspread. By spreading options, net outlays are reduced. Some traders, as with call ratio back-spreads, like to leg into these positions for net credits. For example, if prices rally, the long option leg is established.

FIGURE 5-19
Put ratio backspread

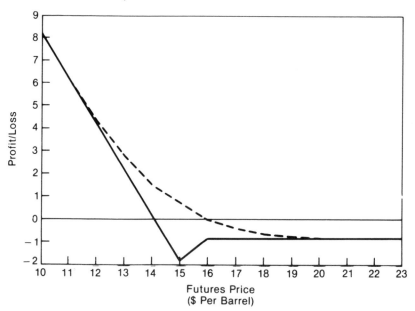

The short option leg is put on when prices decline. The risk, of course, is that a leg is put on and the market keeps moving against that leg.

SYNTHETICS

Synthetic futures and options are based on the following relationship:

$$C - P = e^{-rt}(F - E)$$

where:

C = call premium

P = put premium

F = future price

E = strike price

e^{-rt} = discounting factor

r = risk-free rate of return

t = time until expiration

If the call premium and the futures price are known, then by the foregoing relationship, the put premium can be determined.

Example: based on the following October Swiss franc option settlement prices for September 14, 1987, futures prices can be determined. The October options are options on December futures.

Month	Strike	Call Premium	Put Premium
Oct	.67	.0070	.0081
Oct	.68	.0033	.0143

Applying the equality (ignoring the discount factor for now) gives

$$(1) \ .0070 - .0081 = F - .67$$
$$(2) \ .0033 - .0143 = F - .68$$

Solving for F or the futures price yields $\$.6689$ in (1) and the actual settlement price for December futures is $\$.6688$. Arbitrage profits exist:

Traders will execute conversions or reversal trades to take advantage of mispriced options. (These strategies are discussed in detail in Chapter 10.)

The effect of the discount factor is more evident in options that are deep in or deep out of the money and have a relatively long time to expiration. Consider September 14, 1987 settlement prices for April gold options (in dollars per ounce).

Month	Strike	Call Premium	Put Premium
April	$440.00	$43.70	$ 9.30
April	$520.00	$12.50	$54.60

Using the equality now gives

$$(1) \ \$43.70 - \$9.30 = F - \$440.00$$
$$(2) \ \$12.50 - \$54.60 = F - \$520.00$$

From (1), solving for F yields $474.40; from (2), F equals $477.90. The actual settlement price for that day was $476.20. What is going on?

Consider the trade of buying the April 440 gold call and selling the April 440 put for a net debit of $34.40. If prices are at $400.00 at expiration, the call expires worthless, and the put loses $40.00. Adding the cost of the trade yields a total loss of $74.40 with prices at $400.00. If prices are at $500.00, the put expires worthless, and the call is worth $60.00. Subtracting the cost of the trade yields a total profit of $25.60.

Regardless of where futures trade, buying the 440 call, and selling the 440 put exhibit a profit/loss situation like a long futures contract established at $474.40. In fact, the trade is called a *synthetic* long futures position. The position is "synthetically" long at $474.40, which is lower than the current futures price of $476.20, because of the interest rate effect. Paying a net debit of $34.40 per ounce, a cash outflow, for an April option has an opportunity cost associated with it. That is, the $34.40 could be earning interest. In this example, it looks as if a trader can get synthetically long at a price below the futures price. However, it is an illusion, because when interest and transaction costs are considered, there is usually no profit gained by getting synthetically long using options.

Buying the 520 call and selling the 520 put can be done for a net credit of $32.10, a cash inflow. Now the trade is synthetically long at $477.90, higher than the current futures price. But, now, cash is received and can earn interest. The interest rate effect makes it look as if the trade is long at $477.90, when in fact the options are not mispriced. Because interest is earned on the cash credit, the long positions is actually established at a price below $477.90.

A synthetic short futures position can be established by buying puts and selling calls in the same month and same strike price.

See Figure 5-20. A trader may need to hedge a long cash position by selling futures. The trader might also decide to buy calls to cover the futures hedge, but could get the same effect from buying puts. Synthetic trades are a result of the relationship between options and futures. Traders should familiarize themselves with synthetics to understand this relationship fully.

Further, knowledge of synthetic trades will allow traders to take the most efficient route in translating market opinions into option trades. Usually, the least number of transactions is the most efficient way to trade. If a trader is thinking of selling puts and selling futures, why not just sell calls? Sometimes options are mispriced, and selling overpriced puts and futures may be a slightly better trade, but these mispricings are usually taken advantage of by floor traders who have lower transactions costs and can act much more quickly than nonfloor traders. (See Chapter 10) The profit/loss diagrams in Figures 5-21 through 5-24 illustrate some synthetic positions using crude oil options.

FIGURE 5-20
Summary of synthetic positions

Synthetic long call   = long put + long futures
Synthetic long put   = long call + short futures
Synthetic short call = short put + short futures
Synthetic short put   = short call + long futures
Synthetic long futures = long call + short put
Synthetic short futures = long put + short call

FIGURE 5-21

Synthetic short futures

Position	Premium	Dollar Premium	Delta
Sell 1 $16.00 call	$1.09	$1,090.00	−.53
Buy 1 $16.00 put	$1.09	$1,090.00	−.47
Net debit	0	0	N/A
Net delta	N/A	N/A	−1.00

Maximum Risk:	Unlimited on the upside
Maximum Profit:	Unlimited on the downside
Breakeven Futures Price:	$16.00
Current Price:	$16.00

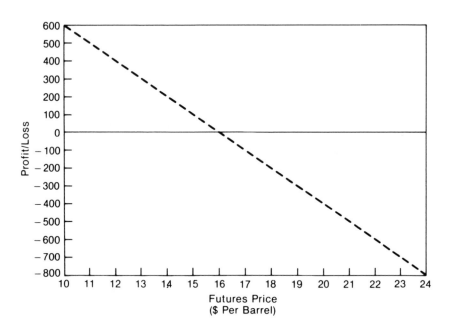

Futures Price
($ Per Barrel)

FIGURE 5-22
Synthetic long futures

Position	Premium	Dollar Premium	Delta
Sell 1 $16.00 put	$1.09	$1,090.00	+.47
Buy 1 $16.00 call	$1.09	$1,090.00	+.53
Net debit	0	0	N/A
Net delta	N/A	N/A	+1.00

Maximum Risk:	Unlimited on the downside
Maximum Profit:	Unlimited on the upside
Breakeven Future Price:	$16.00
Current Price:	$16.00

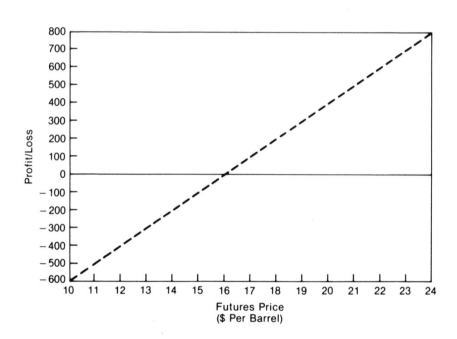

FIGURE 5-23
Synthetic long put

Position	Premium	Dollar Premium	Delta
Sell 1 futures	$16.00	N/A	−1.00
Buy 1 $16.00 call	$ 1.09	$1,090.00	+.53
Net debit	$ 1.09	$1,090.00	N/A
Net delta	N/A	N/A	−.47

Maximum Risk:	$1.09 per barrel or $1,090.00
Maximum Profit:	Unlimited on the downside
Breakeven Futures Price:	$14.91
Current Price:	$16.00

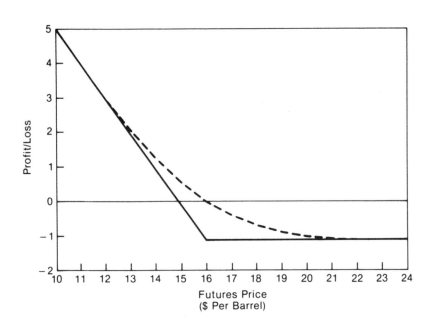

FIGURE 5-24
Synthetic long call

Position	Premium	Dollar Premium	Delta
Buy 1 futures	$16.00	N/A	+1.00
Buy 1 $16.00 put	$ 1.09	$1,090.00	− .47
Net debit	$ 1.09	$1,090.00	N/A
Net delta	N/A	N/A	+ .53

Maximum Risk:	$1.09 per barrel or $1,090.00
Maximum Profit:	Unlimited on the upside
Breakeven Futures Price:	$17.09
Current Price:	$16.00

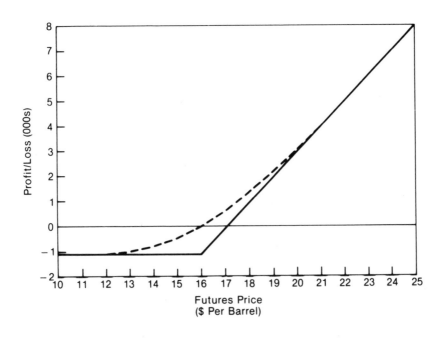

FENCE

A popular hedging strategy that illustrates the flexibility of options is the fence. This strategy is also called a *collar* or a *cap and floor*.

The hedger has a long cash position and needs to establish protection against declining prices. A buy put strategy would do nicely, except that the hedger is not willing to pay that much premium. The hedger could establish a fence by buying a put and offsetting the cost by selling an out-of-the-money call.

Example: The hedger is long futures at $16.00, a proxy for a long cash position. He is also long a $15.00 put and short a $17.00 call. This trade is actually executed at a net credit of $.06, because by selling the call, the hedger receives $70.00 while only paying out $.64 for the put.

Fence

Position	Premium	Dollar Premium	Delta
Buy 1 futures	$16.00	N/A	+ 1.00
Buy $15.00 put	$ .64	$640.00	− .32
Sell 1 $17.00 call	$ .70	$700.00	− .40
Net credit	$ .06	$ 60.00	N/A
Net delta	N/A	N/A	+ .28

Maximum Risk:	$.94 per barrel or $940.00
Maximum Profit:	$1.06 per barrel or $1,060.00
Breakeven Futures Price:	$15.94
Current Price:	$16.00

Refer to Figure 5-_. . .he hedger receives at least $15.06 as a floor price. If prices drop to $13.00 the put is exercised and a short position is established at $15.00. Add to this the $.06 net credit, and the hedger sells crude at $15.06.

Creating a floor price without any cash outlay does have a cost, however. The cost is that if prices rise above $17.00, the hedger no longer participates. For example, at $19.00 the trader earns $3.00 from the cash position ($19.00 − $16.00) plus the $.06 credit. But the short

FIGURE 5-25
Fence

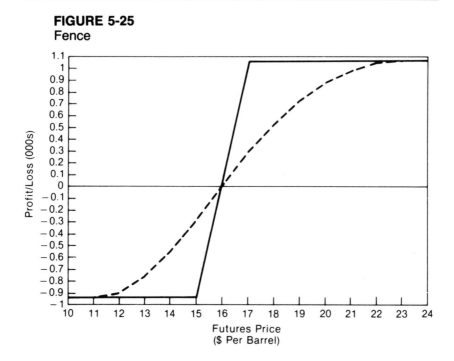

Futures Price
($ Per Barrel)

call loses $2.00 ($19.00 − $17.00) for a total gain of $1.06. The fence establishes a floor selling price and a ceiling selling price.

The hedger effectively has bought and sold extreme price outcomes. If prices rally sharply, the hedger still participates but only up to the strike price of the short call. If prices drop, the hedger has unlimited downside protection in place below the market. The trade-off is that the hedger receives low-cost downside protection in return for giving up some upside protection. In fact, if the long put, short call, and long futures positions are taken together the profit/loss diagram looks exactly like a bull call spread. This is because a long put and a long future is a synthetic long call.

To hedge a short cash position the hedger could create a fence by buying a call and selling a put. This trade might be established by an end user, such as an airline company, trying to put a ceiling on energy costs at little or zero cash outlay.

CHAPTER 6

Hedging with
Options on Futures

Hedging with futures and/or options is the art of managing price risk. Many firms are in business to add value to a product or to provide a service for a profit. In the process, the company may be exposed to potentially volatile changes in commodity prices or in financial asset or liability values that could significantly reduce earnings. These pressures are in addition to the natural risks of conducting business: that is, the risk of a weak economy or recession, the risk of an aggressive competitor, and the like. Consider some examples.

An airline company is in business to provide passengers with a way to get from point A to point B by way of air travel. The airline is exposed to many factors on which it has no direct influence. For example, the economy may slow down, reducing the number of air travelers, or a competing airline might reduce fares on a particular route to increase market share. The airline could take countermeasures. If a recession or a slowdown in the economy is anticipated, the airline might put expansion plans on hold. A reduction in fares by a major competitor may force the firm to also reduce fares to remain competitive. The airline in this example is exposed to the risks natural to a going concern within the air travel industry. However, it also is exposed to price risk of commodities and financial instruments exogenous to the airline industry.

Airlines consume a tremendous amount of jet fuel. If fuel prices rise, costs increase. These increases in costs may not be easily passed on to the consumer, particularly in a highly competitive environment. Thus, airline companies' profits could be sharply reduced based on the results of an OPEC meeting, an escalation of the Gulf war or a general uptrend in energy prices. Further, some foreign airlines' profits are denominated in dollars. A sharp decline in the value of the dollar could significantly affect the firm's bottom line. Thus a meeting of the economic ministers of developed countries could have a significant effect on currency prices, and profits. Further, the airline may have a retirement fund invested in equity and bonds exposed to potentially sharp stock and bond market declines. Or the cost of raising capital is exposed to interest rate moves.

The airline company finds itself in a business that is susceptible to many external shocks. The concept of hedging, then, in this context means reducing the risk of an adverse price shock that cannot be passed along to consumers. This particular company might be more concerned over major moves in commodity prices than smaller day-to-day changes.

A bond dealer, conversely, is in the business of making markets in Treasury and/or other kind of bonds. The dealer earns profits by buying bonds at a low price and selling at a higher price. Profit margins are very small per transaction, but transactions are many. The bond dealer is much more concerned with very-short-term moves in prices and needs much more precision when hedging its portfolio. Treasury bond price risk is the nature of the business.

The bond dealer and the airline both face significant price exposure. However, each will likely take a different approach to reduce this exposure: the bond dealer will likely be a more aggressive hedger than the airline because its margins relative to the instrument being hedged is much tighter.

In this chapter, we will first discuss some issues facing hedgers whether they are using futures or options; then, we outline the thought process that a hedger might follow when confronted with a wide range of hedging strategies.

HEDGING WITH FUTURES

The traditional example of a hedger is the farmer who at planting time sells December corn futures to cover some percentage of the expected crop. The idea is that if prices drop, the farmer has already contracted (by selling futures) to sell his corn at a higher price. If prices rally, the farmer loses money on the hedge, but gains in the cash market offset the losses. The farmer has effectively locked in a selling price for his corn. Unfortunately, there are some potential problems that arise in reality that are not addressed in the traditional example.

Basis Risk

Corn futures call for delivery of #2 yellow corn in Chicago if held to the delivery date. The farmer who sells December corn futures must actually deliver corn if the contract is still outstanding in December. Most futures contracts are offset before the delivery period approaches. In this example, the farmer would sell the corn in the cash market and liquidate the hedge by buying back the December futures contract. The corn futures price is basically a Chicago price of corn. A farmer in North Carolina faces a slightly different corn market from a farmer in the Midwest. Farmers in the Southeast will harvest one to two months earlier than will farmers in the Midwest. Also, much of the corn in Virginia and North Carolina is sold to poultry producers on the eastern shore of Maryland. Although corn prices in both markets will be related, there is potential for prices to diverge because of varying supply/demand relationships for the individual market.

For the farmer in North Carolina, this means that Chicago futures prices will not be perfectly correlated with local cash prices. The effectiveness of the hedge is determined by the degree of price correlation between the commodity being hedged and the hedging instrument. If the farmer in North Carolina sells Chicago futures to hedge, it is possible for losses to accrue on both sides of the transaction. If export activity picks up, tightening supplies in the Midwest, futures prices will move higher. In North Carolina, the harvest might be in full swing, pressuring cash prices. The hedged farmer can lose on the futures and lose in the cash markets.

Any time a hedged commodity is not exactly the same in grade and location as the underlying futures, this correlation problem exists. A mortgage banker hedging GNMAs with T-note futures, a North Sea oil producer using NYMEX West Texas Intermediate crude oil futures, or a bank hedging CDs with Eurodollar futures all face the potential problem that the price of the instrument or commodity being hedged fails to correlate with the futures contract. This problem is called basis risk. The difference between the cash price and the futures price is called the basis. It is important for potential hedgers to understand fully the nature of the underlying futures contract being used and how it relates to their cash instrument.

Some firms will be reluctant to hedge because their cash price does not exhibit a stable basis relationship. However, a less than perfect relationship might still offer good price protection. In this case, the hedger exchanges significant price risk for a lesser basis risk. There is no set rule as to what constitutes a good correlation. It depends on the individual trader and firm. Some firms may refrain from hedging with futures and options because of basis instability, but others might try to take advantage and trade the basis relationship.

STACKING A HEDGE

An oil producer wants to hedge a year's worth of production totaling 12 million barrels. Ideally, the hedger would sell enough futures to cover each month of production: 1 million barrels in January (1,000 futures contracts), 1 million in February, and so on. As monthly production is realized and sold in the cash market, futures are bought back. Unfortunately, liquidity dries up in deferred futures months. The producer must stack the entire hedge in the nearby futures months and continually roll the position over as time passes. This type of hedging has important implications.

First, stacking increases transactions costs. Transaction costs accrue not only through increased commissions but also through the spread between the bid price and offer price. Second, rolling a position from one month to the next involves a spread risk. Prices between two months can narrow or widen adversely for hedgers trying to roll positions. Finally, if an oil producer can stack one year's worth of production, why not stack two years? or five years? The problem is that futures contracts are marked to market on a daily basis. Profits and losses are settled daily. If prices move against the hedge, cash must be paid out and losses accrue immediately. Gains on the cash side are not realized until the cash commodity is sold, which could be one or two years away. Cash flow implications of hedging must be considered. Option strategies do not get around the hedging problems of basis risk, nor do they remove the negative aspects of stacking hedges.

HEDGING VERSUS SPECULATING

Firms should have clear goals when developing a hedging program. What benefits are to be gained from hedging with futures and options? Is the company's objective mainly to stabilize costs or revenues? Or is the firm interested in hedging for some long-range marketing plan? How aggressively will the hedge be managed? How these questions are answered will depend on the leadership of each company. Some companies may be textbook hedgers: a cash position is established, and the entire position is immediately hedged in the futures market. Others might only hedge a portion of the cash position, taking an educated but exposed position in the market. Still others may set up "profit centers" to take positions in futures and options that have absolutely no connection to a cash position.

The optimal hedging strategy will depend largely on the philosophy of the hedging company. How much price risk can the company live with? The more price risk it is able to withstand, the more flexibility it will have in hedging strategies. Once the hedger has determined acceptable levels of price risk, market opinion enters the picture. As we have seen, option strategies allow traders to fine tune market opinions to include time frames and market volatility. The next section lays out various hedging strategies and the trade-offs.

COMPARISONS OF HEDGING STRATEGIES

In Chapter 5, a wide range of options strategies was introduced. We now need to develop a structured model that will help to analyze the trade-offs among the various strategies. The model will help identify the optimal strategy for each hedger based on ability to assume price risk, market opinion, and cash flow.

Example: Let us return to the classic hedging example of the farmer protecting against a decline in soybean prices. In this example our focus is on the March 19 settlement prices for July futures and options. The farmer is faced with many hedging alternatives, summarized in Figure 6-1.

The farmer could sell futures. On March 19, July futures settled at $6.38 per bushel. The farmer could have sold futures, locking in an effective sale price of $6.38 per bushel regardless where prices go. If prices drop, the farmer is hedged because he already has contracted to sell soybeans at $6.38. If prices rally, the farmer does not participate because, again, he has contracted to sell soybeans at $6.38. The results of the futures hedge in Figure 6-1 indicate that no matter where prices

FIGURE 6-1
Comparison of hedging strategies: soybeans ($ per bushel)

July Futures Price at Expiration	Futures	Net Sales Price						
		Buy Puts			Sell Calls			
		$6.25	$6.00	$5.75	$6.50	$6.75	$7.00	Fence[2]
$5.00	$6.38[1]	$6.07½	$5.91½	$5.71½	$5.19½	$5.13	$5.08¼	5.99¾
5.50	6.38	6.07½	5.91½	5.71½	5.69½	5.63	5.58¼	5.99¾
6.00	6.38	6.07½	5.91½	5.96½	6.19½	6.13	6.08¼	5.99¾
6.50	6.38	6.32½	6.41½	6.46½	6.69½	6.63	6.58¼	6.49¾
7.00	6.38	6.82½	6.91½	6.96½	6.69½	6.88	7.08¼	6.99¾
7.50	6.38	7.32½	7.41½	7.45½	6.69½	6.88	7.08¼	6.99¾
Net credit					.19½	.13	.08¼	
Net debit		.17½	.08½	.03½				.00¼

[1]Settlement prices for July futures and options, March 19, 1988.

[2]Buy $6.00 put at $.08½ and sell $7.00 call at $.08¼ for a net debit of $.00¼.

move after the hedge is established the net sales price to the farmer will be $6.38 per bushel. The first column in Figure 6-1 shows varying price assumptions; the second column lists the effective sales price for the farmer using a futures hedge. If prices rally, the farmer must make cash margin payments because the futures hedge will show losses. These must be settled on a daily basis. Conversely, if prices decline, the farmer receives cash.

The only real flexibility the farmer has with a futures hedge is what percentage of the crop should be hedged. The actual percentage that is hedged will be determined by the farmer's risk preference and market opinion.

Example: Consider a farmer who is bullish the market but is risk averse. He is willing and able to live with some decline in market price but couldn't survive a major decline. This farmer might consider a buy put strategy. The buy put strategy provides a floor selling price. It also allows the farmer to participate in market rallies. In Figure 6-1, the farmer establishes a 6.07½ price floor by purchasing the $6.25 put for $.17½ per bushel. If prices decline to $5.00 at expiration, the farmer sells soybeans at a net sales price of $6.07½ per bushel. The long put gives the farmer the right to sell futures at $6.25. The cost of the put is $.17½. Subtracting gives a net sales price of $6.07½. If prices rally to $7.50, the farmer certainly would not exercise the right to sell at $6.25. Thus, the option expires worthless, and the farmer sells soybeans for $7.50 minus the premium $.17½ for an effective sales price of $7.32½. The farmer has set a floor at $6.07½ and can still participate in a bull market. There is an upfront cash payment of $.17½. However, unlike a futures hedge, buy option strategies require no margin.

If prices decline, the futures hedge is superior to the buy put hedge. If prices decline to, say, $5.00, the farmer receives $6.38 per bushel if he hedged using futures and $6.07½ if he hedged using the $6.25 puts. If prices rally, as the farmer expects them to, the long put strategy is superior to the futures hedge. If prices rise to $7.50, the futures hedge yields a net sales price of $6.38 while the option hedge yields at net sales price of $7.32½. If prices remain unchanged, the futures hedge does better yielding a $6.38 sales price, while the buy put strategy yields a price of $6.10½ ($6.38 minus the premium, $.17½).

The long put hedge is effective if prices decline. Floor prices can be established at a fixed cost. But unlike futures, the long put hedge does well when prices rally. A hedger might have a bullish market opinion and still buy puts for protection. Or a U.S.D.A. report on soybean production may be scheduled. The farmer thinks that prices could move sharply in either direction if the report contains surprises. Buying puts to cover a cash position gives the farmer protection against a sharp decline in prices and enables him to participate in a market rally. In fact, the farmer has bought downside price insurance but has the desire that no "accident" occur.

The decision to buy puts versus selling futures will depend on the hedger's ability to assume risk, market opinion, and the cost of the puts. In this example, the farmer must be willing and able to accept a price floor of $6.07½. He must also believe that the cost of this price insurance is reasonable. (One way to determine relative value in an option is to track its implied volatility as discussed in Chapter 7.) Different floors or levels of price insurance can be established with varying costs by examining the different strike prices.

In Figure 6-1, three buy put strategies are summarized: the $6.25 put with a $.17½ premium (already discussed), the $6.00 put with an $.08½ premium, and the $5.75 put with a $.03½ premium. Each establishes a different floor price. Each has a different cost. If prices decline to $5.00 at expiration, the farmer sells soybeans at $6.07½, $59½, or $5.71½, depending on which put was bought. When prices decline, the $6.25 put offers the most protection of the three buy put strategies, while the $5.75 offers the least protection. However, if prices rally, the $5.75 put offers the most participation and the $6.25 offers the least. Further, the most cash is paid out to buy the $6.25 put, and the least cash is paid out for the $5.75 put. These are the trade-offs a hedger must analyze when deciding the optimal strategy. How much risk am I willing and able to assume? How much protection do I need? What cost am I willing to pay? What is my market opinion? The answers determine the optimal strategy.

Our farmer is long soybeans in the cash market and is exposed to a decline in prices. An option strategy that profits when prices decline is a short call strategy. The farmer could sell calls against inventory as a hedge against declining prices. This hedge has risk/reward implictions different from selling futures or buying puts.

On March 19, 1988, our farmer sells $6.50 calls for $.19½ per bushel (Figure 6-1). At expiration, prices decline to $5.00. The farmers effective sales price is $5.19½ per bushel. This is because the maximum profit earned on a short option is the premium or $.19½ in this example. The farmer sells soybeans at $5.00, and the $6.50 call expires worthless for a $.19½ profit to the farmer. Selling calls, therefore, is the least effective strategy to protect against sharply declining prices. However, the strategy does perform better than no hedge at all.

If prices rally to $7.50 the farmer's effective selling price is $6.69½. At $7.50 the farmer loses $1.00 ($6.50 − $7.50) minus the $.19½ net credit or a total of $0.80½ from the short call. The farmer sells soybeans at $7.50, the current price, or 6.69½ after including the loss on the option. If prices rally sharply, a short call strategy outperforms a futures hedge but underperforms the long put hedge (Figure 6-1).

The short call hedge is most effective when prices move relatively sideways. For example, if prices are unchanged at $6.38 at expiration, the short call hedge outperforms the futures hedge and the long put hedge. At $6.38, the $6.50 call expires worthless, and the farmer profits $.19½ on the option. The farmer's effective selling price is $6.57½ ($6.38 plus $.19½). The short futures hedge yields a price of $6.38, and the long $6.25 put yields a price of $6.20½ ($6.38 minus the $.17½ net debit).

The farmer might sell calls against his soybean inventory if he assigns a very low probability that prices will drop sharply. The hedger would expect the most likely outcome to be prices moving sideways to slightly higher. And call premiums are perceived to be relatively high. Short option hedges must be margined.

Depending on which call option is sold, different levels of premium will be received. In this example, selling the $6.50 call receives $.19½, while selling the $7.00 call receives only $.08¼. The more premium received, the more protection received against a downside move in prices. If prices drop to $5.00, the short $6.50 call yields a higher sales price than do the other two short call strategies. However, if prices rally, the hedger who sells the $7.00 call participates more than does the one who sells the $6.50 call.

The farmer in this example might like the idea of establishing a floor selling price by buying puts. However, he might not like the idea of paying out so much cash to buy puts. The farmer could sell calls with strike prices above the market and at the same time buy puts to establish a floor. The premium received from selling calls is used to offset the cost of purchasing the puts. The strategy is called a fence or a collar. The idea is to place a band around prospective selling prices, removing the effects of extremely volatile price moves.

In this example, the farmer buys a $6.00 put for $.08½ and sells a $7.00 call for $.08¼ (Figure 6-1). The farmer pays a net $.00¼ debit for the trade. The effective price floor for this trade is $5.99¾. If prices drop below $6.00, the farmer exercises the put option, which gives him the right to sell soybean futures at $6.00. Only $.00¼ was paid for the trade making the effective floor $5.99¾. This floor is between the floor established by the long $6.25 put, $6.07½, and the floor established by the long $6.00 put, $5.91½.

The cost of the fence is not so much a cash cost as an opportunity cost. The farmer is giving up participation if soybean prices rally above $7.00 because he has sold a $7.00 call. A ceiling of $6.99¾ is realized after accounting for the $.00¼ premium paid. For example, if prices rally to $7.50 and the farmer sells soybeans at $7.50, he loses $.50 on the short $7.00 call and another $.00¼ in premium paid, for an effective sale price of 6.99¾.

The fence gives a hedger a price floor and some upside participation at low cost. The strategy works well for hedgers who are interested in keeping selling prices within a band rather than selling at some specific level. Compare the futures hedge with the fence. If prices rally, the fence hedge can get as much as 6.99¾ per bushel, but the futures hedge yields a selling price of $6.38 throughout.

The exercise through which we have just led our farmer can be repeated for any market and for any kind of hedger. A soybean processor, for example, might be more interested in establishing a net purchase price: Figure 6-1 would show long futures, long calls, short puts, and a fence established by selling puts and buying calls.

Given the variety of strategies and probability of outcomes, the hedger decides on optimal strategy based on risk assessment, market opinion, and initial cost. The increased flexibility which option strategies give to hedgers also complicates the decision process significantly. Now, different parts of the price probability curve can be bought and sold to achieve the desired level of risk.

Hedging with options can reduce overall price risk but not without some trade-off. A put buyer knows that downside price protection is achieved only for a certain period of time. After the option expires, the protection is gone. Changes in expected volatility can work against a hedged position using options. In Chapter 9, we examine in more detail the exact nature of the exposure assumed in return for price protection. Now, we turn to a measure that helps traders determine how expensive or cheap option premiums are.

CHAPTER 7

Evaluating
Option Premiums

A trader is offering a crude oil call at $.50. Should you buy it? Is it cheap or expensive? A cynic might say that an option is cheap if you can buy it today and sell it tomorrow at a higher price. Otherwise, it is expensive. How does a trader know value when trading options?

Some of the information that a trader needs to know to evaluate an option's premium is obvious. First, where is the strike price relative to the futures price? Is the option in, out of, or at the money? Second, for how much time is the option valid? Does the option expire today, tomorrow, or six months from now? Some traders can trade options successfully knowing only this much information.

Example: A $17.00 call with 90 days until expiration is offered at $.50. Futures are now trading at $16.75 per barrel. A trader who has the opinion that prices will trade higher than $17.00 within the next 90 days might purchase the call. The actual transaction will depend on the trader's risk/reward preference. If the trader is willing to risk $.50 per barrel to earn $.50 per barrel (a one-to-one-risk/reward ratio), the trader needs only to have the opinion that prices will reach $18.00 within 90 days.

There is a piece of very important information not considered in the analysis that gives an option value: volatility. How volatile has the market been recently? Is the market expected to trade quietly or violently during the option's life? The option offered in the example may be even more valuable if an OPEC meeting is scheduled within the next 90 days. The OPEC meeting may result in active and volatile markets, giving the limited risk feature of buy option strategies more value. However, in anticipation of higher market volatility due to OPEC, option premiums will begin to be bid higher sometimes several days before the actual event. We need some method of quantifying the effect of volatility on option premiums.

The simplest measure of volatility is to look at the futures' price range. The lowest price of the day is subtracted from the highest price of the day to give the range. Markets that exhibit higher-than-normal price ranges will exhibit higher-than-normal option premiums. This method is of little use to option traders because it considers only futures prices and measures only past market volatility. What is needed is a method to evaluate the market's expectation of future volatility, which is built into the current option quote.

AN EXACT OPTION PRICING MODEL

Option theorists have developed mathematical equations that calculate option premiums as a function of certain variables. The most famous of these is Black-Scholes, or Black for commodity options (a modified version of Black-Scholes). The model makes simplifying assumptions about how the real world works but nonetheless is widely used by market makers and option traders. As traders, we are more interested in how the model is used and its limitations than how the model is derived. However, a brief intuitive description of the Black model is helpful.

Example: Assume that crude oil is trading at $17.00 per barrel, and that, in the next time period can increase or decrease by only $1.00 with equal probability. What is the value of a $17.00 call, which will expire in the next time period?

The price of crude can be either $18.00 or $16.00 in the next time period with equal (.50) probability. If crude oil is priced at $18.00, the $17.00 call is worth $1.00. If the crude is priced at $16.00, the $17.00 call is worthless.

With a 50-50 chance of each outcome, the expected value of the call at expiration is .50 × $1.00 + .50 × $.00 or $.50. Given our restrictive assumptions , the $17.00 call should trade for $.50 (ignoring the discounting factor). Figure 7-1 illustrates the example.

FIGURE 7-1

Option value under restrictive assumptions

Period t Today's price	Period t + 1	Value of $17.00 call		Probability of Occurrence	Option Expected Value
$17.00	$18.00	$1.00	×	.50	$.50
	$16.00	0	×	.50	0
				Expected value of call	$.50

This example can be made more complicated by adding more time periods or more potential price paths. Let's look at what happens in time period $t + 2$ given the same price path of $+/- $1.00. Figure 7-2 illustrates the outcome.

FIGURE 7-2

Option value with two time periods

Period t Today's price	Period t + 1	Period t + 2	Value of $17.00 call		Probability of Occurrence		Option Expected Value
$17.00	$18.00	$19.00	$2.00	×	.25	=	$.50
	$16.00	$17.00	0	×	.50	=	0
		$15.00	0	×	.25	=	0
			Expected value of $17.00 call				$.50

The $17.00 call has a value of $.50 in the example. Ignoring the discounting factors, the probability of prices trading at $19.00 in $t + 2$ is

.50 × .50 or .25. Two price paths reach $17.00. The probability of reaching $17.00 in t + 2 is 2 × .50 × .50 or .50. A $15.00 outcome has .25 likelihood of occurring. The probabilities are multiplied by the value of the option at each price and then summed to calculate the expected value of the option at expiration. This number is then multiplied by a discounting factor to determine today's value of the option.

Now consider a price path in which prices can move by +/− .50 or +/− $1.00 with equal probability. The outcome is illustrated in Figure 7-3.

FIGURE 7-3
Option value with multiple price paths

Period t Today's price	Period t + 1	Value of $17.00 call	Probability of Occurrence	Option Expected Value
	$18.00	$1.00	.25	$.25
	$17.50	$ .50	.25	$.125
$17.00	$16.50	$ 0	.25	0
	$16.00	$ 0	.25	0
		Expected value of $17.00 call		$.375

These examples are gross simplications. Prices certainly do not trade in $1.00 or $.50 increments. Option pricing models are more complicated because they assume a more complicated underlying price path. However, the idea of evaluating the option's value is the same: The models are calculating an option's expected value and discounting it based on assumptions about the expected price path.

Assume that today's crude oil price is $17.00. A $19.00 call has 30 days until expiration. If some probability distribution for future prices is assumed, then a value for the call can be calculated. Figure 7-4 shows an expected price path that exhibits a normal distribution, that is, the well-known bell-shaped curve. Given today's price, the strike price, interest rates, and the probability distribution of futures prices, the expected value of the call can be calculated. The call value is equal to the probability that prices will be below $19.00 at expiration multiplied by zero (because the call expires worthless as long as prices are $19.00 and

FIGURE 7-4
Normal distribution

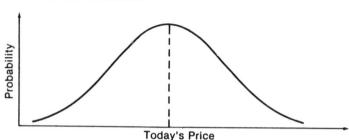

Today's Price

below) plus the summation of the probability that prices are above $19.00 times the difference of the strike price and the futures price evaluated at every point along the price path. This value is then discounted by the risk-free rate of return. In Figure 7-4, in order to determine the current value of the $19.00 call, integral calculus must be used.

The Black model is more complicated because it assumes a price path that the logs of the percentage changes of prices are normally distributed. This implies that prices are log normally distributed instead of normally distributed. Using logs of percentage changes of prices is an attempt to assume an expected price path which more reflects the real world. For example, if prices were really distributed normally, negative prices could exist. Further, prices of commodities are more likely to double (increase by 100 percent) than to go to zero (decrease by 100 percent). The log normal assumption of futures prices is an attempt to reflect real life. (Unfortunately, prices do not seem to move log normally, nor options priced this way.)

The Black model is:

(1) $C = e^{-n} [FN(d_1) - EN(d_2)]$

(2) $P = e^{-n} [EN(-d_2) - FN(-d_1)]$

(3) $d_1 = \dfrac{ln(F/E) + (S^2/2)t}{S\sqrt{t}}$

(4) $d_2 = d_1 - S\sqrt{t}$

where:

$N(d)$ = is the cumulative normal integral

r = risk-free rate of return

S = the standard deviation of logs of percentage changes in prices, annualized

F = futures price

E = strike price

t = time to expiration, annualized

C = call premium

P = put premium

exp = exponent = 2.7183

ln = natural logarithm

Let's calculate a call premium using the following assumptions:

F = futures price ($17.00)

E = strike price ($19.00)

t = 90 days until expiration, or annualized (90/365 = .2466 years)

r = 6.00% annualized, the 90-day Treasury bill rate

S = .35, an estimate of volatility using the standard deviation of logs of percent changes in prices (we will explain this number in detail, shortly).

Plugging these assumptions into the equations gives

(1a) $C = e^{(-.06)*(.2466)} [17\ N(d_1) - 19\ N(d_2)]$

(3a) $$d_1 = \frac{ln\ (17/19) + (.35)^2(.2466)(.50)}{(.35)\sqrt{.2466}} = -.5529$$

(4a) $d_2 = -.5529 - (.35)\sqrt{.2466} = -.7267$

$C = .9853\ [17N(-.5529) - 19N(-.7267)$

Using cumulative normal probability tables which are available in basic statistics texts and interpolating,

$$N(-.5529) = .2902$$
$$N(-.7267) = .2337$$
$$CC = .9853 \ [17(.2902) - 19(.2337)]$$
$$C = .4859 \text{ or } .49$$

Based on this above assumption, the model indicates a call premium for the $19.00 exercise price equal to $.49. The market in our example is offering the call for $.50. Everything that is known was plugged into the option equation: futures price, the strike price, time until expiration, and interest rates. The unknown piece of information is expected volatility or, in the equation, the standard deviation. An estimate of future volatility is required. We used $S = .35$ in our example.

One way to evaluate option premiums is to estimate a measure of future volatility and calculate option premiums based on it using an exact option pricing model. In this example, a trader might estimate future volatility to be $S = .35$, calculate the option premium, and compare the results to the actual market traded premium. If the calculated premiums are higher than market premiums, the trader might lean toward long option strategies to take advantage of "undervalued options." Or, if the calculated option premiums are below market premiums, the trader might sell options to take advantage of "overvalued" options.

Most option traders use option models in a slightly different way. Instead of each trader estimating a measure of volatility to plug into the model, they will let the market calculate volatility. Instead of solving for C or P, the call or put premium, traders plug the currently traded premium into C and P and solve for S, the volatility measure. If, as the model says, a call (or put) value is a function of the futures price, the strike price, time until expiration, interest rates, and volatility, why not plug the currently traded call premium into the model and solve for volatility? By tracking this measure over time, a trader can determine whether option premiums are relatively cheap or expensive. This volatility measure, which is calculated based on currently traded option premiums, is called *implied volatility*.

Since volatility is a key variable in determining option value, we examine two measures of market volatility in more detail: historical and implied volatility.

HISTORICAL AND IMPLIED VOLATILITY

Historical Volatility

In the preceding example we used $S = .35$ as a measure of volatility to plug into the option model. From where did it come? One way to measure market volatility is to measure the standard deviation of past changes in prices. However, the measure must be compatible with the option model that is used. The Black model assumes that the natural logarithms of percentage changes in prices are normally distributed. This means that instead of calculating simple standard deviations of changes in prices, we must use standard deviations of logs of percentage changes in prices.

The simple calculation for a standard deviation is:

$$S = \sqrt{\frac{\sum_{t=1}^{n} (X_t - \bar{X})^2}{n - 1}}$$

where:
S = the standard deviation
X_t = the observation in time t

$\bar{X}$ = the mean or $\sum_{t=1}^{n} \dfrac{X_t}{n}$

n = the total number of observations

To calculate a standard deviation of the logs of percentage changes in prices, historical futures price data must be transformed. In Figure 7-5 the first 30 days of 1987 for May crude oil futures are listed in column 1. Percentage changes in prices are calculated in column 2. In column 3,

FIGURE 7-5
Ten-day historical volatility calculation

May Futures	P_t	P_t/P_{t-1}	$\ln(P_t/P_{t-1})$	Ten-Day Historical Volatility S[1]	Annualized $S\sqrt{255}$[2]
2/12/87	17.82	.9978	− .0022	.0100	15.97
2/11	17.86	.9786	− .0216	.0102	16.26
2/10	18.25	1.0039	.0039	.0074	11.79
2/09	18.18	1.0072	.0072	.0076	12.13
2/06	18.31	.9940	− .0060	.0076	12.13
2/05	18.42	1.0166	.0165	.0075	11.93
2/04	18.12	.9967	− .0033	.0055	8.73
2/03	18.18	.9934	− .0066	.0057	9.10
2/02	18.30	.9946	− .0054	.0064	10.22
1/30	18.40	1.0016	.0016	.0065	10.38
1/29	18.37	1.0038	.0038	.0065	10.38
1/28	18.30	1.0072	.0071	.0064	10.22
1/27	18.17	.9956	− .0044	.0062	9.90
1/26	18.25	.9940	− .0060	.0061	9.74
1/23	18.36	.9951	− .0049	.0061	9.74
1/22	18.45	1.0071	.0071	.0077	12.30
1/21	18.32	1.0044	.0044	.0077	12.30
1/20	18.40	1.0138	.0137	.0079	12.60
1/19	18.15	.9973	− .0028	1/18	18.20
1/18	18.20	1.0005	.0005		
1/15	18.19	.9989	− .0011		
1/14	18.21	.9951	− .0049		
1/13	18.30	.9887	− .0014		
1/12	18.51	1.0065	.0065		
1/11	18.39	1.0099	.0098		
1/8	18.21	1.0185	.0183		
1/7	17.88	1.0028	.0028		
1/6	17.83	1.0154	.0153		
1/5	17.56				

[1]The formula for calculating the standard deviation of a series is:

$$S = \sqrt{\frac{\sum_{t=1}^{n} (X_i - \bar{X})^2}{n - 1}}$$

where:

X_i = $\ln(P_t/P_{t-1})$
$\bar{X}$ = is the mean of the series
n = 9 observations

[2]Assume that there are 255 trading days in a year.

logs of percentage changes in prices are determined. The historical volatility or standard deviation for 10 price days (but nine observations) are calculated. Finally, the 10-day historical volatilities are annualized by multiplying by $N\sqrt{255}$, or the square root of the number of trading days in a year.

This annualized historical volatility number is what was plugged into the option model in the example. Our example assumed a volatility measure of .35. A current 10-day, 20-day or even 30-day volatility measure could have been used. Analogous to a moving average of prices, a 30-day historical volatility measure will be smoother than a 10-day measure. Which one is more appropriate? Neither!

Using an historical volatility measure as an estimate of option value suffers from a major weakness. Historical volatility is based on past movements of prices. Option premiums trade on expected future volatility.

Example: Treasury bond markets sometimes react violently to scheduled economic news when the news is unexpected. An unemployment report released on the first Friday of the month could contain surprising information causing bonds to trade sharply in one direction or the other. Previous to this report, bond markets might trade quietly sideways, as traders await the release before establishing new positions.

Using some historical volatility measure will undervalue option premiums. Historical volatility is capturing the quiet trading ahead of the economic news. However, option premiums are likely to be bid higher as the limited-risk feature of buy option strategies becomes more valuable ahead of the release of new economic data. The model may tell the trader that options are overvalued and should be sold. However, selling options ahead of the economic release could be hazardous to one's health.

Before we discuss a more widely used measure of option value, implied volatility, let's look at some 30-day volatility data for three markets: Treasury bonds, the S&P 500 Index, and crude oil.

Example: Refer to Figure 7-6. Crude oil markets were most volatile during 1986, when OPEC, particularly Saudi Arabia, flooded the world markets with oil. Prices shot down to $10.00 from above $30.00 per barrel in the first quarter of 1986. Listed options on crude oil were

FIGURE 7-6

Volatility comparison (January 1986–December 1987)

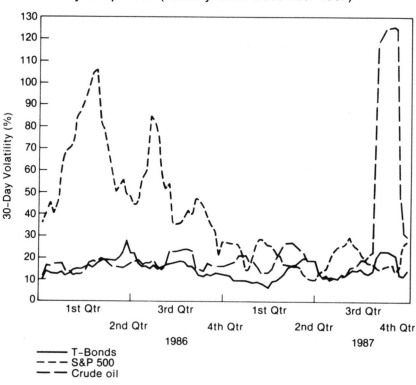

Source: The Options Group.

not trading during this period but would be very expensive in a market with such volatility. A similar impact on the S&P 500 Index volatility was recorded on Black Monday. Option premiums, of course, exploded due to the huge increase in volatility.

Option traders need to get very familiar with their market. An oil option trader should know when the oil market was most volatile and why. A S&P 500 option trader should have a good idea what happened to S&P premiums during its most volatile period. The effect of changing price volatility on option premiums can be significant. (In Chapter 10 we will look at ways to measure the effect of an increase in volatility on option premiums.)

Implied Volatility

Using historical volatility measures to value current option premiums fails to take into account important market information. By definition, historical volatility is based on past market volatility.

Currently traded option premiums are based not only on past market volatility, but also expected future volatility. Option traders track implied volatilities to determine an option's true value. Implied volatility is calculated by inserting the currently traded option premium into an option pricing formula and solving backward for the standard deviation. If the exact option model is of the form of the Black model, then all of the "knowns" (currently traded option premium, strike price, futures price, interest rates, time until expiration) can be used to solve for the "unknown" volatility. By tracking implied volatility measures over time, a trader begins to develop a sense of option value, that is, when options are being bid very high or offered very low.

An implied volatility chart tells a story of market fear. How much is the market willing to pay for price insurance?

Example: In Figures 7-7 and 7-8, implied volatilities for puts and calls from the first day of trading (crude oil options, November 4, 1986) are illustrated. At-the-money puts and calls for the second nearby option are used. (Put and call volatilities for the same strike price must trade at the same volatility. Discrepancies on the chart occur because settlement prices are used. Settlement prices are not the current market.)

During the first few days of trading, crude oil options exhibited implied volatilities between 35 percent and 37 percent (A on Figure 7-7), a high level when compared with options in most other markets. But the oil markets had just gone through one of the most volatile periods in recent history. Prices had gone from over $30.00 per barrel to under $10.00 in a few short months. The market traded quietly into the Thanksgiving holiday, and implied volatility declined to under 32 percent (B, Figure 7-7). However, during early December, OPEC was scheduled to meet. The option market anticipated this by sending option premiums soaring to above 38 percent on the day before the scheduled meeting. During this particular meeting, OPEC agreed on production cuts, sending prices higher and volatility lower into early 1987 (letter D,

FIGURE 7-7
Implied volatility (at-the-money options)

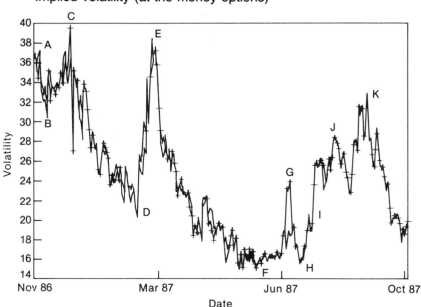

−Calls   +Puts

Figure 7-7). With OPEC back in control of its own production, option premiums were squeezed. Traders expected less volatility ahead, and this was reflected in option premiums.

In early February, however, prices began to weaken on news that OPEC was producing more than the quotas agreed on during the December meeting. Implied volatility, again measuring the willingness of the market to pay up for price insurance, soared from a low of around 21 percent (D) to 38 percent (E). Prices rebounded as evidence revealed that OPEC was no longer overproducing; volatility declined to 15 percent and sat there through June (F). Toward the end of June, OPEC was due to meet. The option market anticipated the potential volatility of the meeting by bidding up premiums to 24 percent on the day before the meeting began (G). The meeting was a success from OPEC's standpoint, and volatility quickly declined to 16 percent (H).

At this time, U.S. warships began to enter the gulf and tension, as

FIGURE 7-8
Implied volatility (at-the-money options)

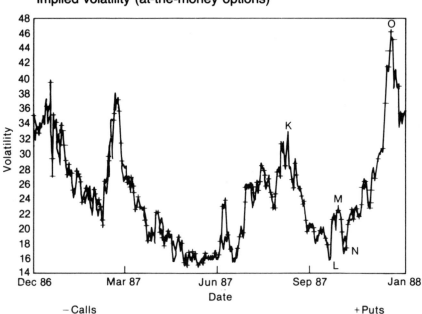

− Calls   + Puts

measured by the option market, rose (I). Volatility increased as prices increased. Highs in prices were made in August during the Mecca riot incident which highlighted tension in the Middle East. Implied volatility peaked, for a short time, at 28 percent (J). Prices subsequently declined, and volatility declined to 23 percent. Prices continued to fall, and as the markets became concerned that OPEC was overproducing, volatility climbed to 32 percent (K). Prices stabilized and began trading in a narrow range; volatility declined to 16 percent (L, Figure 7-8), Iran then attacked a U.S.-flagged ship causing prices to rally and volatility to increase to 22 percent (M). The markets quieted down and volatility retreated to 17 percent (N).

Approaching the December 1987 OPEC meeting, prices declined on talk of OPEC overproducing and discounting and plentiful crude and product supplies. As prices traded below $15.00 a barrel, implied volatility increased to 46 percent.

Based on only little more than a year's data, crude oil options, in general, tend to get more expensive as prices decline and less expensive as prices rally. Increasing price volatility is associated with a lack of OPEC resolve in adhering to production quotas. When OPEC overproduces, volatility picks up and prices decline. Each market has its own tendencies. Precious metals tend to increase in volatility most when prices are rising. Grains also increase in volatility most when prices increase. This is not to say the markets will not trade differently from their tendencies. But if crude volatility has been declining as prices rally, a trader might not use a buy call strategy to establish long positions. Higher prices work in favor of a long call, but declining volatility works against a long option. The trader might instead establish bull call spreads to offset the expected decline in volatility.

The point of tracking implied volatilities is to get a feel for option value in the market you are trading. Knowing option value will steer a trader toward a particular option strategy or away from another strategy. For example, let's say a trader is bearish on the market and wants to take a position. There are an infinite number of strategies, but we can focus on a few general categories. Let's also assume that implied volatility is 45 percent, an extremely high number based on history. The trader can sell futures, buy puts, sell calls, or enter into some bearish spread position. Let us examine each strategy.

Buying puts gives a trader the right to sell futures, a bearish position, at some fixed premium. But at 45 percent volatility the market is charging an extreme amount of money based on experience. Even though the risk of the buy put strategy is limited to the premium, the trader may not want to pay up for an option with a 45 percent implied volatility. If prices drop and volatility declines to 35 percent, the long put could actually decline in value. There are alternatives.

First, the trader could sell futures. Selling futures is profitable if prices go down. No premium is paid or received. The problem, however, is that the risk of selling futures is unlimited. And, if implied volatility is at historically high levels, it is likely that prices will fluctuate wildly in the near future. The trader gets around high premiums by selling futures, but the risk/reward profile is dramatically changed.

Second, the trader could sell calls to take advantage of high premiums. If prices decline or move sideways, the trader could earn the entire premium. In the case of crude oil (currently) if an out-of-the money call is sold at high volatility, profits may be earned even if prices rally. The tendency of oil options is to decline in volatility as prices rally. This decline and the passing of time may offset an increase in price. If prices continue to rally, however, the position has unlimited risk. And, if prices drop sharply, the most the position can earn is the premium.

Third, the trader might like the idea of taking a position with limited risk. The trader could buy a bear put spread to offset the high cost of options. For example, a trader could buy a $16.00 put and sell the $15.00 put to reduce the cost. A bear put spread is a limited-risk trade (Chapter 5) put on at low cost. If prices rally, the trader loses only the net debit of the trade, which is less than the buy put strategy outright. Subsidizing the $16.00 put purchase with a $15.00 put sale removes some of the effects of the high volatility on option premiums. However, if prices decline sharply, the trader no longer participates below $15.00.

Implied volatility is an important concept in option pricing and trading. Some traders will trade the implied volatility chart, selling volatility at the peaks (selling straddles and strangles) and buying volatility in the valleys (buying straddles and strangles). Others will track implied volatility to lean away from straight buy option strategies when implied. Volatility is high and shy away from selling options when implied volatility is low. In the example, the trader was bearish and had many alternatives. Each one may turn out to be profitable. Buying an option at an historically high volatility level does not mean that volatility can't go even higher. The "correct" strategy will be determined by each individual trader based on the level of acceptable risk, market opinion, and volatility opinion. The concept of implied volatility helps to steer a trader into an optimal position. The trader who understands implied volatility will begin to understand an option's value in the marketplace.

MARKET INFORMATION CONTAINED IN IMPLIED VOLATILITY DATA

The implied volatility measure is simply a standard deviation derived from substituting currently traded option premiums into an option pricing formula and solving backward for S. If the underlying assumption of the model is that the logs of percentage changes in prices are normally distributed is correct, we can use the implied volatility measure, or S, to determine market-expected price ranges within certain time periods. If the futures market gives a best guess as to where futures prices will be some time in the future, the options market reveals a range of prices around which futures are likely to trade.

Example: Crude oil is currently priced at $16.50. An option with 90 days left until expiration is trading at an implied volatility level of 35 percent. What does this 35 percent actually mean? From probability theory, we can say that for a price path that is normally distributed, prices would be expected to remain between plus or minus one standard deviation 67 percent of the time. But the 35 percent is a standard deviation relating to the logs of percentage changes in prices, not the absolute price. We need to transform the 35 percent into a price range around $16.50. To do this first solve the following equations:

$$+.35 = ln\ X_1 \quad \text{and} \quad -.35 = ln\ X_2$$

where ln is the natural log can be written as

$$e^{+.35} = X_1 \quad \text{and} \quad e^{-.35} = X_2$$

and solving gives

$$1.4191 = X_1 \quad \text{and} \quad .0747 = X_2$$

The original implied volatility is now in the form of percentage changes in prices. Multiplying 1.4191 by $16.50 and .7047 by $16.50 reveals a price range of $11.63 to $23.42. The option trading at 35 percent implied volatility indicates that the option market expects prices to range between $11.63 and $23.42 with a probability of 67 percent within the next year (recall that time, interest rates, and therefore the standard deviation are annualized in our model).[1] Different volatilities reveal

[1]We could calculate daily expected ranges by transforming the annualized standard deviation into a daily standard deviation. Dividing S by $\sqrt{365}$ or $\sqrt{255}$ will yield the daily standard deviation. The number of calendar days or trading days is used, depending on what is used in the model to calculate implied volatility. Some traders feel that 365 days are a more accurate measure because prices do change over weekends and holidays. However, since the model is mostly used as a filter, consistency is most important.

FIGURE 7-9

Price ranges calculated from implied volatility

Implied Volatility	Expected Price Range[1]		
	(Futures Price)		
	$15.50	$16.50	$17.50
15%	$13.34–18.01	$14.20–19.17	$15.06–20.33
25	12.07–19.90	12.85–21.19	13.63–22.47
35	10.92–22.00	11.63–23.42	12.33–24.83
45	9.88–24.31	10.52–25.88	11.16–27.45

[1]Annualized price range using ± 1 standard deviation.

different expected price ranges around the current futures price (See Figure 7-9).

An option trading at 45 percent volatility, with futures at $16.50, suggests an annual trading range of $10.52 to $25.88 with a 67 percent probability. Option traders establishing volatility positions by buying (long volatility) or selling (short volatility) straddles and strangles are really trading expected prices ranges. A trader who sells straddles or strangles is making a statement that expected volatility currently in the marketplace is too high. The trader believes that prices will trade in a narrower range than implied by current premiums. Conversely, a trader who buys straddles or strangles expects prices to trade in a wider range than implied by market premiums.

IMPLIED VOLATILITY DIFFERENCES
AMONG STRIKE PRICES

To derive an exact pricing formula for puts and calls, simplifying assumptions must be made. Each assumption makes calculating option premiums practical, but each takes the model farther and farther from reality. At the beginning of this chapter we introduced the Black model for commodity options. This model postulates that logs of percentage changes in prices follow a normal distribution. Further, the model assumes that volatility, or the standard deviation, and interest rates do not change for the life of the option, that prices trade in a continuous fashion (i.e., prices do not gap), that there is no early exercise of options. Do these assumptions reflect real life?[2] Of course not. Is the Black model still valid? Yes, but it is important for traders to realize where the model is effective and where it breaks down.

For example, one might expect implied volatilities for different strike prices for options of the same months to be equal. This is not normally the case. Figure 7-10 illustrates a normal pattern of implied volatilities across strike prices for February Deutsche mark options, December 22, 1987. Usually the at-the-money option will exhibit the lowest implied volatility.

From the at-the-money option, implied volatility will rise in both directions, parabola shaped. This occurs because the assumptions used to construct the model have abstracted it from real life. Based on implied volatilities alone, it appears that in-the-money and out-of-the-money options are overvalued relative to the at-the-money options. However, this does not automatically lead to the conclusion that at-the-money options should be bought and out-of-the-money options sold.

Figure 7-10 tells us that markets do not price options as if prices move in a log normal way, assumed in the Black and other models. In- and out-of-the-money options are higher priced based on implied volatilities. The market prices options as if there is a higher probability that prices will end up in the tails of the price distribution. The market, through option premiums, is saying that it is more likely for prices to travel farther away from today's price in either direction than is indicated in a log normal price distribution. Also, there is an early exercise premium that exists in futures' options that is not picked up by the Black

FIGURE 7-10
February Deutsche mark calls,
December 22, 1987

Strike Price	Implied Volatility
64	13.8
63	13.4
62	13.3
60	13.7
Futures price = 61.99	

[2]Some models use less restrictive assumptions to calculate call and put premiums. (See Appendix II.)

model, which assumes no early exercise. Because of the nature of futures' options margining, no cash flow takes place during the life of the option. If a trader buys a call and pays a premium up front, profits and losses are not realized until the position is offset. If the trader's call goes deep in the money, the only way to remove the marked to market cash is to trade out of the option or to exercise the option. Exercising the option converts the option into a futures contract. The trader can remove all excess cash above and beyond initial margin requirements. This cannot be done while the option is still an option. Although most options do not get exercised, there is an early exercise premium which is not captured by the Black model. Hence, deep in-the-money options with a long time until expiration will be undervalued by the model.

Some option models include modifications of the Black-Scholes model to represent real life more accurately. However, these models are usually much more complicated and take much longer to calculate. The trade-off becomes increased accuracy versus speed of calculation. Further, some of the changes made do not add much to accuracy. Thus, many option traders still trade off the basic Black model.

Sometimes the market will exhibit implied volatility levels not so "normal." For example, late November and early December of 1987 the implied volatilities for crude oil options exhibited a strange pattern (see Figure 7-11).

During this period OPEC was due to meet and discuss production quotas. The market was not optimistic as to OPEC's resolve in keeping production within quotas. Prices were under pressure, and the option market through implied volatility was indicating bearish sentiment.

FIGURE 7-11
March crude oil options,
December 3, 1987

Strike Price	Implied Volatility
20	26.6
19	26.6
18	28.1
17	30.0
16	31.1

Futures price = 18.46

The at-the-money option on December 3 could be considered the $18.00 or $19.00 strike price, since the futures price, $18.46, is in the middle. These options should exhibit the lowest implied volatilities with implied volatilities increasing for higher and lower strike prices. The pattern works for lower strikes ($17.00 and $16.00) but not for higher strikes ($19.00 and $20.00). Traders were willing to bid for options with strike prices below the market price but were not willing to bid for options with strike prices above the market. Traders were buying puts (with strikes below the market) aggressively and selling calls or not buying calls aggressively (with strikes above the market). The option market was revealing an awfully bearish sentiment in the crude oil market. Prices, in fact, collapsed to below $15.00 before rebounding.

Much information is gained by tracking implied volatilities. Traders who buy and sell volatility (buy and sell straddles and strangles) are in reality trading expected price ranges with the marketplace. Traders will sell straddles and strangles when they think that option premiums are too rich; that is, the market expects a wider price range than does the trader during the life of the option. Or traders will buy and sell straddles and strangles expecting a wider price range than what is built into the market.

A trader who tracks implied volatility can make a more informed decision on whether to buy or sell options. For example, a trader who is bearish and thinks volatility will decline might sell calls rather than buy puts. Another trader who is bullish and thinks that volatility will increase might buy calls instead of selling puts or buying futures. Option traders tracking implied volatilities will learn tendencies of markets. Implied volatilities in crude options tend to increase on downward price moves. Soybeans and gold act oppositely: implied volatility increases with price increases. In the next chapter we will learn a more precise way to measure the effect of a change of volatility on option premiums.

CHAPTER 8

Delta, Gamma, Vega, Theta

Exact option pricing formulas yield much useful information in addition to implied volatilities. Important risk parameters are calculated from the formula's partial derivatives. In this chapter we examine four of the more widely used measures: delta, gamma, vega (sometimes called sigma), and theta.

If, as we have said in Chapter 4, an option's value is a function of the current futures price, the strike price, interest rates, time until expiration, and expected volatility, then, as each factor changes, the premium will change. If futures prices change, a week goes by, or volatility increases, the option's premium will also change. What option traders would like to know is by how much. We know that if a week goes by, option premiums will decline in value (everything else remaining unchanged). But how much of a decline should we expect? If volatility increases from 25 percent to 35 percent how will that effect a particular option premium? The partial derivatives help to quantify how changes in each option pricing factor effect option premiums.

DELTA

The first partial derivative we examine is delta. An option's delta is defined as the change in the option's premium due to a change in the futures price.

Example: An $18.00 crude oil call option has a delta of .45. If the futures price moves up by $.10, the option premium should move by 45 percent of the $.10 tick or up by $.04 to $.05. A put option with a delta of .45 would be expected to show a premium decline equal to 45 percent of the upward futures move. A put trading at $.50 might trade at $.45 if prices moved a dime higher.

Option premiums for D mark options are listed in Table 8-1, and deltas are listed in Table 8-2. The January $.62 call settled at $.0068 (Table 8-1) with a delta of .503 (Table 8-2). If D mark futures move from $.6199 up to $.6209 or 10 ticks higher, the call premium would be

TABLE 8-1

Option premiums for D mark options on June futures, December 22, 1987

	Option Expiration					
	Jan 1/9		Feb 2/6		Mar 3/5	
Strike Price	Call	Put	Call	Put	Call	Put
.64	.0015		.0048		.0075	.0273
	(13.4)[1]		(13.8)		(13.7)	(13.7)
.63	.0032	.0132	.0075	.0175	.0104	.0204
	(12.6)	(12.5)	(13.4)	(13.3)	(13.3)	(13.4)
.62	.0068	.0069	.0113	.0114	.0146	.0147
	(12.2)	(12.2)	(12.9)	(12.9)	(13.2)	(13.2)
.61	.0131	.0033	.0172	.0074	.0201	.0103
	(12.7)	(12.8)	(13.3)	(13.3)	(−11.4)	(−11.6)
.60	.0213	.0015	.0243	.0046	.0266	.0070
	(13.6)	(13.8)	(13.7)	(13.8)	(−10.1)	(−10.6)

Underlying futures = .6199

[1]Implied volatilities in parentheses.

TABLE 8-2
Option deltas for D mark options on June futures, December 22, 1987

| | Option Expiration | | | | | |
| | Jan 1/9 | | Feb 2/6 | | Mar 3/5 | |
Strike Price	Call	Put	Call	Put	Call	Put
.64	.151		.267		.315	.686
.63	.292	.709	.377	.623	.406	.594
.62	.503	.497	.508	.492	.511	.489
.61	.716	.286	.641	.359	.616	.384
.60	.857	.146	.754	.247	.714	.288

Underlying futures = .6199

expected to increase to .0073, 5 ticks higher based on a .503 delta. The $.62 put, with a delta of .497, would be expected to trade 5 ticks lower.

Deltas allow option traders to convert option positions into futures equivalent positions for risk measurement purposes. For example, an option trader who is long 10 January $.62 calls has a futures equivalent position of long 5.03 futures contracts (10 options × .503 delta = 5.03 equivalent futures). The trader knows that being long those 10 calls is similar to (but not exactly the same as) being long 5 futures.

Signs are attached to option deltas to denote bullish or bearish positions. Long futures, long calls, and short puts have positive deltas. Short futures, short calls, and long puts have negative deltas. This allows traders to sum all option and futures positions and derive an overall delta exposure. Delta exposure gives the trader an indication of how long or how short the entire position is.

Delta is a dynamic concept and is constantly changing as futures prices move, as time ticks away and as volatility changes. In mathematical terms an option's delta is calculated as follows:

For a call;

$$\frac{\Delta C}{\Delta F} = \frac{\text{change in call premium}}{\text{change in futures price}} = e^{-rt}[N(d_1)]$$

For a put;

$$\frac{\Delta P}{\Delta F} = \frac{\text{change in put premium}}{\text{change in futures price}} = e^{-rt}[1 - N(d_1)]$$

where:
$N(d)$ = the cumulative normal integral
$\ \ r\ \ $ = interest rate, annualized
$\ \ S\ \ $ = standard deviation of logs of percent changes in prices, annualized
$\ \ F\ \ $ = futures price
$\ \ E\ \ $ = strike price
$\ \ t\ \ $ = time to expiration, annualized
$\ ln\ $ = natural logarithm
$\ \ e\ \ $ = exponent = 2.7183

The main point to get from this somewhat complicated formula is that an option's delta is a function of the futures price, strike price, time, volatility, and interest rates. As each one of these factors change, the delta's change.

Example: Let's examine Table 8-2 more closely with respect to each factor.

First, as an option moves deeper and deeper in the money, the delta approaches one. As the option moves deeper and deeper out of the money, the delta approaches zero. This is illustrated by comparing the delta of the January $.64 out-of-the-money call (.151) with the delta of the January $.60 in-the-money call (.857). In fact, the $N(d_1)$ term in the call delta formula and the $N(d_1) - 1$ term in the put delta formula can be interpreted as the probability that the particular option will expire, in the money. A deep in-the-money option has a high probability that it will expire in the money while a deep out of the money option has a low probability that it will expire in the money. At-the-money options are the most uncertain as to whether they will expire in or out of the money. Thus, at-the-money options will exhibit deltas of around .5. (Actually, at-the-money calls will exhibit deltas of slightly more than .5, while puts will exhibit deltas slightly less than .5, reflecting the log normal price distribution underlying the option model). Note, again, that at-the-money options also contain the most time value.

As volatility changes, option deltas change. An increase in volatility, under normal circumstances, will have the effect of moving options that are in and out of the money toward the at-the-money option. That is, the delta of an out-of-the money option will increase in absolute value as volatility increases while the delta of an in-the-money option will decrease. If volatility increases, the out-of-the money option has a better chance to expire in-the-money while the in the money option has less of a chance to expire in the money. The deltas approach a delta of about .50 (an at-the-money option) as volatility increases. Determining delta risk during volatile periods can be quite difficult not only because futures prices are moving around, but also because volatility as a variable in the delta equation is volatile.

As time passes, deltas change. Consider an extreme situation, when zero time is left. An option in the money will exhibit a delta of one because it will trade entirely on intrinsic value or tick for tick with the futures contract. An option out of the money will exhibit a delta of zero because it is about to expire worthless. On expiration day, option deltas become so volatile as to become a virtually useless measure of risk. For example, if futures are trading near a strike price at expiration, the option delta could go from zero to one with just a small move in prices. The option is at zero when it looks as if the option will expire worthless and increase to one when it looks as if the option will expire in the money and thus be converted into a futures contract. The point is that within the last few days of trading, an option's delta becomes too volatile to use as a measure of market risk.

Example: Table 8-2 illustrates the effects of time option deltas. For all three months, the at-the-money options' deltas are roughly .5. The .62 call delta differs from the .63 call delta by .211 in January, .131 in February, and only .105 in March. More time has a similar effect on option deltas as does more volatility: in-the-money option deltas decline and out-of-the-money option deltas increase in absolute value.

It is important for traders to understand the strengths and weaknesses of using delta as a measure of market risk. The concept is very powerful because it lets option traders aggregate complex positions into a single measure of market exposure. When volatility is changing rapidly, or expiration is near, however, delta can be a misleading indicator of market risk. We need to look at other measures to get an overall picture of risk.

GAMMA

The major weakness in using only deltas as a risk measure is illustrated by examining a short selling straddle strategy.

Example: An option trader is short 100 February $.62 straddles. The delta for this trade is calculated using the option deltas listed in Table 8-2.

Strategy	Option Delta	Position Delta
Short 100 Feb $.62 calls	− .508	− 50.8
Short 100 Feb $.62 puts	+ .492	+ 49.2
Short 100 Feb $.62 straddles		− 61.6

The trader is short a total of 200 options, and yet the overall delta position shows a futures equivalent position of short only 1.6 futures. Does this mean that any two-lot trader can sell 100 straddles? Certainly not! If prices rally sharply, the puts go farther and farther out of the money, which means the delta moves toward zero. The short calls, however, move more into the money, and their deltas approach minus one per option. That is, the position gets more and more bearish as prices rally. It is possible for this trade to move from a − 1.6 delta to a − 90 to − 100 delta position if prices rally sharply. Similarly, the position gets longer and longer (more bullish) the market as prices go lower: the call deltas approach zero, while the puts approach one. The short strangle gets more exposed as prices move away from the strike price in either direction. This kind of exposure is called gamma exposure.

Gamma is the change in an option's delta due to a change in the underlying futures price. It is a measure of the volatility or stability of the option's delta. Like delta, gamma is only good for small changes in futures prices because it also is constantly changing.

Example: Option gammas are listed in Table 8-3. The $.62 February call has a gamma of .139. This means that if prices move 20 ticks

TABLE 8-3

Option gammas for D mark options on June futures, December 22, 1987

| | Option Expiration | | | | | |
| | Jan 1/9 | | Feb 2/6 | | Mar 3/5 | |
Strike Price	Call	Put	Call	Put	Call	Put
.64	.124		.107		.092	.092
.63	.193	.193	.128	.128	.104	.103
.62	.231	.232	.139	.139	.107	.107
.61	.189	.187	.126	.126	.102	.102
.60	.117	.118	.103	.103	.090	.089

Underlying futures = .6199

higher, the delta will increase from .508 to .536 (.139 × 20 = .0278, .028 + .508 = .536). Recall that delta signs are positive for bullish positions and negative for bearish positions. Gamma signs are positive for long options (long puts, long calls) and negative for short options (short puts, short calls). In this example, a long call delta is moving from +.508 to +.536. The delta exposure is moving in the same direction as the price. The position gets longer and longer the market as prices go up. Thus, gamma is positive. If the trader is short the call in this example, the delta position is moving from −.508 to −.536 (a higher number to a lower number when signs are included). Now, the delta exposure is moving against the market. As the market moves higher, the position gets shorter and shorter the market. Long options equal long gamma and short options equal short gamma.

Our short 100 February $.64 straddle example has more risk associated with it than implied by the −1.6 delta position. Calculating gamma exposure gives a better picture of market risk.

Strategy	Option Gamma	Position Gamma
Short 100 Feb $.62 calls	−.139	−13.9
Short 100 Feb $.62 puts	−.139	−13.9
Short 100 Feb $.62 straddles		−27.8

If prices move 10 ticks higher, the trader could expect the position to get shorter the market by about three futures equivalents.

Option market makers are very concerned about gamma exposure. In fact, many market makers require their floor traders to stay gamma neutral as well as delta neutral. This is achieved by selling options (straddles) when gamma exposure is too positive and buying options (straddles) when gamma is too negative.

In mathematical terms the options gamma is the second derivative of the option pricing formula with respect to the futures price or:

$$\text{Gamma} = \frac{\Delta \text{ in delta}}{\Delta \text{ in futures price}} = \frac{e^{(-rt - .5d_1^2)}}{FS\sqrt{2\pi t}}$$

Gamma is the same for puts and calls.

The math is illustrated here not to confuse anyone but to illustrate the fact that gamma is dependent on the futures prices, the strike price, volatility, time, and interest rates. If any one of these factors changes (which they do constantly), gamma exposure changes. Gamma, like delta, is a dynamic concept.

An option's delta becomes most volatile around expiration. This should be reflected in gamma.

Example: Table 8-3 lists option gammas for three different months. Notice that the highest gamma for each month is exhibited by the at-the-money option. This is the option that is most uncertain as to whether it will expire in the money. The highest gamma of all three months is contained on the January at-the-money option. A higher gamma implies a less stable delta. The lowest gamma of all three months is located on the March at-the-money option. At times, option traders will take advantage of gamma being higher in nearby months and lower in farther out months by buying nearby options and selling options farther out. The idea is that a price move will affect the nearby options at a greater rate (the options deltas are changing much more rapidly) than the deferred month options.

Gamma strategies are covered in greater detail in the next chapter. For now, suffice it to say that gamma exposure helps option traders to determine what their positions will be like when prices blow out in either direction. The trader needs to be sure that negative gamma exposure is not too great in case prices do move sharply.

VEGA

Vega measures the change in an option's premium due to a change in volatility. In Chapter 7, we had showed how crude oil implied volatility ranged between 15 percent and 45 percent. What does that mean in dollar terms to an option premium? Vega gives option traders a way to quantify volatility exposure.

Vega calculated for puts and calls use the same formula:

$$\text{Vega} = \frac{\Delta \text{ in premium}}{\Delta \text{ in volatility}} = \frac{e^{(-rt - .5d_1^2)} F\sqrt{t}}{\sqrt{2\pi}}$$

Note again that all the partial derivates or risk measures are functions of futures prices, strike prices, time to expiration, interest rates, and volatility. Vega, like gamma and delta, is dynamic. As any one of the factors changes, vega changes.

Example: Option vegas are listed in Table 8-4. In this table, an 11.1 vega means that an increase in volatility of .1 will increase the option premium by $11.10, or an increase in implied volatility from 12.9 percent (Table 5-1) to 13.0 percent for the February $.62 call, will increase the option premium from .0113 to .0114 (one tick in D mark options is worth $12.50). In markets that are known to move in full percentage points, volatility exposure can be significant.

Let's return to our earlier example of a short straddle strategy:

Strategy	Option Vega	Position Vega
Short 100 Feb $.62 calls	−11.1	−1,110
Short 100 Feb $.62 puts	−11.1	−1,110
Short 100 Feb $.62 straddles		−2,220

TABLE 8-4

Option vegas for D mark options on June futures,
December 22, 1987

	Option Expiration					
	Jan 1/9		Feb 2/6		Mar 3/5	
Strike Price	Call	Put	Call	Put	Call	Put
.64	4.1		9.1			
.63	6.1	6.1	10.6	10.6	13.6	13.6
.62	7.1	7.1	11.1	11.1	14.0	14.0
.61	6.0	6.0	10.4	10.4	13.4	13.4
.60	4.0	4.0	8.8	8.8	12.0	12.0

Underlying futures = .6199

Obviously, this position is very exposed to an increase in volatility. It is aggressively short volatility. This position will lose $2,220.00 for every increase in implied volatility of .1 and will earn $2,220.00 for every .1 percentage point decline.

Vega exposure underlines the problems that traders face when selling deep out-of-the money options. A false sense of security exists for the trader who sells $.60 D mark puts when the market is at $.6199. It appears that the option will expire worthless, and the trader will profit the entire premium. And the trader might sell a few more deep outs than normal because it looks like a safe trade. But what happens if the market drops sharply? Obviously, the option will trade higher. Compounding the price effect could be a sharp increase in volatility. The trader could see an option trading two to three times for what it was sold. Now, the trader must decide to take the loss or cover with futures. But covering with futures introduces another risk, that of being whipsawed. Traders must be careful not to sell more options just because they are deep out of the money and look safe.

Example: Notice in Table 8-4 that vegas are highest on options that have the most time left until expiration. Changes in volatility have a much greater effect on longer dated options than on nearby options. In fact, the vega on the March $.62 put is twice that of the January $.62 put. Traders who are taking pure volatility positions would tend to establish positions in outer months, assuming of course, that outer-month bid offer spreads aren't too prohibitive. Selling nearby options takes advantage more of the effect that time has on option premiums.

THETA

Theta is the time derivative. That is, the change in option premium due to a change in time. How fast is the option wasting away? For hedgers, how much is price insurance costing on a daily basis? Theta helps traders determine where exactly their position is along the time decay curve.

Example: Option thetas are listed in Table 8-5. The February $.62 call has a theta of -15.0. This means that the option is losing $15.00 overnight, with all other factors remaining unchanged. Theta shows a deterioration of option premium at a much greater rate for the January options when compared with the February or March options. This effect, of course, was illustrated in Chapter 4 as a time decay curve (Figure 4-1).

A constant tug of war is played out between time and volatility. Time always wins out and has a much greater effect on nearby options. An increase in volatility has a similar effect as adding time to the option's life, but has a much greater effect on options that have not yet entered time's vice like grip.

Example: Continuing our short straddle example yields the following:

Strategy	Option Theta	Position Theta
Short 100 Feb $.62 calls	+14.9	+1,490
Short 100 Feb $.62 puts	+15.0	+1,500
Short 100 Feb $.62 straddles		+2,990

TABLE 8-5
Option thetas for D mark options on June futures,
December 22, 1987

| | Option Expiration | | | | | |
| | Jan 1/9 | | Feb 2/6 | | Mar 3/5 | |
Strike Price	Call	Put	Call	Put	Call	Put
.64	− 14.5		− 13.2		− 11.1	
.63	− 20.2	− 19.8	− 14.8	− 14.6	− 11.8	− 11.6
.62	− 22.8	− 22.7	− 14.9	− 15.0	− 11.9	− 11.9
.61	− 19.9	− 20.4	− 14.4	− 14.5	− 11.4	− 11.6
.60	− 13.8	− 14.6	− 12.2	− 12.7	− 10.1	− 10.1

Underlying futures = .6199

Short options have positive thetas because time works in favor of short option positions. The position theta indicates that this trade earns $2,990.00 per day. If the trade had been a long straddle, the position would be losing $2,990.00 per day.

The math looks like this:

$$\text{Theta} = \frac{\Delta \text{ in call premium}}{\Delta \text{ in time}} = -rc + \frac{e^{(-rt - .5d_1^2)}FS}{\sqrt{8\pi t}}$$

and

$$\frac{\Delta \text{ in put premium}}{\Delta \text{ in time}} = \text{call theta} - [re^{-rt}(E - F)]$$

Trading options involves buying and selling various parts of a probability distribution that is always changing. Changes in time, volatility, futures prices, and interest rates all affect option premiums. This chapter examined some measures that quantify position exposures to changes in those key factors. Before a trader establishes any position in the marketplace, it is crucial to know the risks involved. Using deltas, gammas, vegas, and thetas as risk management tools helps a trader to recognize unwanted exposures. Each of the risk parameters discussed in this chapter is dependent on the usual factors: the futures price, strike price, time, volatility, and interest rates. Theta also is a dynamic concept and changes as any one of the factors change. The complicated nature of options can sometimes lead to situations and positions that do not reflect the trader's market opinion or risk preference.

In the next chapter, we will examine the risk parameters of specific positions. As cash futures and option positions become more and more complex, risk assessment becomes more and more important.

PART III

SETTING THEORY TO PRACTICE

CHAPTER 9

Portfolio Analysis

As options are introduced into a hedger's or speculator's trading program, the nature of risk management is changed significantly. A hedger buys puts to protect against declining prices. However, buying put strategies, while reducing downside price risk, introduces volatility risk and time risk. If prices drift slowly down to the strike price until after the option expires, and then decline some more, the hedger loses the premium without receiving protection. A speculator may have a complicated position established to take advantage of a particular market and volatility opinion. It is important for the speculator to understand where and when the worst case scenario occurs. As option positions become more complex, the risks are not always clear, nor are they only risks involving price movement.

In the last chapter we described four risk parameters that option traders track to measure total exposure: delta, gamma, vega, and theta. In this chapter we look at the parameters from an overall portfolio perspective. Option traders usually do not hold positions until expiration. Profit/loss diagrams discussed in Chapter 5 are informative as to price risk/reward at expiration. But now we are interested in what happens to the portfolio throughout the life of the option.

HEDGING A LONG CASH POSITION

Buying Puts

A simple buy put strategy illustrates how traders could go about analyzing a portfolio.

Example: An oil company is long 100,000 barrels of oil in the cash market and wants to establish a price floor by buying $17.00 puts at $.48. (Settlement prices are for May 19, 1988. See the appendix to this chapter.) As a proxy for the cash position, assume that the company is long 100 September futures contracts at the current price of $17.91. The options expire in 86 days. Using a pricing model, the risk parameters are calculated in Table 9-1.

The position delta at current prices is +68.5. Or this position, long 100 $17.00 puts and long 100 futures, is equivalent to being long 68.5 futures. The individual option delta is −.315. Multiplying by 100 options yields an option position delta of −31.5. Add to this the futures delta, +100 to get the overall position delta of +68.5. This information tells the hedger that this position profits if prices increase.

How is the delta going to change if prices change? The position gamma is +15.9. This means that if prices move up, the position gets longer the market or adds deltas. If prices go down, the position gets shorter the market or loses deltas. If prices move up by $.10, the position delta should increase by 1.59 deltas. A long gamma position also means that no defensive action must be taken if prices begin to move violently in either direction.

Downside price protection is created from the long put position, but the position profits when prices increase. The hedger is bullish the market, but can't afford to be too wrong. In Table 9-1, position deltas and gammas are calculated over $.50 price increments. As prices go up, the delta increases; as prices go down, the delta decreases. The hedger already knows this from looking at a positive gamma.

This position is exposed to declining volatility expectations. The position vega, +$3,090.00, indicates a loss of $3,090.00 if volatility moves lower by one percentage point (in the previous chapter, vega was described in terms of tenths of percentage points because implied volatility for options is normally half to a third of crude oil volatility). If volatility increases, the puts will increase in value by $3,090.00, for every percentage point increase. Recent history shows crude oil implied volatility for the money options ranging from 15 percent to 45 percent. In dollar terms, this could be career ending for the trader who sells volatility at 15 percent and covers at 45 percent.

Owning price insurance has its costs. On a daily basis, this position is losing $448.00 (position theta). The lower half of Table 9-1 indicates losses of $3,187.00 if nothing changes after a week. If prices remain unchanged for the life of the option, losses are $48,000.00.

This is a bullish position that gets more bullish as prices go up and less bullish as prices go down. In return for downside price protection, the hedger is exposed to declining volatility and the passing of time. If implied volatility declines from 25.7 to 24.7 for the $17.00 put, the position loses $3,090.00. The position loses $448.00 the first day, but increasing amounts as the option approaches expiration. The hedger has substituted volatility and time risk for some downside price protection. By applying portfolio analysis, the option trader can track how the portfolio reacts to changing market conditions on a daily basis.

TABLE 9-1
Portfolio analysis: long puts

| Position: | Long 100 Sept. $17.00 puts at $.48 | | | | |
| | Long 100 Sept. futures at $17.91 | | | | |

Futures price:	16.91	17.41	17.91	18.41	18.91
Position delta	50.8	60.0	68.5	75.8	82.0
Position gamma	18.9	17.8	15.9	13.6	11.1
Position vega	3,270	3,260	3,090	2,790	2,410
Position theta	− 468	− 471	− 448	− 405	− 351

Days Elapsed	Profit/Loss ($)				
1	− 60,960	− 32,884	− 448	35,918	75,641
7	− 63,837	− 35,772	− 3,187	33,452	73,524
14	− 67,348	− 39,290	− 6,501	30,501	71,026
16	− 139,000	− 98,000	− 48,000	27,000	52,000

Delta-Neutral Hedging. Table 9-1 shows portfolio losses if prices drop.

Example: The losses are limited, eventually, because the hedger has bought 100 $17.00 puts against the long 100 futures. A minimum selling price is established at $16.52 ($17.00 − $.48), but the hedger might want protection against any drop in prices. A delta-neutral position could be created by purchasing more than 100 $17.00 puts. The amount of options required to create a delta-neutral position is equal to the reciprocal of the option's delta. Two options with deltas of .5 could cover one futures position. The option's delta is also referred to as the *hedging ratio*.

The oil company could buy 317 $17.00 puts to cover the long 100 futures position exactly in delta terms ($317 \times -.315 = 100$). Table 9-2 summarizes the risk parameters.

The delta position is zero at the current price. However, if prices change, the delta position will also change. The position exhibits a gamma of 50.4. The gamma exposure is much higher compared with the long 100 put position. If prices increase by $.10 the position gets more

TABLE 9-2
Portfolio analysis: long puts, delta neutral

| Position: | Long 317 Sept. $17.00 puts at $.48 | | | | |
| | Long 100 Sept. futures at $17.91 | | | | |

Futures price:	16.91	17.41	17.91	18.41	`18.91
Position delta	− 56.0	− 26.8	0	23.4	43.0
Position gamma	59.9	56.4	50.4	43.1	35.2
Position vega	10,380	10,350	9,800	8,840	7,630
Position theta	11,485	− 1,492	− 1,420	− 1,285	− 1,111

Days Elapsed	Profit/Loss ($)				
1	23,756	4,259 −	1,420	5,631	22,783
7	14,636 −	4,898 −	10,102 −	2,456	16,070
14	3,506 −	16,050 −	20,607 −	11,812	8,153
16	− 223,630	− 202,160	− 152,160	− 102,160 −	52,160

bullish by 5 futures equivalents. If prices decline by $.10, the position gets bearish by 5 futures.

If prices move away from the current price in either direction within the next few days, the position profits. However, there is much time and volatility exposure. If volatility declines by one percentage point, the position loses $9,800.00. The position deteriorates at a rate of $1,420.00, which is the cost of price insurance for one day.

The hedger has turned a long cash position into a long volatility position getting delta neutral from buying puts. The position greatly increases time and volatility exposure. A hedger might get delta neutral with long put options ahead of an OPEC meeting, expecting volatility to increase sharply. Another way to get delta neutral without increasing time and volatility exposure, of course, is to trade futures. Selling long 100 futures against a 100,000-barrel cash position is delta neutral. The hedger needs to decide what level of delta exposure is appropriate for current market conditions.

Using an option pricing model to analyze the portfolio, the hedger knows how exposed to price changes the company is. If prices change in either direction, the hedger can reassess the portfolio. If prices rally, the hedger might decide to increase protection by selling futures, buying more puts or selling calls. If prices decline, the hedger could sell the $17.00 puts and take profits, or could sell $16.00 puts. The hedger can continually reassess market opinion and adjust the market exposure accordingly.

In fact, a hedger could replicate a long put option by selling enough futures to cover the put's delta.

Example: The $17.00 put has a delta of .315. To replicate 100 long $17.00 puts, the hedger could sell 31 or 32 futures. To continue replicating the $17.00 put, futures positions must adjust to changing deltas. If prices dropped by $.50 the option's delta is now − .40. An additional 9 futures must be sold to replicate the option. Replicating options in this manner causes the hedger to sell more and more futures as prices go lower and to buy more and more futures as prices go higher.

Any strategy that uses futures to replicate options is eventually doomed to fail. For delta hedging strategies to work, markets must trade continuously. That is, prices must move in an orderly fashion without gaps. The futures hedges must be implemented to accommodate changing deltas. If the market gaps open, the replicated option's delta changes, but futures hedges aren't able to be adjusted accordingly. Most markets at some time have gone through extremely volatile periods thwarting attempts to replicate options. Further, if a market exhibits high volatility, delta risk is difficult to assess; recall that an option's delta is also a function of volatility. If volatility is changing violently, deltas are changing also. The result is that delta-neutral hedging strategies, portfolio insurance, or replicating option strategies fail when they are needed the most—during times of high volatility and uncertainty.

Selling Calls

Example: The hedger is long 100,000 barrels of oil in the cash market (or long 100 September futures at $17.91 as a proxy). In the buy put example, the hedger was bullish the market but still needed some price protection at lower levels. Now, the market opinion is that prices are likely to go slightly higher and that option premiums are expensive. The hedger sells 100 $19.00 calls for $.40.

The option delta is $-.323$; the position delta is -32.3 or short 32.3 futures equivalents (Table 9-3). Add to this 100 long futures gives an overall position delta of $+.67.7$, a bullish position. If delta risk were the only risk, this position would be equivalent to being long 100 $17.00 puts in our first example. The delta risk of that strategy was $+68.5$.

TABLE 9-3
Portfolio analysis: short calls

| Position: | Short 100 Sept. $19.00 calls at $.40 | | | | |
	Long 100 Sept. futures at $17.91				
Futures price:	16.91	17.91	17.91	18.41	18.91
Position delta	83.2	76.1	67.7	58.7	49.4
Position gamma	-13.0	-15.6	-17.5	-18.5	-18.5
Position vega	$-2,060$	$-2,620$	$-3,120$	$-3,480$	$-3,660$
Position theta	275	350	415	461	482

Days Elapsed	Profit/Loss ($)				
1	− 75,938	− 35,841	415	32,349	59,753
7	− 74,290	− 33,721	2,945	35,171	62,708
14	− 72,373	− 31,206	5,994	38,603	66,314
86	− 60,000	− 10,000	40,000	90,000	140,000

Comparing the two significantly different strategies illustrates the weakness of looking only at deltas as an indicator of market risk. Much more is revealed by gamma.

Example: The position gamma is − 17.5. This means that rising prices cause the position to lose deltas (or get shorter the market) and declining prices cause the position to gain deltas (to get longer the market). If prices move $.10 higher, the delta position would decline by 1.75. A $.10 lower move would increase the delta position by 1.75. This is the opposite of what happens to the buy put strategy, which adds deltas in rising markets and subtracts deltas in declining markets.

Negative gamma (short options) tells a trader that defensive action may be required if prices move sharply away from today's price. In this case, a sharp move upward is covered: profits from 100 long futures eventually will offset equal losses from 100 short calls. If prices move sharply lower, a defensive decision might be made to sell more calls, buy puts, sell futures, or liquidate the cash position, depending on the new market opinion. Understanding the nature of gamma risk reveals the inner workings of option pricing and portfolio risk.

Market makers strive for gamma neutrality as well as delta neutrality. To get gamma neutral in this example, a trader would buy options to increase a − 17.5 gamma to zero. Puts or calls could be bought because long options have positive gammas and short options have negative gammas. The choice of options to buy or sell will be determined by cheapness, gamma levels, and stability of gamma. For example, deep out-of-the-money calls may be cheap, but many must be bought to reduce gamma exposure. One way to reduce positive gamma exposure is to sell straddles or strangles. By selling straddles or strangles, the portfolio's delta position will be changed, but only slightly. The market maker can get delta neutral simply by buying or selling futures. (Futures, of course, have no gamma, vega, or theta exposure.) The option with the highest gamma will be the at-the-money option of the nearest option month. This may not be a good option to buy or sell because it expires soon and its gamma is volatile.

Selling options has opposite volatility and time exposure compared with buying options. In this example, selling 100 calls earns $415.00 overnight. Time works in favor of short option strategies. However, the position is exposed to increasing volatility. If volatility increases by 1 percent point, this position loses $3,120.00.

Volatility exposure can cause problems for traders who are short options.

Example: A trader is short 100 $19.00 calls naked. Prices begin to rally, the $19.00 calls are bid higher. Panic buying bids up the calls (implied volatility increases) an additional 10 ticks. The trader has two factors going against the short call position: higher prices and higher volatility. If the trader covers by purchasing back the short call position, a high price must be paid, but this is usually the best thing to do.

The trader could also buy futures to cover the short calls. The problem with this strategy is that she could get whipsawed: prices move higher, volatility moves higher, and the trader buys futures. Now prices move sharply lower, the trader sells futures at a lower price and prices move higher. Defensive actions used when trading options should be similar to those used when trading futures: set maximum risks before establishing positions. If premiums reach the maximum risk points, get out.

Example: Our hedger now thinks that option premiums are expensive and desires a delta neutral position. The $19.00 calls exhibit a delta of $-.323$. Selling 310 (1 $\div$ .323) calls achieves a short 100 delta position (Table 9-4). What kind of risks does the position now have?

The delta position is flat at current prices. But we know that delta is a dynamic concept. How will delta change over changes in price? Gamma exposure is -54.4. If prices move $.10 higher, the positions become 5.44 futures equivalents shorter the market. If prices move $.10 lower, the position gains 5.44 deltas (gets longer the market).

The position earns $1,285.00 overnight, everything else equal.

TABLE 9-4
Portfolio analysis: short calls delta neutral

| Position: | Short 310 Sept. $19.00 calls at $.40 | | | | |
| | Long 100 Sept. futures at $17.91 | | | | |

Futures price:	16.91	17.41	17.91	18.41	18.91
Position delta	48.0	25.8	0	− 28.1	− 56.9
Position gamma	− 40.3	− 48.4	− 54.4	− 57.4	− 57.3
Position vega	− 6,380	− 8,130	− 9,670	− 10,790	− 11,350
Position theta	852	1,084	1,285	1,429	1,494

Days Elapsed	Profit/Loss ($)				
1	− 25,409	− 6,106	1,285	− 4,720	− 24,766
7	− 20,298	464	9,131	4,031	− 15,605
14	− 14,356	8,261	18,581	14,669	− 4,427
86	24,000	74,000	124,000	174,000	224,000

However, if volatility moves higher by one percentage point the position loses $9,670.00. In Table 9-4, the profit/loss profile shows large profits if prices stay where they are or move slightly higher. Losses accrue if prices move sharply in either direction. The hedger has turned an exposed long cash position into a position that is exposed to higher volatility.

This example illustrates the downside of ratio spreads. A ratio spread usually involves selling more options than buying options. For example, two $18.00 calls are sold for every $18.00 call bought. The idea is to establish the position for little or no cash outlay. The trader feels that position can be liquidated before the market reaches the strike price of the short option. This is not always the case as option traders on days such as October 19, 1987 have experienced. The advantages of selling many options to cover fewer long options or futures positions are offset by the increased risk of being short options during a highly volatile period.

The hedger could remain delta neutral by selling more calls as prices decline and by buying calls as prices increase. The delta-neutral position could be maintained by trading futures or puts also. However, because of transaction costs, and the difficulty in maintaining delta neutrality during volatile times, hedgers normally do not strictly maintain delta neutral positions. Further, most hedgers are in business to assume some kind of risk. A total reduction in price risk is likely not attainable nor desirable.

LONG STRADDLES

Buying puts and calls with the same strike price (straddles) or with different strike prices (strangles) enable a trader to take advantage of sharp swings in futures prices. The trader is not concerned with the direction of the price move but with the magnitude of the move. The idea is that profits accruing on the long calls (long puts) more than offset losses accruing on the long puts (long calls). Long straddles are popular trades ahead of scheduled economic events. For example, a trader might buy bond straddles ahead of an unemployment report, crude oil straddles ahead of an OPEC meeting, or currency straddles ahead of a merchandise trade number. The increased demand for buy option strategy ahead of these scheduled events causes option premiums to be bid higher. The degree of the increase in demand is detected by tracking implied volatility.

Traders also buy straddles to take advantage of changes in implied volatility. For example, a trader might anticipate the fact that options will begin to bid higher as an OPEC meeting approaches. The trader might buy straddles at 25 percent volatility expecting to sell them back at 30 percent volatility. Many times, novice option traders are surprised when a particular option declines in value, even though prices have moved in the right direction. What usually happens is that the option is bought a day or two before an economic report is due, that is, when implied volatility is very high. After the release, the market digests the new information, and implied volatility collapses; the demand for buy option strategies declines.

Example: A long straddle strategy is summarized in Table 9-5. September futures prices are at $17.91. The trader is long 100 $18.00 puts and long 100 $18.00 calls. The position delta at current prices is

TABLE 9-5

Portfolio analysis: long straddles

Position:	Long 100 Sept. $18.00 calls at $.87				
	Long 100 Sept. $18.00 puts at $.87				

Futures price:	16.91	17.41	17.91	18.41	18.91
Position delta	− 34.5	−16.6	1.7	19.3	35.6
Position gamma	34.7	36.5	36.2	34.2	30.8
Position vega	5,930	6,600	6,930	6,920	6,580
Position theta	−833	−932	− 983	−980	− 927

Days Elapsed	Profit/Loss ($)				
1	15,528	2,813	− 983	4,309	17,978
7	10,448	− 2,900	−7,013	− 1,698	12,306
14	4,321	− 9,849	−14,371	− 9,016	5,435
86	− 65,000	− 115,000	− 165,000	− 133,000	− 83,000

+ 1.7, slightly bullish. This particular straddle has a delta exposure because the straddle is not at the money. The trader could create an at the money straddle in this example by selling 2 futures contracts.

Gamma is highly positive at + 36.2 at current prices. If prices move higher, the position gets longer the market; if they go lower, the position gets shorter the market at a rate of 3.6 futures equivalents for a $.10 move in prices. Recall that gamma is higher for options at the money and closer to expiration (that is, delta is most unstable for at the money options as expiration nears). A trader who is buying straddles to take advantage of a sharp move in prices might tend toward buying straddles of nearby months. For example, long 100 August $18.00 calls and long 100 August $18.00 puts yield a gamma of + 51.1. The trade-off, of course, is that time decay is more rapid on the August options. We will examine a gamma strategy in more detail in a later section.

Long straddles do not necessarily require price movement to show profits. At current prices, this position has a dollar vega exposure of $6,930.00. This means that if implied volatility moves higher by 1 percentage point, the position earns $6,930.00. Crude oil implied volatility as we have shown has moved from a low of 14 percent to 16 percent to a high of 45 percent or a difference of 30 percentage points. Volatility exposure is not something to be ignored. Traders might buy straddles at 24 percent volatility, expecting to sell at some higher level of volatility. If OPEC is due to meet, the trader knows that the demand for price insurance (demand for buy option strategies) will increase some time before the meeting. The trader tries to anticipate the bottom of implied volatility. Because volatility is likely to decline after the meeting, or after a major economic number is released, the trader might get out of the long volatility position the day before the major event takes place. Because volatility has a bigger effect on deferred month options, a trader might tend to buy straddles in months with more time until expiration.

The major downside to buying straddles is the negative effect of time decay on the position.

Example: Premium is lost at a rate of $983.00 per day. If prices are unchanged and volatility is unchanged, the position loses $7,013.00 after a week and $-14,371.00$ after two weeks. A trader who buys straddles at 24 percent might not earn any profits selling straddles at 26 percent if the position was held for weeks.

Another way to get long volatility is to buy one leg of the straddle and use futures to get delta neutral.

Example: The oil producer found that buying puts against a cash position to achieve a delta-neutral position was the same as establishing a long volatility position. Buying only 100 $18.00 puts would yield a position delta of -49.4. If the trade now included a long 49 futures position, the trader would be long volatility.

The premium paid out is less, but so is the gamma exposure. If volatility increases, or prices move sharply in either direction, the position will not earn as much profit as the long straddle position. However, the long puts and long futures position is not as exposed to declining implied volatility and time decay, as is the long straddle position.

Short Straddles

It is most important for option traders to understand the nature of risk. Traders can sometimes get overly enthusiastic when shorting options. Selling deep out-of-the-money options because "prices will never get there in two weeks" usually means prices will "get there" in two days. Focusing only on delta exposure is an almost sure way to economic ruin. Some option traders have learned only parts of risk analysis. One trader "understood" theta and set up a position that earned $10,000.00 per day. Unfortunately for this particular trader, theta is a measure of time decay only when other factors are held constant. When are other factors ever held constant?

Selling straddles is a good example of the potential risks of selling options. We have mentioned that the best outcome for a short straddle to earn profits is for prices to trade quietly around the strike price. Our risk measures tell a more detailed story.

Example: Table 9-6 summarizes a short straddle position which is exactly the same as that in Table 9-5, except the signs are different.

TABLE 9-6

Portfolio analysis: short straddles

Position:	Short 100 Sept. $18.00 calls at $.87				
	Short 100 Sept. $18.00 puts at $.87				
Futures price:	16.91	17.41	17.91	18.41	18.91
Position delta	+ 34.5	+ 16.6	− 1.7	− 19.3	− 35.6
Position gamma	− 34.7	− 36.5	− 36.2	− 34.2	− 30.6
Position vega	− 5,930	− 6,600	− 6,930	− 6,920	− 6,580
Position theta	+ 833	+ 932	+ 983	+ 980	+ 927

Days Elapsed	Profit/Loss ($)				
1	− 15,528	−2,813	983	−4,309	− 17,978
7	− 10,448	2,900	7,013	1,698	− 12,306
14	−4,321	9,849	14,371	9,016	−5,435
86	65,006	115,000	165,000	133,000	83,000

One weakness of using only delta as a risk measure is illustrated here. The delta exposure is only − 1.7 or short 1.7 futures equivalents at current prices. This position includes selling 100 $18.00 puts and 100 $18.00 calls, and yet the delta is only showing − 1.7 futures equivalents. It is possible for the trader who is short these straddles to end up with a long or short 100 futures positions against which the market is moving.

The other risk measures are more revealing. Gamma exposure is − 36.2. If prices move higher by $.10, this position becomes 3.6 futures equivalents shorter the market. If prices move lower by $.10, this position gains 3.6 futures equivalents. Gamma indicates that this position gets more exposed as prices move away from today's price. Gamma is a much better indicator of potential risk of a position than is delta. This position is also exposed to increasing implied volatility at the rate of $6,930.00 for one percentage point.

A major problem for traders covering a short option position is that a violent futures price move is usually accompanied by an increase in volatility. For example, a trader is short out-of-the-money calls naked. Prices begin to rally, and the calls increase in value. Prices continue to rally and volatility increases. The trader may pay a high implied volatility to liquidate the position. An alternative is to buy futures. This introduces the problem of being whipsawed by the market if the trader buys futures and prices then decline.

A trader who believes that implied volatility will decline might tend to sell straddles in months with long expirations.

Example: A decline of one percentage point of the August $18.00 straddle will earn $50.00 per straddle, while a similar decline in volatility in the October $18.00 straddle will earn $80.00 per straddle.

Another way to sell volatility is to sell an option and then trade futures to maintain a delta-neutral position.

Example: Selling 10 September $18.00 calls would yield a delta position of − 5.1. To lock in volatility position, five futures are bought. If prices move, the trader must adjust the futures position to stay delta neutral.

All the pitfalls of maintaining delta neutral positions apply here as well.

CALENDAR SPREADS

A *calendar spread* is an option trade that tries to take advantage of rapid premium decay in nearby month options. An example would be selling August $18.00 calls and buying September $18.00 calls. The August calls lose more premium per day than do the September options.

When a portfolio analysis is applied to calendar spreads, a much clearer picture of risk is revealed.

Example: Table 9-7 provides a risk analysis of a calendar spread, in which 10 $18.00 July calls are sold and 10 $18.00 August calls are bought. Based on the analysis, this position profits most if prices remain around $18.00 for the life of the July contract. However, if prices remain around $18.00 through July expiration, it is likely that implied volatility will decline. Volatility exposure of this trade is $110.00 for each percentage point decline in volatility. If implied volatility increases, the position profits, but, usually, high implied volatility is accompanied by volatile prices that may go against this position.

TABLE 9-7
Portfolio analysis: calendar spread

Position:	Sell 10 Jul. $18.00 calls at $.16				
	Buy 10 Aug. $18.00 calls at $.55				
Futures price:	16.91	17.41	17.91	18.41	18.91
Position delta	2.0	2.2	1.3	−0.1	−1.2
Position gammas	−1.0	−0.7	−2.6	−2.8	−1.3
Position vega	150	150	110	100	120
Position theta	−36	−17	13	19	−4

Days Elapsed	Profit/Loss ($)				
1	−2,018	−919	13	302	−104
7	−2,271	−1,055	128	467	−147
14	−2,636	−1,396	394	914	−362
16	−2,744	−1,523	403	1,098	−486

Delta exposure is +1.3 at current prices. If prices drop, losses begin to accrue on the long August options at a greater rate than had profits made on the short July options. This is because there is simply more premium to lose on the August option. The trade also has significant spread risk. Position delta is +1.3 at current prices; short 10 July $18.00 calls has a delta of −3.5, while long 10 August $18.00 calls has a delta of +4.8.

A change in the spread values of July and August could work against this position.

Example: July futures could trade higher while August futures remain unchanged. This could be a much larger problem when the two option months are old crop/new crop months in grains and soybeans. Some intramonth commodity spreads can be more volatile than the outright futures contract.

Another trade illustrates other problems with calendar spreads.

Example: In another calendar spread a trader sells $18.00 July straddles and buys $18.00 August straddles (Table 9-8). The profit/loss profile shows a window of profits around the $18.00 level.

TABLE 9-8
Portfolio analysis: calendar spread

Position:	Sell 10 Jul. $18.00 straddles at $.63				
	Buy 10 Aug. $18.00 straddles at $1.25				

Futures price:	16.91	17.41	17.91	18.41	18.91
Position delta	4.0	4.2	2.5	−0.2	−2.3
Position gamma	1.9	−1.4	−5.0	−5.4	−2.5
Position vega	300	290	220	200	240
Position theta	−69	−28	32	43	−2

Days Elapsed	Profit/Loss ($)				
1	−3,948	−1,788	32	623	−111
7	−4,435	−2,019	302	993	−151
14	−5,157	−2,660	910	1,960	−522
16	−5,363	−2,906	966	2,381	−759

First, this position is, again, long volatility. If prices remain around $18.00, volatility will likely decline. The losses from lower volatility may, in fact, more than offset profits from time decay.

Second, four option positions are established. If commissions are included in the profit/loss profile, the window of profitability gets even smaller.

Third, establishing four option positions means facing four bid/offer spreads. Our examples use settlement prices that are unrealistic for actual trade prices. If bid/offer spreads are wide, the profitability of the trade is less.

Finally, the position earns the most profits when it is the most risky. That is, a calendar spread takes advantage of the rapid time decay of nearby options. This occurs mostly within the last week of the options' life. But this is also the time when being short options can be most risky. If prices remain at current levels at expiration (everything else remaining equal) the position earns $966.00. If prices drop by $.50, the position loses $2,906.00, a swing of $3,972.00 in one day.

In the next section we examine long gamma strategies that take advantage of prices moving sharply.

LONG GAMMA STRATEGIES

The simplest long gamma strategy is a long straddle. Long gamma strategies attempt to take advantage of the rate of change in delta. If prices move higher, the position becomes very long the market automatically. If prices decline, the position gets very short the market. As we have shown, at-the-money options of nearby options is a play that takes advantage of sharp price swings as opposed to changes in implied volatility. Changes in implied volatility will of course affect the nearby option's premium, but not as much as it will affect the premium of a deferred option. There are other ways to establish long gamma positions.

Example: Table 9-9 illustrates the opposite trade of a calendar spread. This position includes buying nearby straddles and selling deferred straddles. The delta of this position is −2.5. If we wish to center the trade around current prices rather than the $18.00 strike price, we could buy two or three futures contracts. Gamma is +5.0 for every $.10 increase (decrease) in price, and the position will gain (lose) .5 delta.

The position is short volatility. If volatility ticks up by one percentage point, the position loses $220.00. Situations can occur when prices move sharply and volatility actually contracts. This happens often after a scheduled economic event or an OPEC meeting. The new information causes market prices to move, but the market is no longer nervously anticipating the result. The outcome is a sharp move in prices and a decline in volatility.

The downside to this trade is that it loses $32.00 overnight if nothing happens and more as each day passes. Recently, a postponement of an OPEC meeting by three days and a rumor of a two-week postponement caused much more consternation in the options pit than in the futures pit.

This type of long gamma trade explains why implied volatility of nearby options tends to move higher than that of deferred options ahead

TABLE 9-9
Portfolio analysis: long gamma

Position:	Buy 10 Jul. $18.00 straddles at $.63				
	Sell 10 Aug. $18.00 straddles at $1.25				
Futures price:	16.91	17.41	17.91	18.41	18.91
Position delta	−4.0	−4.2	− 2.5	0.2	2.3
Position gamma	−1.9	1.4	5.0	5.4	2.5
Position vega	− 300	− 290	− 220	− 200	− 240
Position theta	69	28	−32	−43	2

Days Elapsed	Profit/Loss ($)				
1	$3,948	1,798	−32	− 623	111
7	4,435	2,019	− 302	− 993	151
14	5,157	2,660	−910	−1,960	522
16	5,363	2,906	− 966	−2,381	759

of scheduled major market events. As traders establish long gamma trades, nearby options are bid higher while longer-term options are offered lower.

A trader may have a market opinion that prices will likely trade sharply higher. One way to take advantage of this outcome is to buy twice as many nearby options as longer-term options are sold.

Example: Table 9-10 summarizes this position, which can be established usually with little or no cash outlay. The trader sells 5 August $18.00 calls and buys 10 July calls.

The delta is +1.1, a bullish position. Gamma is +3.9. If prices increase by $1.00 overnight, the position earns $3,049.00. If prices decline by $1.00, the trade profits $240.00. A $.50 decline in price shows a $139.00 loss. The risk/reward profile of this trade is excellent, if prices move overnight. As time goes by, and prices remain unchanged, this position loses. Overnight, the position loses $48.00.

At current prices, the position is only slightly long volatility. If implied volatility increases by one percentage point, the position's value increases by $10.00.

TABLE 9-10

Portfolio analysis: long gamma

Position:	Long 10 Jul. $18.00 calls at $.16				
	Short 5 Aug. $18.00 calls at $.55				
Futures price:	16.91	17.41	17.91	18.41	18.91
Position delta	−0.9	−0.4	1.1	3.2	4.8
Position gamma	0	1.9	3.9	4.0	2.3
Position vega	−60	−30	10	20	−10
Position theta	11	−15	−48	−53	−26

Days Elapsed	Profit/Loss ($)				
1	240	−139	−48	1,003	3,049
7	338	−200	−381	662	2,900
14	514	−105	−926	−100	2,878
16	572	−38	−1,001	−349	2,943

With little cash outlay, the trader can establish somewhat larger positions using options rather than futures. The beauty of this kind of trade is that large profits can accrue if the market moves in the right direction. If not, only small losses are sustained. The problem, of course, is that most traders like to hang on to positions until they become profitable. And that's when this position loses most.

Two other potential problems with this trade should be mentioned. First, spread risk between the two months exists. If July futures remain unchanged and August futures rally, the position will show losses. Second, the market usually anticipates long gamma strategies. That is, ahead of major economic releases nearby options will be bid up; long-term options will not increase as much.

Appendix: Settlement Prices/Implied Volatility of Crude Oil Options[1]

	Futures Settlement							
	July *17.70*		*August* *17.84*		*September* *17.91*		*October* *17.95*	
Strike	*Call*	*Put*	*Call*	*Put*	*Call*	*Put*	*Call*	*Put*
$20	.01		.08		.20		.28	
	(26.6)		(25.7)		(24.0)		(23.5)	
19	.03	1.33	.23	1.38	.40	1.48	.51	
	(22.6)	(24.8)	(25.7)	(25.6)	(23.5)	(23.7)	(23.2)	
18	.16	0.47	.55	.70	.87	.87	.88	.92
	(19.2)	(20.3)	(25.2)	(25.1)	(26.0)	(24.2)	(23.0)	(22.8)
17	.78	0.08	1.16	.31	1.40	.48	1.54	.58
	(22.1)	(21.8)	(27.6)	(26.9)	(26.4)	(25.7)	(26.5)	(25.6)
16	1.72	.02	1.97	.12	2.17	.25	2.26	.30
	(29.2)	(28.8)	(30.6)	(28.8)	(29.3)	(27.6)	(27.9)	(26.1)

[1]As of May 19, 1988 for purposes of the crude oil options scenario.

CHAPTER 10

Making Markets in Futures Options

Anyone trading commodity futures options will eventually face certain well-capitalized floor traders who work for themselves or for option trading companies. These traders are called market makers because they will bid and offer on virtually all option months and all option strike prices listed by the exchange. The goal of market makers, obviously, is to buy low and sell high as many times as possible. In doing so, they provide much liquidity to the options markets as well as to the futures markets. This section examines how market makers trade and their impact on options and futures markets.

AN ILLUSTRATIVE MARKET MAKING SCENARIO

Example: Trader A calls the exchange floor to get the current market on $18.00 December crude oil puts. The phone clerk informs trader A that the market is $.32 bid and $.37 offered and that it is a market makers' market. Trader A now knows that she can buy puts for $.37 or $370.00 per option or sell the same put for $.32 or $320.00 per option. Trader A also knows that this market is good for size because it is a market makers' market and not a market given by locals. (Market makers are usually better capitalized than are locals and can take larger positions.) How did the market maker arrive at a $.32 bid and $.37 offer for the $18.00 puts?

Let us first examine an ideal situation for XYZ Options Company, a market maker. XYZ is willing to buy $18.00 puts at $.32 and sell the same puts at $.37. The ideal situation for XYZ is if traders continually hit XYZ's bid and take XYZ's offer at the same rate. For instance, if trader A decides to buy 1,000 $18.00 puts from XYZ at $.37 and trader B soon after sells 1,000 $18.00 puts at $.32, XYZ has made a large profit:

XYZ sells 1,000 options at	$	.37	
XYZ buys 1,000 options at		.32	
	$	.05	per barrel profit
×	1,000.00		barrels
	$	50.00	per contract
×	1,000.00		contracts
	$50,000.00		profit

XYZ Options will try to set bids and offers so that half the trades hit bids and half hit offers. If XYZ bids $.32 and offers $.37 and very quickly has bought thousands of options while selling none, the market is set too high. Conversely, if the trader bids $.32 and offers $.37 and has attracted a crowd willing to buy unlimited quantities at $.37, it is most likely a good time to raise the bid and offer.

Market makers cannot control the level of prices, so they must continually adjust their bids and offers to the level that trades are executed equally on the bid side and offer side.

Example: XYZ knows that options have been trading recently around the 27 percent volatility level. December crude oil futures prices are trading at $19.15 per barrel. Using an exact option pricing model such as Black-Scholes, XYZ can determine where bids and offers should be placed for each option. Figure 10-1 is a sample trading sheet that an option trader might use on the trading floor. Premiums are

FIGURE 10-1
Sample trading sheet

1900	1600	1600	1700	1700	1800	1800	1900	1900	2000	2000	2100	2100	2200	2200	2300	2300	2400	2400
	Call	Put	Call	Put	Call	Put	Call	Put	Call	Put	Call	Put	Call	Put	Call	Put	Call	Put
29.0%	303 $_{94}$	6 $_6$ 216 $_{85}$	18 $_{15}$ 142 $_{70}$	43 $_{30}$ 86 $_{52}$	86 $_{48}$ 47 $_{35}$	146 $_{65}$ 24 $_{21}$	222 $_{79}$ 11 $_{11}$	308 $_{89}$ 5 $_5$	401 $_{95}$ 2 $_2$	500 $_{98}$
28.0%	302 $_{95}$	5 $_5$ 214 $_{86}$	16 $_{14}$ 140 $_{71}$	41 $_{29}$ 83 $_{52}$	83 $_{48}$ 45 $_{34}$	144 $_{66}$ 22 $_{20}$	220 $_{80}$ 10 $_{10}$	307 $_{90}$ 4 $_5$	400 $_{95}$ 1 $_2$	500 $_{98}$
27.0%	301 $_{95}$	4 $_5$ 213 $_{86}$	15 $_{14}$ 137 $_{71}$	38 $_{29}$ 80 $_{52}$	80 $_{48}$ 42 $_{33}$	141 $_{67}$ 20 $_{19}$	218 $_{81}$ 8 $_9$	305 $_{91}$ 3 $_4$	400 $_{96}$ 1 $_2$	500 $_{98}$
26.0%	301 $_{96}$	3 $_4$ 211 $_{87}$	13 $_{13}$ 135 $_{72}$	36 $_{28}$ 77 $_{52}$	77 $_{48}$ 39 $_{33}$	138 $_{67}$ 18 $_{18}$	216 $_{82}$ 7 $_8$	304 $_{92}$ 3 $_4$	400 $_{96}$ 1 $_1$	500 $_{99}$
25.0%	300 $_{96}$	3 $_4$ 209 $_{88}$	11 $_{12}$ 132 $_{72}$	33 $_{28}$ 74 $_{52}$	74 $_{48}$ 37 $_{32}$	136 $_{68}$ 16 $_{17}$	214 $_{83}$ 6 $_8$	303 $_{92}$ 2 $_3$	400 $_{97}$ 1 $_1$	500 $_{99}$
	V 0.75	G 0.049	V 1.64	G 0.108	V 2.56	G 0.168	V 2.99	G 0.197	V 2.73	G 0.180	V 2.03	G 0.133	V 1.25	G 0.082	V 0.66	G 0.044	V 0.31	G 0.020

1905	1600	1600	1700	1700	1800	1800	1900	1900	2000	2000	2100	2100	2200	2200	2300	2300	2400	2400
	Call	Put	Call	Put	Call	Put	Call	Put	Call	Put	Call	Put	Call	Put	Call	Put	Call	Put
29.0%	308 $_{94}$	6 $_6$ 220 $_{85}$	17 $_{15}$ 146 $_{71}$	42 $_{29}$ 89 $_{53}$	84 $_{47}$ 49 $_{36}$	143 $_{64}$ 25 $_{21}$	218 $_{79}$ 12 $_{12}$	304 $_{88}$ 5 $_6$	396 $_{94}$ 2 $_3$	495 $_{97}$
28.0%	307 $_{95}$	5 $_5$ 219 $_{86}$	16 $_{14}$ 143 $_{71}$	39 $_{29}$ 86 $_{53}$	81 $_{47}$ 46 $_{35}$	140 $_{65}$ 23 $_{20}$	216 $_{80}$ 10 $_{11}$	303 $_{89}$ 4 $_5$	395 $_{95}$ 2 $_2$	495 $_{98}$
27.0%	306 $_{95}$	4 $_5$ 217 $_{87}$	14 $_{13}$ 141 $_{72}$	37 $_{28}$ 83 $_{53}$	78 $_{47}$ 44 $_{34}$	138 $_{66}$ 21 $_{19}$	214 $_{81}$ 9 $_{10}$	301 $_{90}$ 3 $_4$	395 $_{96}$ 1 $_2$	495 $_{98}$
26.0%	305 $_{96}$	3 $_4$ 215 $_{88}$	12 $_{12}$ 138 $_{73}$	34 $_{27}$ 80 $_{53}$	75 $_{47}$ 41 $_{34}$	135 $_{66}$ 19 $_{18}$	212 $_{82}$ 8 $_9$	300 $_{91}$ 3 $_4$	395 $_{96}$ 1 $_1$	495 $_{99}$
25.0%	305 $_{97}$	3 $_4$ 214 $_{89}$	11 $_{11}$ 136 $_{73}$	32 $_{27}$ 77 $_{53}$	72 $_{47}$ 38 $_{33}$	132 $_{67}$ 17 $_{17}$	210 $_{83}$ 6 $_8$	299 $_{92}$ 2 $_3$	395 $_{97}$ 1 $_1$	495 $_{99}$
	V 0.72	G 0.047	V 1.60	G 0.105	V 2.53	G 0.165	V 2.99	G 0.196	V 2.77	G 0.181	V 2.07	G 0.136	V 1.30	G 0.085	V 0.69	G 0.045	V 0.32	G 0.021

1910	1600	1600	1700	1700	1800	1800	1900	1900	2000	2000	2100	2100	2200	2200	2300	2300	2400	2400
	Call	Put	Call	Put	Call	Put	Call	Put	Call	Put	Call	Put	Call	Put	Call	Put	Call	Put
29.0%	312 $_{95}$	5 $_5$ 224 $_{86}$	16 $_{14}$ 149 $_{72}$	40 $_{28}$ 91 $_{54}$	81 $_{46}$ 51 $_{37}$	140 $_{63}$ 26 $_{22}$	214 $_{78}$ 12 $_{12}$	299 $_{88}$ 5 $_6$	391 $_{94}$ 2 $_3$	490 $_{97}$
28.0%	311 $_{95}$	4 $_5$ 223 $_{87}$	15 $_{13}$ 147 $_{72}$	38 $_{28}$ 88 $_{54}$	78 $_{46}$ 48 $_{36}$	137 $_{64}$ 24 $_{21}$	212 $_{79}$ 11 $_{11}$	298 $_{89}$ 4 $_5$	391 $_{95}$ 2 $_2$	490 $_{98}$
27.0%	311 $_{96}$	4 $_4$ 221 $_{87}$	13 $_{13}$ 144 $_{73}$	35 $_{27}$ 85 $_{54}$	75 $_{46}$ 45 $_{35}$	134 $_{65}$ 22 $_{20}$	210 $_{80}$ 9 $_{10}$	297 $_{90}$ 3 $_4$	390 $_{95}$ 1 $_2$	490 $_{98}$
26.0%	310 $_{96}$	3 $_4$ 220 $_{88}$	12 $_{12}$ 142 $_{74}$	33 $_{26}$ 82 $_{54}$	72 $_{46}$ 43 $_{35}$	132 $_{65}$ 20 $_{19}$	208 $_{81}$ 8 $_9$	295 $_{91}$ 3 $_4$	390 $_{96}$ 1 $_1$	490 $_{99}$
25.0%	310 $_{97}$	2 $_3$ 218 $_{89}$	10 $_{11}$ 139 $_{74}$	31 $_{26}$ 79 $_{54}$	69 $_{46}$ 40 $_{34}$	129 $_{66}$ 18 $_{18}$	206 $_{82}$ 7 $_8$	294 $_{92}$ 2 $_3$	390 $_{97}$ 1 $_1$	490 $_{99}$
	V 0.69	G 0.045	V 1.56	G 0.102	V 2.50	G 0.163	V 3.00	G 0.195	V 2.80	G 0.182	V 2.12	G 0.138	V 1.34	G 0.087	V 0.72	G 0.047	V 0.34	G 0.022

1915	1600	1600	1700	1700	1800	1800	1900	1900	2000	2000	2100	2100	2200	2200	2300	2300	2400	2400
	Call	Put	Call	Put	Call	Put	Call	Put	Call	Put	Call	Put	Call	Put	Call	Put	Call	Put
29.0%	317 $_{95}$	5 $_5$ 229 $_{86}$	16 $_{14}$ 153 $_{72}$	39 $_{28}$ 94 $_{55}$	79 $_{45}$ 53 $_{37}$	137 $_{63}$ 27 $_{23}$	210 $_{77}$ 13 $_{12}$	295 $_{88}$ 6 $_6$	387 $_{94}$ 2 $_3$	485 $_{97}$
28.0%	316 $_{95}$	4 $_5$ 227 $_{87}$	14 $_{13}$ 150 $_{73}$	37 $_{27}$ 91 $_{55}$	76 $_{45}$ 50 $_{37}$	134 $_{63}$ 25 $_{22}$	208 $_{78}$ 11 $_{12}$	293 $_{88}$ 5 $_6$	386 $_{95}$ 2 $_2$	485 $_{98}$
27.0%	315 $_{96}$	4 $_4$ 226 $_{88}$	13 $_{12}$ 148 $_{74}$	34 $_{26}$ 88 $_{55}$	73 $_{45}$ 47 $_{36}$	131 $_{64}$ 23 $_{21}$	206 $_{79}$ 10 $_{11}$	292 $_{89}$ 4 $_5$	385 $_{95}$ 1 $_2$	485 $_{98}$
26.0%	315 $_{96}$	3 $_4$ 224 $_{89}$	11 $_{11}$ 146 $_{74}$	32 $_{26}$ 85 $_{55}$	70 $_{45}$ 44 $_{36}$	128 $_{64}$ 21 $_{20}$	204 $_{80}$ 9 $_{10}$	291 $_{90}$ 3 $_4$	385 $_{96}$ 1 $_2$	485 $_{98}$
25.0%	315 $_{97}$	2 $_3$ 223 $_{90}$	10 $_{10}$ 143 $_{75}$	29 $_{25}$ 82 $_{55}$	67 $_{45}$ 42 $_{35}$	126 $_{65}$ 19 $_{19}$	202 $_{81}$ 7 $_9$	289 $_{91}$ 3 $_4$	385 $_{96}$ 1 $_1$	485 $_{99}$
	V 0.67	G 0.043	V 1.52	G 0.099	V 2.47	G 0.160	V 2.99	G 0.194	V 2.84	G 0.183	V 2.17	G 0.141	V 1.39	G 0.090	V 0.76	G 0.049	V 0.36	G 0.023

1920	1600	1600	1700	1700	1800	1800	1900	1900	2000	2000	2100	2100	2200	2200	2300	2300	2400	2400
	Call	Put	Call	Put	Call	Put	Call	Put	Call	Put	Call	Put	Call	Put	Call	Put	Call	Put
29.0%	322 $_{95}$	5 $_5$ 233 $_{87}$	15 $_{13}$ 157 $_{73}$	38 $_{27}$ 97 $_{56}$	77 $_{44}$ 55 $_{38}$	134 $_{62}$ 28 $_{23}$	206 $_{77}$ 13 $_{13}$	291 $_{87}$ 6 $_6$	382 $_{94}$ 2 $_3$	480 $_{97}$
28.0%	321 $_{96}$	4 $_4$ 231 $_{88}$	14 $_{12}$ 154 $_{74}$	35 $_{26}$ 94 $_{56}$	74 $_{44}$ 52 $_{38}$	131 $_{62}$ 26 $_{23}$	204 $_{77}$ 12 $_{12}$	289 $_{88}$ 5 $_6$	381 $_{94}$ 2 $_2$	480 $_{98}$
27.0%	320 $_{96}$	3 $_4$ 230 $_{88}$	12 $_{12}$ 152 $_{74}$	33 $_{26}$ 91 $_{56}$	71 $_{44}$ 49 $_{37}$	128 $_{63}$ 24 $_{22}$	202 $_{78}$ 11 $_{11}$	288 $_{89}$ 4 $_5$	380 $_{95}$ 1 $_2$	480 $_{98}$
26.0%	320 $_{97}$	3 $_3$ 228 $_{89}$	11 $_{11}$ 149 $_{75}$	30 $_{25}$ 88 $_{56}$	68 $_{44}$ 46 $_{36}$	125 $_{64}$ 22 $_{21}$	200 $_{79}$ 9 $_{10}$	286 $_{90}$ 3 $_4$	380 $_{96}$ 1 $_2$	480 $_{98}$
25.0%	320 $_{97}$	2 $_3$ 227 $_{90}$	9 $_{10}$ 147 $_{76}$	28 $_{24}$ 85 $_{56}$	65 $_{44}$ 43 $_{36}$	123 $_{64}$ 19 $_{20}$	198 $_{80}$ 8 $_9$	285 $_{91}$ 3 $_4$	380 $_{96}$ 1 $_1$	480 $_{99}$
	V 0.64	G 0.041	V 1.48	G 0.095	V 2.44	G 0.157	V 2.99	G 0.193	V 2.87	G 0.184	V 2.22	G 0.143	V 1.43	G 0.092	V 0.79	G 0.051	V 0.38	G 0.024

1925	1600	1600	1700	1700	1800	1800	1900	1900	2000	2000	2100	2100	2200	2200	2300	2300	2400	2400
	Call	Put	Call	Put	Call	Put	Call	Put	Call	Put	Call	Put	Call	Put	Call	Put	Call	Put
29.0%	326 $_{95}$	4 $_5$ 237 $_{87}$	15 $_{13}$ 160 $_{74}$	36 $_{26}$ 99 $_{57}$	75 $_{43}$ 57 $_{39}$	131 $_{61}$ 29 $_{24}$	203 $_{76}$ 14 $_{13}$	286 $_{87}$ 6 $_7$	378 $_{93}$ 3 $_3$	475 $_{97}$
28.0%	326 $_{96}$	4 $_4$ 236 $_{88}$	13 $_{12}$ 158 $_{75}$	34 $_{25}$ 96 $_{57}$	72 $_{43}$ 54 $_{39}$	128 $_{61}$ 27 $_{23}$	200 $_{77}$ 12 $_{12}$	285 $_{88}$ 5 $_6$	377 $_{94}$ 2 $_2$	475 $_{97}$
27.0%	325 $_{96}$	3 $_4$ 234 $_{89}$	12 $_{11}$ 155 $_{75}$	32 $_{25}$ 94 $_{57}$	69 $_{43}$ 51 $_{38}$	125 $_{62}$ 25 $_{22}$	198 $_{78}$ 11 $_{12}$	283 $_{88}$ 4 $_5$	376 $_{95}$ 2 $_2$	475 $_{98}$
26.0%	325 $_{97}$	3 $_3$ 233 $_{90}$	10 $_{10}$ 153 $_{76}$	29 $_{24}$ 91 $_{57}$	66 $_{43}$ 48 $_{37}$	122 $_{63}$ 23 $_{21}$	196 $_{79}$ 10 $_{11}$	282 $_{89}$ 4 $_5$	375 $_{95}$ 1 $_1$	475 $_{98}$
25.0%	325 $_{97}$	2 $_3$ 232 $_{90}$	9 $_{10}$ 151 $_{77}$	27 $_{23}$ 88 $_{57}$	63 $_{43}$ 45 $_{37}$	119 $_{63}$ 20 $_{20}$	194 $_{80}$ 8 $_{10}$	281 $_{90}$ 3 $_4$	375 $_{96}$ 1 $_1$	475 $_{99}$
	V 0.62	G 0.039	V 1.44	G 0.092	V 2.46	G 0.154	V 2.99	G 0.191	V 2.90	G 0.185	V 2.27	G 0.145	V 1.48	G 0.095	V 0.82	G 0.053	V 0.40	G 0.026

Courtesy of, and copyright © by, D. Isbister.

calculated using the Black-Scholes model modified for commodity options. Strike prices are located across the top, volatilities down the left hand side, futures prices are located in the upper left corner. Finding the block of option premiums for futures at $19.15, a trader would know that a $19.00 put that just traded at $.73 went off at 27 percent volatility.

215

A market maker bidding $19.00 puts at 26 percent volatility and offering at 28 percent would make a market $.70 bid at $.76. By tracking implied volatilities, the market maker can determine where to buy and sell options based on volatility measures and then translate volatilities into actual premiums using the option models.

By bidding 26 percent and offering 28 percent, XYZ has determined that this market will give it the best opportunity to realize half the trades on the bid side and half on the offer. What happens to the bid/offer spread if the futures price drops to $19.00? Finding the block of option premiums that correspond to a futures price of $19.00, XYZ now bids the $19.00 put at $.77 and offers it at $.83. XYZ is still bidding at 27 percent and offering at 29 percent but because the futures market has moved, the actual option premiums must move as well.

An idealized case will help to illustrate the process.

Example: Futures prices are at $19.25. XYZ is bidding $19 puts at 26 percent and offering 28 percent. This translates into a market of $.66 at $.72 for the $19.00 put. XYZ is willing to sell $19.00 puts for $.72 and buy them for $.66. Trader A wants to buy 100 puts and takes XYZ's offer. XYZ sells 100 puts for $.72 each and is now exposed to a market move. If futures trade lower, XYZ will lose. XYZ immediately neutralizes the short put position from a market move by hedging in the futures market. From the trading sheets, XYZ knows that the $19.00 put has a delta of .43. (Recall that an option's delta is the change in option premium due to a change in futures price. Deltas are located to the right and slightly below the option premium on the trading sheet.) By selling 100 puts with a delta of .43, XYZ has established a position equivalent to being long 43 futures. XYZ immediately sells 43 futures to get delta neutral and insulate the position against a move in futures prices. The hedge effectively locks in a sale of 28 percent volatility.

The market drops to $19.00. XYZ is still buying $19.00 puts at 26 percent and selling them at 28 percent. But, now, that translates into a market of $.77 at $.83. See Figure 10-1. Trader B enters the market and sells 100 puts at $.77 to XYZ. XYZ has bought back 100 puts at $.77 and gets out of the futures hedge by buying 43 futures at $19.00.

Summary of XYZ's transactions

Step 1.	Sells 100 $19 puts at $.72 (28% volatility)		
	Sells 43 futures at $19.25		
Step 2.	Buys 100 $19 puts at $.77 (26% volatility)		
	Buys 43 futures at $19.00		

Options:	Sells 100 puts at	$	.72	
	Buys 100 puts at	$	.77	
		− $	.05	per barrel loss
		×	1,000.00	barrels per contract
		$	50.00	per contract loss
		×	100.00	contracts
		− $	5,000.00	loss
Futures:	Sells 43 futures at	$	19.25	
	Buys 43 futures at	$	19.00	
		$	.25	per barrel profit
		×	1,000.00	barrels per contract
		$	250.00	per contract profit
		×	43	contracts
		+ $	10,750.00	profit
Total Trade:	$10,750	futures hedge		
	− 5,000	options trade		
	$ 5,750	profit		

XYZ never held a market view that prices would move in one direction or the other. By hedging each option trade with futures, XYZ is able to remove the effect of a price change on its option positions. The only view that XYZ has is that it will be able to buy options at 26 percent and sell options at 28 percent. XYZ may lose money on the actual option trade as in the example and still profit overall because the profits earned on the futures hedge more than offset the losses on the option position.

Our textbook example is too simple because trading does not occur in such a favorable manner to the market markers. Many months, many strike prices, and two kinds of options (puts and calls) are traded on the exchange. Market makers trade based on the economic supply and demand for options. A market maker's first trade of the day may be a sale of $19.00 November calls, but the next trade may be a different month, a different strike, or a different type of option. The market maker begins to carry an inventory of option positions, and the goal is to turnover the inventory continually, always buying at a lower volatility and selling at a higher volatility.

Let's now turn to some problems that are faced by market makers, specifically:

- Getting the hedge off efficiently
- Changing volatility
- Getting pinned

Getting the Hedge off Efficiently

A major problem market makers face, which cuts into profit margins, is not getting the futures hedge off efficiently. As our textbook example indicated, the bid/offer spread of the market maker not only depends on volatility levels but also on current futures price. The trader must know at what price futures hedges can be established to quote an options market. Once the option trade is executed, the market maker immediately signals a clerk (market makers constantly communicate with their clerks through a series of hand signals), and the clerk tells the futures broker what month and how many futures to buy or sell. Although this process takes just a few seconds, futures prices can change. A trader making markets on options based on a $19.15 futures may find the futures hedge executed at $19.10 or $19.20. A bad hedge can seriously cut into a trader's profit margin.

Further, assessing an option's delta risk is made more difficult in volatile markets. An option's delta is partly a function of volatility. If volatility is changing and prices are changing, overall delta exposure is also changing. The market makers may end up with a position exposed to a move in prices, which is not the way they earn profit. When markets become volatile, it is no surprise that option bid/offer spreads get wider. It is the market makers' way to compensate for the uncertainty of the price of the futures hedge and of the added risk of miscalculating delta risk.

A related problem that market makers face occurs during very quiet or thinly traded markets. Futures prices may be relatively stable, but if volume is low, a market maker laying of risk in the futures may move prices. The market maker sees a $19.15 futures market but gets a $19.20 purchase price because his large market buy order pushed prices higher. (The large future buy order would be offsetting a large option transaction.) For this reason, options on futures with light volume (which include differed futures months of some otherwise liquid futures contracts) exhibit wide bid/offer spreads for large-volume traders. An option market is only as good as the underlying futures market.

Note that market makers not only provide liquidity in option markets by bidding and offering an options, but also help to increase liquidity in the underlying futures via the hedging transaction. The constant laying off of risk in futures markets by option market markers provides additional volume and liquidity in the underlying futures.

Changing Volatility

What happens if volatility suddenly changes? Or what happens if the market maker bids or offers at volatility levels different from the rest of the market? A market maker bidding 26 percent and offering 28 percent is going to own many contracts if the rest of the market is offering 26 percent.

The trader must be experienced to know when there has been a fundamental shift in volatility or if volatility is being distorted temporarily by some large transaction. If a shift has occurred, the market maker must adjust bid/offer spreads accordingly. If bidding 29 percent is too aggressive, the market maker will lower bids and offers. If offering 28 percent is too aggressive, bids and offers will be raised.

Sometimes, a shift in market volatility may be subtle. A market maker may be bidding or offering just slightly too aggressively and buying or selling too many options over time (remember, the markets makers' ideal situation is when half the trades hit the bid and the other half take the offer). If the market maker buys too many options, an exposed position is established even though the trader may be delta neutral. The market maker will now be exposed to changes in volatility, the passage of time, and moves in futures prices large enougl. to change delta exposure. If volatility drops, the options will have to be sold at a lower volatility than they were bought. The passage of time is an enemy to a long option position as premiums lose value when expiration nears. The risk of a position due to a change in the delta position is called gamma risk.

Delta neutrality does not imply gamma neutrality. (Recall that gamma is the change in an option's delta due to a change in futures prices.) What is delta neutral at, say, $19.00 might become delta positive at $19.20. Option deltas are always changing. If a market maker is net long too many options or net short too many options, the position will be gamma exposed. If prices change suddenly, the market maker's overall position will become net long or net short the market. The market maker opens profits from bid/offer spreads and not from taking market positions. Gamma exposure is therefore not desirable for market makers.

Example: Selling large quantities of out-of-the-money options entails gamma risk. XYZ is bidding 25 percent and offering 27 percent for $22.00 calls.

Futures are trading at $19.00, so XYZ's market is bid $.06 offered $.08 (Figure 10-1). Trader A buys 100 calls from XYZ at $.08. Immediately XYZ hedges in the futures market. Selling 100 $22 calls is equivalent to being short 9 futures (100 × a delta of .09). XYZ buys 9 futures at $19.00.

The following day, crude oil opens $.90 higher, at $19.90, and volatility ticks up one percentage point. Figure 10-2 shows that XYZ is now underhedged. Short 100 $22.00 calls when futures are at 19.90 is equivalent to being short 19 futures (at 27 percent volatility). But XYZ hedged as if it were short 9 futures. If XYZ buys back the $21.00 calls at 26 percent or $.19 (a $.90 move overnight in crude could push volatility at least one percentage point higher and probably more), a loss is realized. Gamma risk is the change from a relatively delta-neutral position to a delta-exposed position due to a change in price. The market maker was exposed to gamma risk in this example. A large move in futures prices caused XYZ to have a market position. XYZ was net short too many options. Deltas are always changing and sometimes are quite volatile, particularly as expiration day approaches. To reduce gamma exposure in the preceding example, a market maker could have bought puts or calls.

FIGURE 10-2
Sample trading sheet (the next day)

```
1965   1600   1600   1700   1700   1800   1800   1900   1900   2000   2000   2100   2100   2200   2200   2300   2300   2400   2400
 x    Call   Put   Call   Put   Call   Put   Call   Put   Call   Put   Call   Put   Call   Put   Call   Put   Call   Put
29.0% 365 97   3  3 273 91  10  9 191 79  27 21 123 64  59 36  73 46 108 54  40 30 174 70  20 18 253 82   9  9 341 91   4  5 435 95
28.0% 365 97   2  3 271 91   9  9 188 80  25 20 120 64  56 36  70 46 105 54  37 29 171 71  18 17 251 83   8  9 340 91   3  4 435 96
27.0% 365 98   2  2 270 92   8  8 186 81  23 19 118 64  53 36  67 46 102 54  35 28 169 72  16 16 249 84   7  8 339 92   3  3 435 97
26.0% 365 98   2  2 269 93   7  7 184 82  21 18 115 65  50 35  64 45  99 55  32 28 166 72  15 15 247 85   6  7 338 93   2  3 435 97
25.0% 365 98   1  2 268 94   6  6 182 83  19 17 112 65  48 35  61 45  96 55  30 27 163 73  13 14 245 86   5  6 337 94   2  2 435 98
   V 0.44 G0.027  V 1.14 G0.070  V 2.11 G0.130  V 2.89 G0.178  V 3.08 G0.189  V 2.63 G0.162  V 1.87 G0.115  V 1.13 G0.069  V 0.59 G0.036

1970   1600   1600   1700   1700   1800   1800   1900   1900   2000   2000   2100   2100   2200   2200   2300   2300   2400   2400
 x    Call   Put   Call   Put   Call   Put   Call   Put   Call   Put   Call   Put   Call   Put   Call   Put   Call   Put
29.0% 370 97   3  3 277 91  10  9 195 80  26 20 127 65  57 35  76 47 105 53  42 31 170 70  21 18 249 81  10 10 337 90   4  5 430 95
28.0% 370 97   2  3 276 92   9  8 192 81  24 19 124 65  54 35  73 47 102 53  39 30 168 70  19 17 247 83   9  9 335 91   4  4 430 96
27.0% 370 98   2  2 275 92   7  8 190 82  22 19 121 65  52 35  70 46  99 54  36 29 165 71  17 16 245 84   8  8 334 92   3  3 430 97
26.0% 370 98   1  2 274 93   6  7 188 82  20 18 118 66  49 34  67 46  96 54  34 28 162 72  15 15 243 85   6  7 333 93   2  3 430 97
25.0% 370 98   1  2 273 94   5  6 186 83  18 17 115 66  46 34  63 46  93 54  31 28 160 72  13 14 241 86   5  6 332 94   2  3 430 97
   V 0.42 G0.026  V 1.11 G0.068  V 2.07 G0.127  V 2.88 G0.176  V 3.09 G0.189  V 2.68 G0.164  V 1.92 G0.117  V 1.17 G0.071  V 0.62 G0.038

1975   1600   1600   1700   1700   1800   1800   1900   1900   2000   2000   2100   2100   2200   2200   2300   2300   2400   2400
 x    Call   Put   Call   Put   Call   Put   Call   Put   Call   Put   Call   Put   Call   Put   Call   Put   Call   Put
29.0% 375 97   3  3 282 91   9  9 199 81  25 19 130 65  55 35  78 48 103 52  43 32 167 68  22 19 245 81  10 10 332 90   5  5 425 95
28.0% 375 97   2  3 280 92   8  8 196 81  23 19 127 66  53 34  75 48 100 52  40 31 164 69  20 18 243 82   9  9 331 91   4  5 425 96
27.0% 375 98   2  2 279 93   7  7 194 82  21 18 124 66  50 34  72 47  97 53  38 30 162 70  18 17 241 83   8  8 330 92   3  4 425 96
26.0% 375 98   1  2 278 93   6  7 192 83  19 17 121 67  47 33  69 47  94 53  35 29 159 71  16 16 239 84   7  8 328 92   2  3 425 97
25.0% 375 99   1  1 277 94   5  6 191 84  17 16 118 67  44 33  66 47  91 53  32 28 156 72  14 15 237 85   6  7 327 93   2  3 425 97
   V 0.40 G0.024  V 1.07 G0.065  V 2.03 G0.124  V 2.86 G0.174  V 3.11 G0.189  V 2.72 G0.165  V 1.97 G0.120  V 1.21 G0.074  V 0.65 G0.039

1980   1600   1600   1700   1700   1800   1800   1900   1900   2000   2000   2100   2100   2200   2200   2300   2300   2400   2400
 x    Call   Put   Call   Put   Call   Put   Call   Put   Call   Put   Call   Put   Call   Put   Call   Put   Call   Put
29.0% 380 97   2  3 286 92   9  8 203 81  24 19 133 66  54 34  80 49 100 51  45 32 164 68  23 19 241 81  11 11 328 89   5  5 421 95
28.0% 380 98   2  2 285 92   8  8 201 82  22 18 130 67  51 33  77 49  97 51  42 32 161 68  21 18 239 82   9 10 326 90   4  5 420 95
27.0% 380 98   2  2 284 93   7  7 198 83  20 17 127 67  48 33  74 48  94 52  39 31 158 69  19 18 237 82   8  9 325 91   3  4 420 96
26.0% 380 98   1  2 283 94   6  6 197 84  18 16 125 67  45 33  71 48  91 52  37 30 155 70  17 17 235 83   7  8 324 92   3  3 420 97
25.0% 380 99   1  1 282 94   5  6 195 84  16 16 122 68  43 32  68 48  88 52  34 29 153 71  15 15 233 85   6  7 323 93   2  3 420 97
   V 0.38 G0.023  V 1.04 G0.063  V 1.99 G0.121  V 2.83 G0.171  V 3.12 G0.189  V 2.76 G0.167  V 2.02 G0.122  V 1.25 G0.076  V 0.68 G0.041

1985   1600   1600   1700   1700   1800   1800   1900   1900   2000   2000   2100   2100   2200   2200   2300   2300   2400   2400
 x    Call   Put   Call   Put   Call   Put   Call   Put   Call   Put   Call   Put   Call   Put   Call   Put   Call   Put
29.0% 385 97   2  3 291 92   8  8 207 82  23 18 136 67  52 33  83 50  98 50  46 33 160 67  24 20 237 80  11 11 328 89   5  5 416 95
28.0% 385 98   2  2 290 93   7  7 205 83  21 17 133 67  49 33  80 49  95 51  44 33 157 67  22 19 235 81  10 10 322 90   4  5 415 95
27.0% 385 98   2  2 289 93   6  7 203 83  19 17 131 68  47 32  77 49  92 51  41 32 155 68  20 18 233 82   9  9 321 91   3  4 415 96
26.0% 385 98   1  2 288 94   5  6 201 84  18 16 128 68  44 32  74 49  88 51  38 31 152 69  18 17 231 83   7  8 319 92   3  4 415 96
25.0% 385 99   1  1 287 94   4  5 199 85  16 15 125 69  41 31  71 49  85 51  35 30 149 70  16 16 229 84   6  7 318 93   2  3 415 97
   V 0.36 G0.022  V 1.01 G0.061  V 1.95 G0.118  V 2.81 G0.169  V 3.13 G0.188  V 2.80 G0.168  V 2.07 G0.124  V 1.30 G0.078  V 0.71 G0.042

1990   1600   1600   1700   1700   1800   1800   1900   1900   2000   2000   2100   2100   2200   2200   2300   2300   2400   2400
 x    Call   Put   Call   Put   Call   Put   Call   Put   Call   Put   Call   Put   Call   Put   Call   Put   Call   Put
29.0% 390 98   2  2 295 92   8  8 211 82  23 18 136 68  51 32  85 51  95 49  48 34 157 66  25 21 233 79  12 11 319 89   5  6 411 94
28.0% 390 98   2  2 294 93   7  7 209 83  21 17 137 68  48 32  82 50  92 50  45 33 154 67  23 20 231 80  10 11 317 89   4  5 410 95
27.0% 390 98   1  2 293 94   6  6 207 84  19 16 134 69  45 31  79 50  89 50  42 33 151 67  21 19 229 81   9 10 316 90   4  4 410 96
26.0% 390 98   1  1 292 94   5  6 205 85  17 15 131 69  42 31  76 50  86 50  40 32 149 68  19 18 226 82   8  9 315 91   3  4 410 97
25.0% 390 99   1  1 291 95   4  5 203 86  15 14 129 70  39 30  73 50  83 50  37 31 146 69  17 17 224 83   7  8 314 92   2  3 410 97
   V 0.35 G0.021  V 0.97 G0.058  V 1.91 G0.115  V 2.79 G0.167  V 3.14 G0.188  V 2.83 G0.170  V 2.12 G0.127  V 1.34 G0.080  V 0.74 G0.044

1995   1600   1600   1700   1700   1800   1800   1900   1900   2000   2000   2100   2100   2200   2200   2300   2300   2400   2400
 x    Call   Put   Call   Put   Call   Put   Call   Put   Call   Put   Call   Put   Call   Put   Call   Put   Call   Put
```

Courtesy of, and copyright © by, D. Isbister.

Market makers will constantly monitor their option positions to detect unwanted exposure. Usually, someone off the floor, a risk manager, is assigned to one or more floor traders. If the floor trader gets too

Summary of XYZ's Transactions

Step 1. Sells 100 $22.00 calls at $.08   28%
Buys 9 futures at $19.00

Step 2. Buys 100 $22.00 calls at $.19   26%
Sells 9 futures at $19.90

Options:	Sells 100 $22.00 calls at	$	.08	
	Buys 100 $22.00 calls at	$	.19	
		− $	.11	per barrel loss
		×	1,000.00	barrels per contract
		− $	110.00	per contract loss
		×	100.00	contracts
		− $11,000.00		loss
Futures:	Buys 9 futures	$	19.00	
	Sells 9 futures	$	19.00	
		$	.90	per barrel profit
		× − 1,000.00		barrels per contract
		$	900.00	per contract profit
			9.00	contracts
		$ 8,100.00		profit
Total Trade:	$ 8,100.00	futures hedge		
	− 11,000.00	options trade		
	$ 2,900	loss		

gamma exposed, the risk manager will offset the exposure by buying or selling options. However, when a market maker buys or sells options to reduce gamma exposure, he must face someone else's market, thus paying up to reduce gamma exposure.

The ideal way to keep gamma exposure to a minimum is to hedge options purchases with option sales, and vice versa. Recall the time value chart in Chapter 4 (Figure 4-1). If a large sell order comes into the ring for a particular option, it may pressure that particular option's premium lower. The market maker could buy the option and then sell options around it.

Example: Figure 10-3, illustrates the normal shape of the graph of call options' time value (solid line). A large sell order temporarily

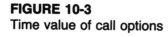

FIGURE 10-3
Time value of call options

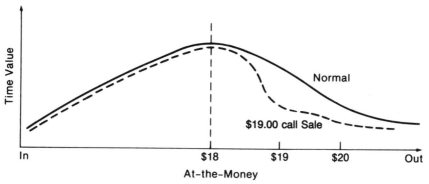

pushes the $19.00 call premiums a few ticks lower. Market makers could buy these cheaper options and sell $20.00 and $18.00 call options that are still "normally" priced. By hedging options with options, the market maker reduces the chance of getting gamma exposed. However, if "cheap" options are bought, expensive options can't always be found to sell.

GETTING PINNED

As expiration day approaches, the market maker is faced with more potential problems, specifically the risk of being caught—or "pinned"—in a losing position.

Example: If XYZ is *short* 1,000 $19.00 puts on expiration day and futures settle at $18.99, will the puts be exercised? Even though the $19.00 put is $.01 in the money, many of the traders who are long the put may decide not to exercise. First, transaction costs most likely won't be covered by buying futures at $18.99 and exercising puts. Second, the trader holding $19.00 puts may not want to be exposed with a short futures position over the weekend.

If prices settle slightly above $19.00, there are no guarantees that the puts won't be exercised. It may be easier for a trader to establish short positions in the futures markets at $19.00 by exercising the puts than to sell futures at slightly above $19.00. If the position established is large, selling futures may push the price below $19.00. The trader is not certain the price at which the futures position will be executed. However, the trader knows for certain that short positions will be established at $19.00 if the puts are exercised.

The problem for XYZ is that there is uncertainty as to whether all or some or none of the $19.00 puts will be exercised. On Friday, XYZ will not know exactly how many long futures should be held to cover the $19.00 put exercises because assignments of futures positions from option exercises don't occur until Saturday morning. XYZ may have a large exposed futures position over a weekend. This goes against the goal of the market maker which is to make money from the bid/offer spreads and not from futures price moves. Usually a market maker or local trader will pay up and trade out of short option positions days before the last day of trading to reduce the exposure of getting pinned.

Another example of getting pinned is when a trader is short straddles, and futures settle near the strike price. Many new option traders originally think that the best thing to happen to a short straddle position is for futures to expire right on top of the strike. Both puts and calls would expire worthless, and the trader earns the entire premium.

One way to get around this problem is to reduce short option positions to a reasonable level if it looks as if the futures may settle near or on the strike price. Of course, XYZ will now have to face another market maker and will have to pay up to reduce the potential market exposure.

It is difficult to perceive pure market markers (those who profit only from bid/offer spreads) on the floor of futures exchanges. Many will take volatility positions in addition to providing the market making function. Some trade volatility across markets, buying volatility in abnormally quiet markets and selling volatility in abnormally volatile markets. Some offer customized over-the-counter options extending their "book" beyond the floor the exchange. Floor transactions by market makers, then, can be offsetting some over-the-counter option exposure, establishing a volatility position, or just providing the pure market maker function by bidding and offering options.

ARBITRAGE STRATEGIES

Arbitrageurs serve important market functions. They add liquidity to options markets and maintain economic relationships between options and futures. Futures markets also gain liquidity from risk transference of options positions.

Local traders, acting as arbitrageurs, take advantage of temporary market inefficiencies in option premiums through arbitrage trading. They constantly monitor specific economic relationships between the option contract and the underlying instrument for profit opportunities. Floor traders have advantages over off-the-floor traders because arbitrage opportunities disappear quickly and transaction costs are much lower for floor traders.

Options are related to the underlying futures contract through the exercise feature. The simplest example of options arbitrage illustrates the relationship.

Example: Arbitrage opportunities exist if a December $17.00 crude oil call is trading at $2.20 and December crude oil futures are trading at $19.22. A trader could buy the call option, sell the futures, and immediately exercise for a profit of $.02:

Short futures	$19.22
Exercise option: Long futures	19.00
Profit	$ .22
Cost of $19.00 call option	.20
Net profit	$ .02

Call options will continue to be bid higher and futures offered lower until no arbitrage profits remain. This activity forces options to trade at values at least equal to their exercise values.

More complex arbitrage strategies are based on the following relationship:

$$C - P = e^{-rt} (F - E)$$

where

    C = call premium
    P = put premium
    F = futures price
    E = strike price
  e^{-rt} = discounting factor
    r = risk-free rate of return
    t = *time until expiration*

Options and futures must be the same month; puts and calls must have the same strike price. If a market maker knows where the put (or the call) is bid or offered, he knows the value of the corresponding call (or put). (In the following example, financing costs and transaction costs are excluded.)

Example: On September 14 the following situation exists:

Dec crude oil futures	$19.22
Dec $19.00 put	.63
Dec $19.00 call	.85

The relationship holds:

$$\$19.22 - \$19.00 = \$.22$$
$$\$.85 \; - \; \$.63 \; = \$.22$$

What would happen if a large supply of buy put orders enters the market suddenly, bidding up premiums to $.66? The relationship is now:

$$\$19.22 - \$19.00 = \$.22$$
$$\$.85 \; - \; \$.66 \; = \$.19$$

Arbitrage profits exist. A trader could sell puts, buy calls, and sell futures to lock in the following profit:

Sell futures $19.22		
Buy $19.00 calls	$.85	debit
Sell $19.00 puts	$.66	credit
	$.19	net debit

Consider how this position locks in profits. If futures are trading at $18.00 expiration, the futures position earns $1.22, the call loses $.85, and the put loses $.34 [$.66 − ($19.00 − $18.00)], for a total gain of $.03 (see Table 10-1, Case 1). If futures prices are trading at $20.00 at expiration (Case 2), the futures position loses $.78, the $19.00 call earns $.15 [($20.00 − $19.00) − $.85], and the $19.00 put earns $.66 for a total gain of $.03.

TABLE 10-1

Arbitrage strategies: reverse conversions

		Expiration Profit (Loss)			
		Case 1		Case 2	
	Actual Trade	At Expiration	Profit/Loss	At Expiration	Profit/Loss
Sell futures	$19.22	$18.00	$ 1.22	$20.00	$(.78)
Buy $19.00 calls	$ .85	0	(.85)	1.00	.15
Sell $19.00 puts	$ .66	1.00	(.34)	0	.66
Net debit	$ .19				
Net result			$ .03		$ .03

Regardless where futures trade, the value of the arbitrageur's position is $.03 at expiration. The strategy of selling futures, buying calls, and selling puts is called a reversal or reverse conversion.

What happens if many buy call orders enter the market and bid premiums to $.89? Floor traders will then execute conversions by selling calls, buying puts, and buying futures. See Table 10-2. This time the market maker has locked in $.04 regardless where futures trade.

In both cases (buy put or buy call orders), arbitrage will continue until no profits exist. Note that conversions and reversals force the options/futures relationship to hold and increase liquidity in both the options and futures markets. Arbitrage profits are locked in without exposure to market moves. In reality, however, the arbitrageur must overcome some potential problems not addressed in our textbook examples. Some of these problems are similar to the ones market makers face described earlier.

TABLE 10-2
Arbitrage strategies: conversions

| | | Expiration Profit (Loss) | | | |
| | | Case 1 | | Case 2 | |
	Actual Trade	At Expiration	Profit/Loss	At Expiration	Profit/Loss
Buy futures	$19.22	$18.00	$(1.22)	$20.00	$ .78
Sell $19.00 calls	$ .89	0	.89	1.00	(.11)
Buy $19.00 puts	$ .63	1.00	.37	0	(.63)
Net credit	$ .16				
Net result			$ .04		$ .04

Legging In and Out

Conversions and reversals have three components: two options and one futures contract. An arbitrageur must trade quickly; otherwise, the position could be exposed to a market move, and expected profits could turn into losses. Many option traders address this problem by teaming up with a trader in the futures pit. However, even if the option trader does the option side of a conversion and signals to the futures trader, the market may have moved, eliminating an already slim profit margin.

Getting "Pinned"

Locals who take conversions and reversals into expiration run the risk of getting "pinned," as explained in the previous section. If futures settle very close to the strike price on expiration day, a decision must be made whether to exercise the long option leg, while trying to guess what the trader holding the long side of the short option will do. A long option holder will have some time after the markets close before deciding about the exercise.

Example: If futures settle at $16.00, a holder of a $16.00 call or put might watch the cash market during that time before deciding whether to exercise. However, because crude oil options expire on Fridays, an exercise of options brings the risk of a substantially higher or lower opening Monday morning.

If futures settle at $19.00 on expiration day, traders who hold, for example, conversions (long futures, short $19.00 calls, long $19.00 puts) must guess what the other side holding the short call will do. If a trader exercises the long puts to offset the long futures, the long call may decide to exercise also. This would leave that trader with a significantly exposed market position (i.e., a short futures position) from Friday to Monday morning.

Market markers will sometimes pay a little extra to unwind conversions and reversals, so as not to get "pinned." Traders unwind by offsetting option positions in the options market and futures positions in the futures market. For example, a conversion executed with a $19.00 strike is liquidated by a reversal with the same $19.00 strike. However, not all conversions and reversals require a trader to hold the position to expiration to earn profits, nor will futures always settle on a strike price at expiration.

Margin Calls

An option position is not margined like a futures position. Unlike a futures trade, the only cash exchanging hands between a buyer and a seller of an option occurs when the trade is put on and when the trade is taken off.

Example: If a trader buys a call for $1.50 and the next day it settles at $1.75, profits of $.25 are not realized until the trade is liquidated. On the other hand, futures positions are marked to market on a daily basis—cash from market losses is transferred to those positions that have increased in value.

The problem facing an arbitrageur is that a potential negative cash flow from a futures margin is not offset by the option leg until the trade is liquidated. The arbitrageur, seeking to profit from a market inefficiency, may have to wait days or weeks before options and futures move back in line. If the market moves against the futures side of the conversion or reversal, considerable cash flow problems could develop.

Some traders simply borrow cash to pay margin and incorporate interest charges into their cost structure. Others will "tail" the conversion or reversal. The details of "tailing" are beyond the scope of this book, but the general idea is to adjust the futures position to account for the disparity in cash flows. Discounting cash flows may reveal that buying 99 futures contracts will cover 100 long puts and 100 short calls. Using slightly fewer futures contracts than options addresses the discrepancy between futures cash flow that occurs daily versus option cash flow that occurs only at execution and liquidation.

To circumvent potential margin calls on reversals or conversions, arbitrageurs will complete a box trade. For instance, if a conversion is held on a $19.00 strike, a reversal can be executed on a $19.00 strike or a $20.00 strike, and the futures positions drop out.

Example: A market maker is long futures, short $19.00 calls, and long $19.00 puts (conversion). Selling futures, buying $18.00 calls, and selling $18.00 puts removes the futures side and any corresponding margin issues.

Arbitrage strategies: Box

Conversion	+	Reversal	=	Box
Long futures		Short futures		
Sell $19.00 calls		Buy $18.00 calls		
Buy $19.00 puts		Sell $18.00 puts		

The arbitrageur originally puts on the conversion to lock in profits, then executes the reversal to remove the futures die. The reversal may not necessarily earn profits, but it serves the trader by eliminating the futures leg and margin calls. The resulting position is called a *box*.

In addition to margin-related cash flow shortfalls, arbitrageurs must closely watch interest expenses. Sometimes what may look like a profitable arbitrage strategy is only profitable before interest charges are taken into account.

Example: A reversal executed on a $16.00 strike price for a five-month option with futures trading at $19.00 will require a large cash payment. A reversal involves buying the call, selling the put, and selling the future. In this case, the call will be trading for at least $300.00. A trader may see $.02 or $.03 reversals available, but the profits disappear when interest charges on the cash flow are considered.

CHAPTER 11

Practical Considerations

In the preceding chapters, we have introduced a long menu of strategies, which, to the new option trader, can be overwhelming. The strength of using options in a trading program lies in the ability of an option strategy to reflect the market opinion of a trader. Profits are earned if the opinion is a correct one. In this chapter, we will examine what thought processes a trader might go through before establishing a position. Further, once the position is established, and markets move, the trader is confronted with more choices. If prices move against the position, how could the trader take defensive action? If prices move in favor of the position, how might the trader react?

ORGANIZING A MARKET OPINION

Option traders consider not only market direction opinions but also the intensity and time frame of the expected move.

Example: Trader A feels that oil prices will drop by $1.00 within the next week. Trader B thinks prices will drop by $1.00 but over a longer period of time. Even though each believes prices will drop by $1.00, they may establish two very different positions in the option market. Trader A is looking for a violent move downward, that is, $1.00 lower in one week. Trader B expects the market to drift lower. Trader A could buy puts outright, to take advantage of a downward move and an increase in volatility. Trader B might lean toward selling calls to take advantage of a declining market and lower volatility. Trader B could also buy bear put spreads, buying puts with higher strikes than the puts that are sold.

Put spreads reduce the effect of changes in volatility and time decay because one option is bought and one is sold. As we have illustrated in previous chapters, selling calls and bear put spreads have significantly different profit/loss outcomes. The bear put spread buyer has limited risk, and the short call buyer has unlimited risk. Both have maximum profit potential. The short call will benefit from lower volatility; the bear put spread will lose if volatility declines, but not as much as the outright long put position.

Option traders need to be very familiar with the market they are trading. Each market has volatility tendencies.

Example: Crude oil option implied volatility tends to increase when prices decline and decrease when prices increase. When crude prices decline, out-of-the-money puts implied volatility becomes much higher relative to out-of-the-money call implied volatility. This means that a bear put spread, which normally is slightly long volatility, may in fact be a short volatility trade. Consider prices at $16.25. The $16.00 put is bought and the $15.00 put is sold. Price moves down to $15.25. The $15.00 puts are bid up sharply as prices decline and volatility increases. The $16.00 calls are now out of the money and are sold aggressively. The aggressive selling of the $16.00 calls limits the upside potential of the $16.00 puts (recall the arbitrage strategies discussed in Chapter 7). The $16.00 puts increase in value because prices are moving downward but do not participate in the volatility move as much as do the $15.00 puts.

The opposite occurs in precious metals and grain markets. Bull call spreads, which are normally thought of as slightly long volatility, can actually be a short volatility trade in these markets.

Price opinions, when combined with views on volatility, help a trader to locate the optimal position that best fits his or her overall market opinion. By monitoring implied volatility, the trader is constantly assessing the value of option premiums with the goal always to buy low and sell high.

Example: Trader A believes that, after the OPEC meeting, price will jump in one direction or the other and volatility will decline sharply. The trader would like to be set up for this. From Chapter 7, we know that volatility has a greater effect on options that have more time until expiration. And price moves in the underlying futures have a greater effect on nearby options (everything else equal, nearby options have higher gammas.) Trader A could buy nearby-month straddles or strangles and sell deferred-month straddles or strangles. The overall position is long gamma and short volatility. Ideally, this trade would be put on the day before the OPEC meeting when implied volatility is high. But the market may anticipate these kind of trades to be established and bid up nearby options. This effect can be monitored by tracking implied volatility of all option months.

Trader A is slightly bullish and thinks that implied volatility is extremely high. Selling puts is long the market and short volatility. However, if the unlimited risk feature of short option strategies does not fit into trader A's program, bull call spreads will reduce the effect of declining volatility.

DEFENSIVE STRATEGIES

Options are different from futures positions in terms of taking a defensive posture toward prices or volatility moving against the position. Stop orders are generally used to reduce or eliminate exposure to adverse price moves on futures positions. Buy option strategies already have a built in stop because the risk is limited to the premium paid. If prices move sharply against a buy call strategy, the risk is automatically reduced because the option's delta is getting less positive (that is, the position's gamma is positive). This feature makes buy option strategies effective when trying to pick market tops or bottoms. Picking tops and bottoms with futures can sometimes be trying because positions can be stopped out if the exact top or bottom is missed. Buying options gives the trader much more staying power because of the natural stop built into the strategy.

Buy option strategies, of course, do have a time limitation. For at-the-money options, time decay is an important consideration. There is no ''correct'' time for rolling into a later month. Salvaging what premium is left before the last couple of weeks is not a bad idea if the price outlook for the particular option looks bleak. Unfortunately, many traders will allow options to expire worthless hoping and praying for a last-minute reprieve.

Buy option strategies are used sometimes to protect a futures position. For example, a trader sells futures, and prices go down sharply. The trader is looking for a further decline in price but does not want to give up profits already earned. The trader uses some of the profits to buy out-of-the-money calls. If prices turn around and go up, the trader has coverage. The trader has effectively turned a short futures position into a synthetic long put (see Chapter 5), which has limited risk.

Selling options is a different story. Risk is potentially unlimited. If prices move against a short option position, defensive action should be taken. As in trading futures, the trader should determine how much risk is acceptable before establishing the position. When the risk level is reached, the trader liquidates the position and eats the losses. What often happens is that prices move against the position and volatility increases. The traders begin to look at the intrinsic value of the option and say, ''If I cover this position with futures, I will actually show a profit at expiration.'' Expiration may be two months away.

Covering a losing short call (put) position by getting long (short) futures can easily backfire if the market begins to chop and trade lower after the futures are bought. If the market trades lower and the trader liquidates the futures, prices could then trade higher. While the trader is being jerked around by a volatile, choppy market, new trading opportunities are being missed. The best way to take defensive positions when selling options is to liquidate the trade as the maximum risk level is reached. The old adage "cut your losses" is appropriate here.

Some traders like to roll positions into higher or lower strikes. For example, a trader who is short $16.00 calls when prices rally can buy back the $16.00 calls, sell $17.00 calls and try again. Traders must be careful when rolling positions defensively because they may tend to become stubborn about their price and volatility expectations. Most of the time, it is better to step back and release the market when maximum risk levels are exceeded rather than rolling positions.

OFFENSIVE STRATEGIES

Rolling positions offensively is an effective way to take profits and maintain a market position.

Example: A trader buys $16.00 calls and the market moves higher. The trader sells out the $16.00 calls for $.75 profit and purchases $17.00 or $18.00 with part of the profit. The trader has guaranteed a profit of $.75 minus the premium of the purchased calls. And if the market continues to rally, the trader still participates.

Rolling options positions in the direction of the price move is an effective strategy when a major price move has occurred. The market may look overbought or oversold based on some technical indicators, so the trader books a profit. However, markets have been known to make significant price moves higher during an overbought situation, and lower during an oversold position: The aggressive trader is trying to capture these final blow-offs by rolling the position. Rolling into out of the money options takes advantage of tremendous leverage offered by these options.

Let's examine the potential increase in out-of-the-money options.

Example: Look at the July 1 settlements for October crude oil options, Table 11-1. In one week, prices rise by $1.00. The largest percent increase occuring in the $18.00 call. This analysis, of course, ignores the possibility of a change in volatility. The $18.00 calls yields the highest return for an equal dollar investment. The option trader is trying to hit a home run by purchasing deep out-of-the-money options. However, if the purchase is fully funded by recently booked profits, the trade becomes the option version of "let your profits run."

TABLE 11-1

Comparison of option strike prices

	Settlement Dates of October Crude Oil Options		
	July 1[1]	July 8[2]	% Change
October Futures	$15.27	16.27	+6.6
$15 call	.89	1.52	+70.8
$16 call	.47	.91	+93.6
$17 call	.21	.47	+123.8
$18 call	.10	.24	+140.0

[1]Actual settlement prices for July 1, 1988.

[2]Estimated settlements for illustrative purposes only.

TRADING FUTURES AGAINST OPTIONS

An option trader buys calls, and prices immediately move higher. The trader could take profits. Or she may decide to trade futures aggressively against the option position. The trader's long-term position is still bullish. But prices have moved up quickly, and a short-term correction is due. The trader could sell futures and buy them back after the short-term correction takes place. The idea is to establish longer term positions with options and scalp the market with futures in an effort to fund the position.

For a speculator, options offer more leverage in volatile markets.

Example: A trader who could buy 10 contracts of currency futures might buy 20 out-of-the-money currency options. If the option has a few months until expiration, and prices move at some point in favor of the option position, the speculator can now trade 20 futures contracts.

The long option position acts as a hedge if the market moves against the futures position. Huge profits can be earned in this way at relatively low risk.

The risks include the initial purchase of the options. Prices need to move in favor of the position before the trader can become more aggressive. If not, the trader risks losing some or all of the premium. The other risk is that prices move against the futures position and never allow the trader to get out of the futures side.

Ideally, a few correct market calls will more than finance the entire original long call position.

Example: A trader buys 10 T-bond calls. Prices move sharply higher. The trader sells 10 T-bonds futures. Prices drop. The trader buys 10 T-bond futures. Prices rally. The trader sells—and so on.

Some traders like to "take profits" by selling options.

Example: A trader buys crude oil futures at $16.00. Prices go up to $17.00. Instead of selling futures, the trader sells a $17.00 call. Now the position is a simple covered call strategy. The trader needs prices to move sideways to higher.

The problem with this kind of trade is that time must go by for the trader to earn the maximum amount from the call. While the trader is waiting for time to work on the call, the trend may reverse.

Covered calls have unlimited risk on the downside and a winning position may turn into a loser.

Example: The initial trade could have been a long $16.00 call. Prices rally and the $17.00 call is sold. Now the trader has established a bull call spread at low cost. But, if prices turn and go down, losses may accrue.

Personally, I would rather book the profit and buy an out-of-the-money option, as described in the previous section. Profitable trades are guaranteed not to turn into losers, and a market position is maintained.

RATIO SPREADS

Some traders like to buy options and finance them with multiple option sales.

Example: Crude prices are at $16.00 and a trader buys one $14.00 put and sells three $13.00 puts for a net debit of $.01. The most this trade can earn is $1,000 ($14 − $13 = $1 × 1,000 barrels) minus $10 ($.01 × 1,000 barrels), or $10.00. Losses accrue if prices drop below $13.00. The trader assumes that prices will drop to a level where the trade becomes profitable. The trader also assumes that the position will be the end of the option trader.

Ratio spreads are potential money makers at low initial cost. But the trader must be careful not to focus all positions as ratio spreads.

One hundred successful option traders will offer one hundred different ways to approach options markets. Each has found some particular niche that personally fits the individual trader. Some traders make money from predicting price direction and getting long or short in the most efficient way. Others will trade vega, or volatility, anticipating periods when premiums will be bid up or offered down. Some traders like getting long gamma: losing a little premium each day awaiting a sharp move in the futures price. Still others focus on option spreads across strikes.

This book introduces beginning option traders to the terms and concepts that most professionals inherently understand. However, advanced training takes place in the trading arena. Who can tell you whether it is time to get out of a straddle because time decay is beginning to take its toll? Market opinions are as varied as market traders.

Each market has its own tendencies. Each position has its own risks. "Options allow traders to translate any market opinion into market action." This is a commonly heard line. The key is still to have enough correct market opinions: whether they are price or volatility or spread value opinions. Without a correct view on the market, option traders can lose as much as futures traders. Options allow more freedom of expression, nothing more. Options are more complicated than futures. The option trader needs to know what is the maximum risk. Selling 100 options with a combined delta of −1 is more risky than being short one future.

The next step is actually to begin trading. Experiment with small positions until a level of real confidence is built. Try bull call spreads, buy options outright, track volatility. Nothing burns a lesson into memory as well as a profit or loss; paper trading just isn't worth the paper. What decisions will be made when real money is ticking away? This can only be answered doing real trading, using real money. But start out slowly and know the risk.

Implied Volatility of
Selected Markets*

*Charts courtesy of PaineWebber.

CBT T-BOND OPTIONS

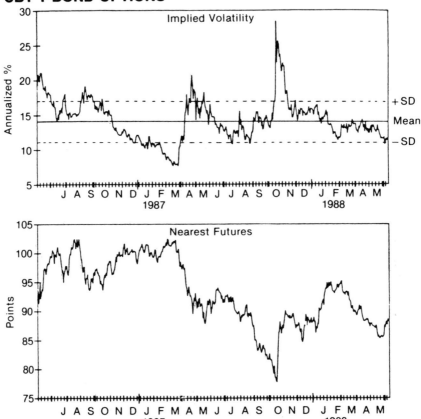

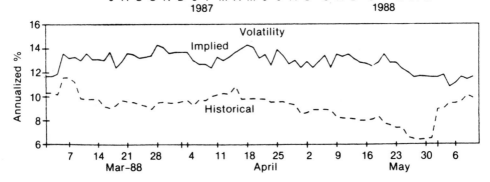

CBT T-NOTE OPTIONS

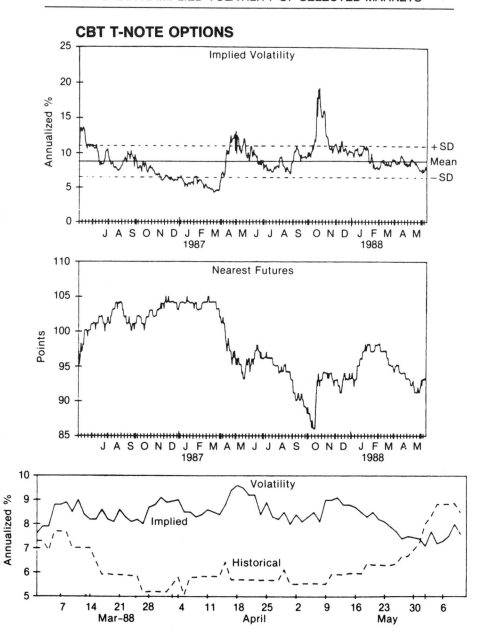

CME EURODOLLAR OPTIONS

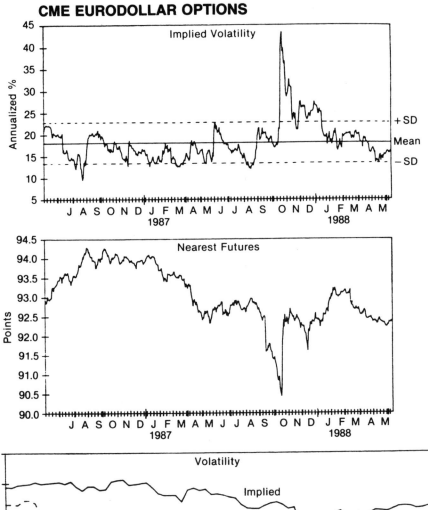

CME S&P 500 OPTIONS

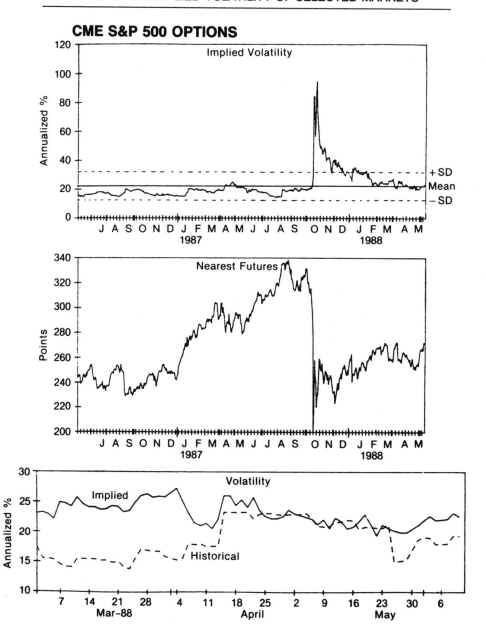

COMEX GOLD OPTIONS

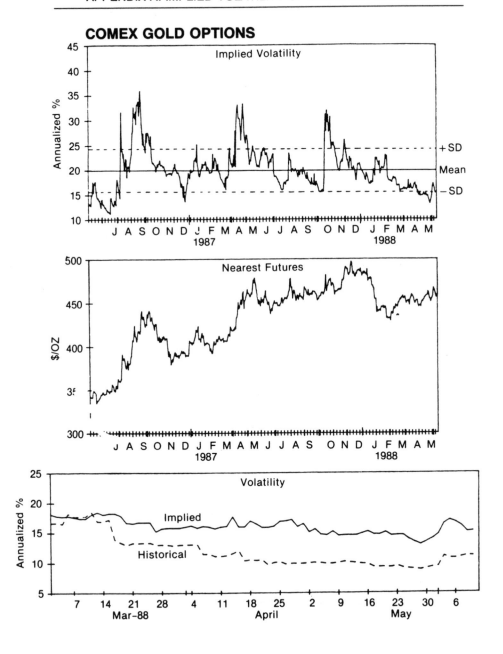

COMEX SILVER OPTIONS

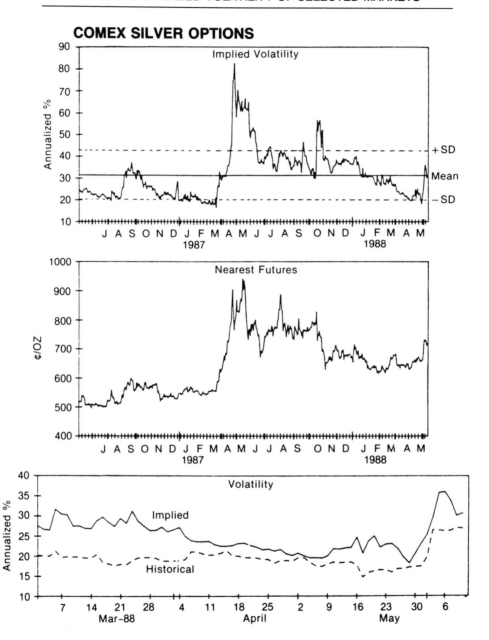

COMEX COPPER OPTIONS

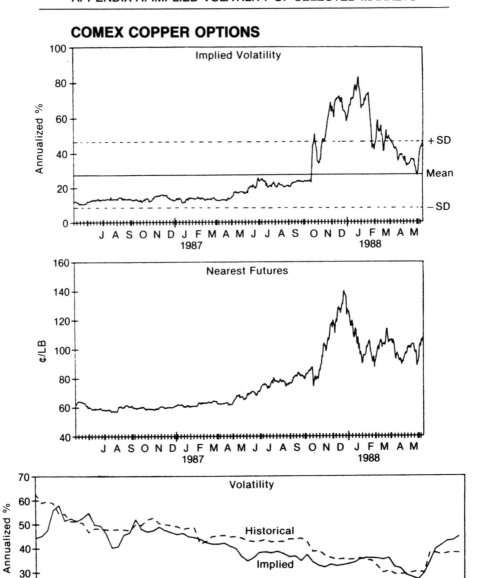

CME SWISS FRANC OPTIONS

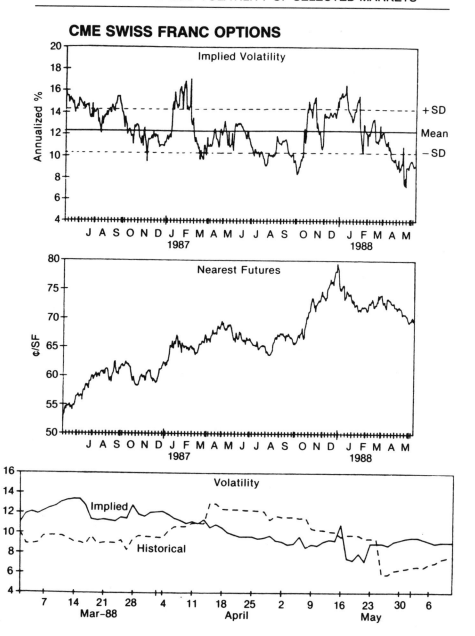

CME DEUTSCHE MARK OPTIONS

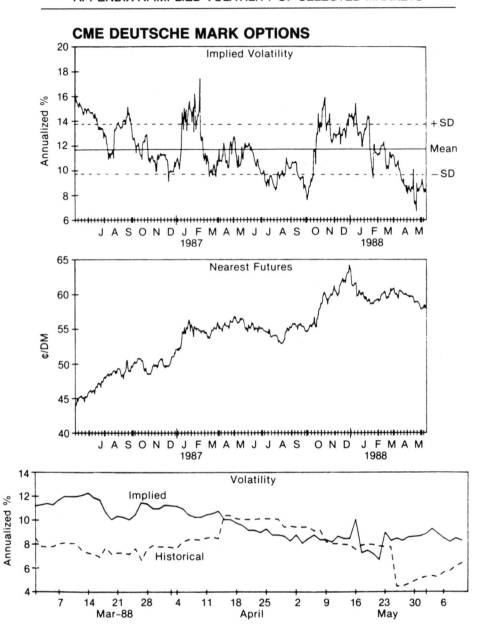

CME JAPANESE YEN OPTIONS

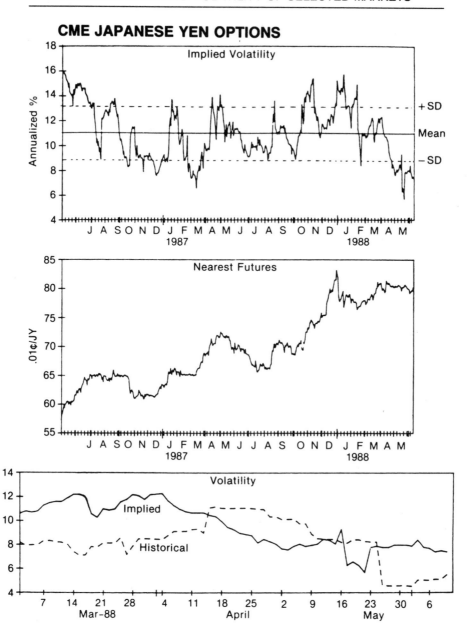

CME BRITISH POUND OPTIONS

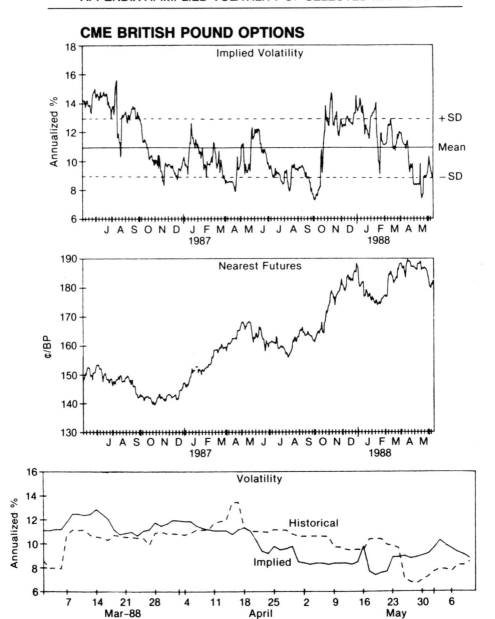

NYMEX CRUDE OIL OPTIONS

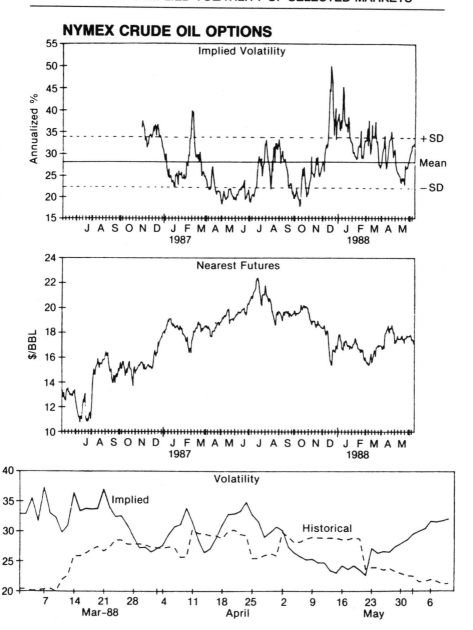

CBT CORN OPTIONS

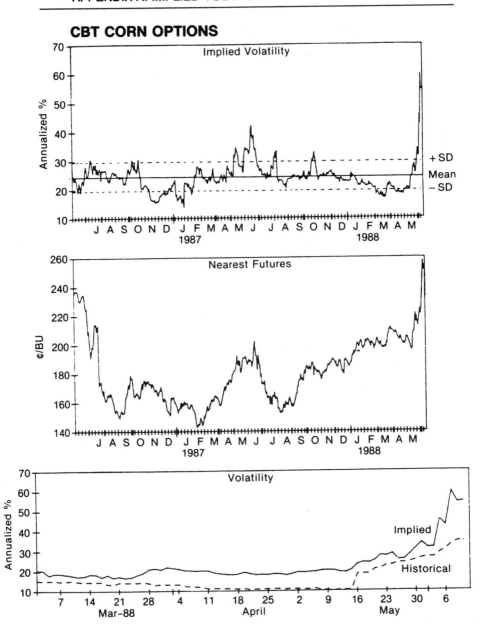

CBT SOYBEAN OPTIONS

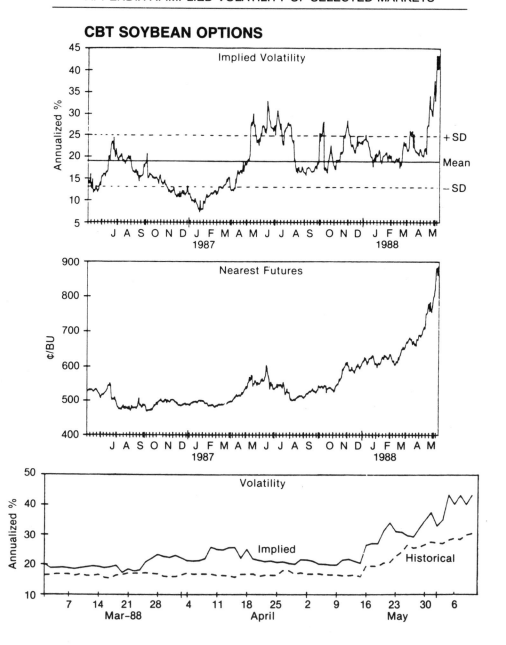

CME LIVE CATTLE OPTIONS

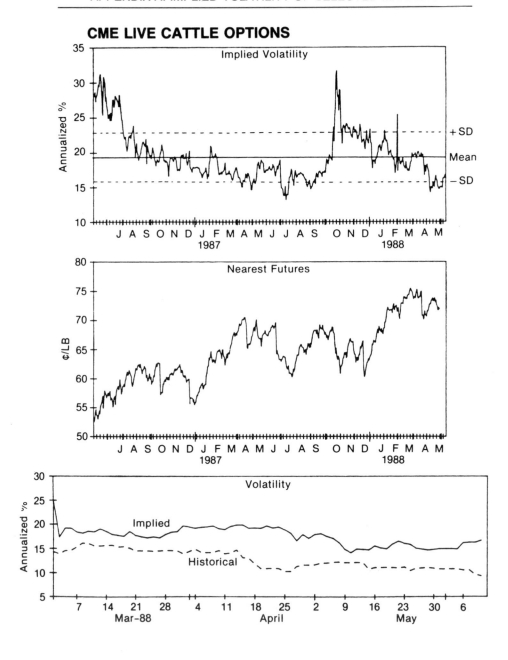

CSCE SUGAR OPTIONS

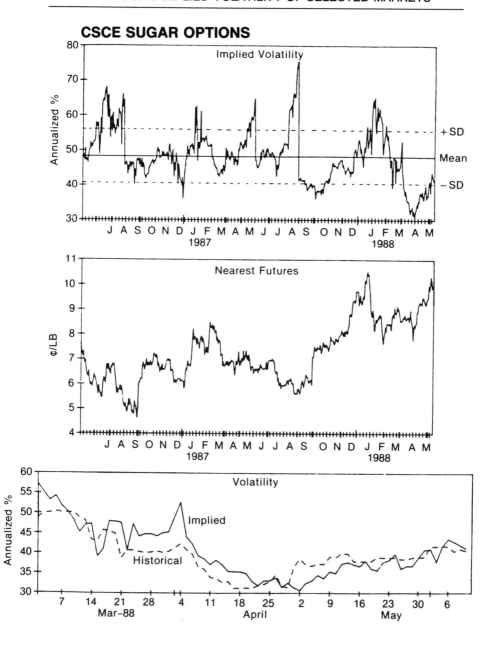

Glossary

AMFOD

An acronym for Association of Member Firm Option Departments, a division of the SIA dedicated to improving the option market.

Arbitrage

The simultaneous purchase and sale of the same or equal securities or futures contracts in such a way as to take advantage of price differences prevailing in separate markets, with relatively low risk.

See Bona Fide Arbitrage; Risk Arbitrage

Arbitrageur

One who engages in arbitrage.

As Agent

The role of a broker/dealer firm when it acts as an intermediary, or broker, between its customer and another customer, a market market, or a contrabroker. For this service the firm receives a stated commission or fee. This is an "agency transaction."

See As Principal

As Principal

The role of a broker/dealer firm when it buys and sells for its own account. In a typical transaction, it buys from a market maker or contrabroker and sells to a customer at a fair reasonable markup; if it buys from a customer and sells to the market maker at a higher price, the trade is called a markdown.

See As Agent

Assign

See Early Exercise; Exercise

Association of Member Firm Option Departments (AMFOD)

A division of the Securities Industry Association dedicated to improving the option market.

Automatic Exercise

To protect the holder of an expiring in-the-money option, the Options Clearing Corporation automatically exercises the option for the holder. Only the owner can instruct to do otherwise.

Back Month

A remote deferred month in futures contract trading.

Backspread

See Reverse Strategy

Bearish

An adjective used to describe an opinion or outlook where one anticipates a decline in price of the general market, of an underlying interest, or of both.

See Bullish

Bear Market

A market characterized by declining prices.

See Bull Market

Bear Spread

An option spread so designed that a profit will result if the underlying security declines in the market. The trader buys (long) the higher strike price and sells (writes) the lower strike price.

Beta

A measurement that quantifies the correlation between the movement of the stock and the movement of the stock market as a whole. Not to be mistaken with volatility.

See Volatility

Black-Scholes Model

A formula used to calculate theoretical option prices from stock price, strike price, volatility, and time to expiration. A by-product of the model is the exact calculation of the delta.

See Delta

Bona Fide Arbitrage

Arbitrage transactions by professional traders that take profitable advantage of prices for the same or convertible securities in different markets. The risk is usually minimal and the profit correspondingly small.

See Risk Arbitrage; Special Arbitrage Account

Box Spread

An option arbitrage. A bull spread and a bear spread are combined to create a profit with no risk.

Bullish

Describing an opinion or outlook that a rise in price is expected either in the general market or in an individual security.

See Bearish

Bull Market

A securities market characterized by rising prices.

See Bear Market

Butterfly Spread

An option strategy combining both limited risk and limited profit potential. It is a combination of a bull spread and a bear spread where striking prices are involved. The lower two prices are utilized in the bull spread and the higher two in the bear spread. Puts and calls can form this strategy with four different ways of combining options to construct the same basic position.

Buyer's Option

See Call

Calendar Spread

An option strategy using the sale of a short-term option and the purchase of a longer-term option, both having the same striking price. Either puts or calls may be used.

A *calendar combination* is a strategy combining a call calendar spread and a put calendar spread, with the strike price of the calls being higher than the strike price of the puts.

A *calendar straddle* combines the selling of a near-term straddle and the purchase of a longer-term straddle, both with the same striking price.

Calendar Straddle or Combination

See Calendar Spread

Call

An option giving its holder (buyer) the right to demand the purchase of 100 shares of stock at a fixed price any time within a specified period (the lifetime of the option). Also sometimes referred to as a buyer's option.

See Put

Cap and Floor

See Fence

CBOE

See Chicago Board Options Exchange, Inc.

Chicago Board Option Exchange, Inc. (CBOE)

The first national exchange to trade listed stock options.

Class

All put and call contracts on the same underlying security.

Collar

See Fence

Commodities Futures Trading Commission (CFTC)

Formed in 1976 by Congress, the CFTC oversees all matters of disclosure and information, registration of firms and individuals, fair trading procedures, and the maintenance of the options and futures market.

Commodity

A bulk good that is grown or mined, such as grains or precious metals.

See Futures

Condor

An options position involving two short options at different middle strike prices, one long option at a lower strike price, and one long option at a higher strike price.

Contract Grade

A commodity grade that an exchange officially designates as acceptable for delivery in a futures contract settlement.

Contract Market

A board of trade that the Commodity Futures Trading Commission specifies as the market for a given commodity.

Conventional Option

An option contract entered into by two parties that is not standardized as to striking price and/or expiration date and is not cleared through the Options Clearing Corporation.

An over-the-counter or unlisted price option.

Converted Put

See Synthetic Put

Cover (Covering)

To buy back an initially written option as a closing transaction.

To buy a security previously sold short to eliminate that open position.

Covered Straddle Write

The strategy in which an investor owns the underlying security but also writes a straddle on that security.

Covered Write

The writing or selling of a call option or put against a position in the underlying stock or its equivalent.

A *short call* is covered if the underlying stock is owned.

A *short put* is covered if the underlying stock is also short in the account.

Currency Futures

Futures contracts on foreign currencies, such as U.S. dollars, British pounds, French francs, Deutsche marks, Swiss francs, or Japanese yen. They provide hedging capability to corporations who sell their products internationally.

Cycle

The cyclical four-month expiration dates applied to various classes of options, such as January/April/July/October (JAJO).

Daily Trading Limit

A maximum that many options or commodities are permitted to fall or rise in one trading day. Most exchanges impose a daily trading limit on each contract.

Day Trading

The act of buying and selling a position during the same day.

Dealer

An individual or firm in the securities business acting as a principal rather than as an agent.

See As Agent; As Principal

Deep in the Money

A term used to describe a securities option with a strike price that is already profitable and relatively far from the market price of the underlying security. The option has intrinsic value.

In certain regulatory contexts, more than 5 points in the money.

Deep Out of the Money

A term used to describe a securities option with a strike price that is unprofitable and relatively far from the market price of the underlying security.

In certain regulatory contexts, more than 5 points out of the money.

Deliver

In options trading, transferring securities from one individual's or firm's account to another individual's or firm's account. The assigned call writer must deliver the stock to the exercised call holder. An exercised put holder must deliver the stock to the assigned put writer.

Delivery (Deliverable) Grade

See Contract Grade

Delivery Notice

The date on a futures contract when the actual commodity is to be delivered to the buyer.

A formal notice documenting when the goods will be delivered.

Delta

The amount that an option's price will change for a corresponding change in price of the underlying stock. Call options have positive deltas, while put options have negative deltas. The delta can be altered for even fractional changes in the underlying stock. The terms *up delta* and *down delta* describe the option's change after a full one-point change in price by the underlying security either up or down. The up delta may be larger than the down delta for a call option, while the reverse is true for put options.

See Hedge Ratio

Delta Spread

A ratio spread established as a neutral position. This neutral ratio is found by dividing the delta of the purchased option by the delta of the written option.

See Ratio Spread; Delta

Diagonal Spread

Any spread created in which (1) the purchased options have a longer maturity than do the written options and (2) both options have different striking prices. Some types of diagonal spreads are diagonal bull spreads, diagonal bear spreads, and diagonal butterfly spreads.

Discount Arbitrage

An arbitrage in which a discount option is purchased while an opposite position is taken in the underlying security.

Basic Call Arbitrage: The arbitrageur can buy a call at a discount and simultaneously sell the underlying stock.

Basic Put Arbitrage: The arbitrageur buys a put at a discount and simultaneously buys the underlying stock. Both positions are considered riskless.

See Discount

Down and Out Option

A block of at least ten call options with the same strike price and expiration date that carries a provision for immediate cancellation of the exercise privilege if the underlying stock declines by a predetermined, agreed-upon amount in the marketplace.

Down Delta

See Delta

Downside Protection

In the case of a covered call, the cushion against loss if the underlying stock declines in price. Alternatively, it may be expressed in terms of the distance the stock could fall before the total position becomes a loss or an amount equal to the option premium. It can also be expressed as a percentage of the current stock price.

See Covered Call Write

Dynamic

A term used to describe option strategies analyses made during the course of changing stock prices over time, as opposed to an analysis made at expiration of the options used in the strategy. A dynamic breakeven point or a dynamic follow-up action changes as time passes.

See Breakeven Point; Follow-Up Action

Early Exercise (Assignment)

Exercising (assigning) an option contract before the expiration date. Most options are exercised at or very close to their expiration date.

Exercise (Assign)

The requirement by an option holder for the seller of the option to perform the agreed-upon securities transaction. The seller (writer) of a call option must deliver (sell) stock to the option holder, whereas the seller (writer) of a put option must purchase it from the holder.

Exercises of index options are settled through the payment of cash. The cash settlement amount is the difference between the exercise price of the option and the current index value at the close of trading on the day of exercise, multiplied by the applicable index multiplier.

Exercise Date

The date when the sale or purchase of an option takes place according to the contract.

Exercise Limit

The limit on the number of contracts that a holder can exercise in a given period, as set by the appropriate option exchange. It is designed to prevent an investor or group of investors from cornering the market in a stock.

Exercise Notice

A document delivered to the Options Clearing Corporation for listed options, or to the guarantor of a conventional option, legally requiring the writer of an option to perform his or her contracted obligations.

Exercise of Call

The full or partial retirement of a bond issue through the use of a call privilege provided for in the terms of that security. The redemption price is usually higher than the face value if the option is exercised in the early years after the distribution.

The action of the owner of a call option when the option is exercised (when delivery of the underlying security is demanded).

Exercise Price

See Strike (Striking) Price

Expiration Date

The date an option contract becomes void. The expiration date for listed stock options is the Saturday after the third Friday of the expiration month. All holders of options who wish to exercise must indicate their desire to do so by this date.

See Expiration Time

Expiration Time

The time of day on the expiration date when all exercise notices must be received. The expiration time is currently 5:00 P.M. on the business day preceding the expiration date.

See Expiration Date

Extrinsic Value

The amount by which the market price of an option exceeds the amount that could be realized if the option were exercised and the underlying commodity liquidated. Also known as time value.

Fair Value

A term describing the worth of an option contract as determined by a mathematical model or used to indicate intrinsic value.

See Intrinsic Value; Model

Farther Out, Farther In

The act of extending or retracting maturity or expiration dates on options.

Fast Market

Term used to describe fast-paced activity in a class of listed options. If the exchange cannot control the market, new orders may be delayed.

Fence

A hedging strategy by which a hedge, who is long cash, buys a put and offsets the cost by selling an out-of-the-money call.

Follow-Up Action

Any option trading that takes place after a position is established. It is generally used to limit losses or to take profits.

Forward Pricing

The means of determining purchase of redemption prices after receipt of a mutual fund order from a customer.

Futures

Short for futures contract, which is an agreement to make or take delivery of a commodity at a specified future time and price. The contract is transferable and can therefore be traded like security. Although futures contracts were once limited to commodities, they are now available on financial instruments, currencies, and indexes. Noncommodity futures contracts often differ from their predecessors in important respects; for example, "delivery" on an index is irrelevant.

Hedge Ratio

A mathematical quantity equal to the delta of an option. It is useful in facilitation because a theoretically riskless hedge can be established by taking offsetting positions in the underlying stock and its call options.

See Facilitation; Delta

Horizontal Spread

The term used to describe an options strategy where the options have the same striking price but different expiration dates.

See Calendar Spread

Implied Volatility

The volatility of the underlying stock, as determined by the price currently existing in the market at the time, rather than historical data on the price changes of the underlying stock.

See Volatility

Index Options

Options on stock indexes.

Intercommodity Spread

A spread consisting of a long position and a short position in different but related commodities, in which the investor hopes to profit from the changing prices between commodities.

Interdelivery Spread

A trading technique in futures or options whereby an investor buys one month of a contract and, in turn, sells another month in the same contract. The investor is hoping to profit from the price differences between the two months. For example, an investor buys a June wheat contract and simultaneously sells a September wheat contract for a higher price.

Interest Rate Futures

A futures contract on an interest rate. The contract calls for delivery of an instrument that will mature some time after the delivery date. It is based on the market's expectation of interest rates for the period in the contract.

Interest Rate Option

An option on an interest rate. The option must be prepaid based on the interest rate. The grantor must receive higher premiums during higher interest rates to compensate for the higher cost of capital.

Intermarket Spread

See Interdelivery Spread

In the Money

An expression used to denote a securities option with a strike price that is profitable in comparison with the current market value of the underlying stock—that is, an option with intrinsic value.

A *call option* is considered in the money if the underlying stock is higher than the striking price of the call.

A *put option* is considered in the money if the stock is below the striking price.

See Out of the Money; Intrinsic Value

Intracommodity Spread

A spread in which the trader buys and sells futures contracts in the same commodity, on the same exchange, but for differing months.

Intraday

Meaning "within the day," this term is most often used to describe daily high and low prices of a security or commodity.

Intrinsic Value

The immediate value of an option if it were to expire with the underlying stock at its current price, or the amount by which an option is in the money.

For *call options,* it is the difference between the stock price and the strike price if that difference is a positive number. If the difference is not positive, it is considered zero.

For *put options,* it is the difference between the strike price and the stock price if the difference is positive, and zero otherwise.

See In the Money Time Value Premium; Parity

Lapsed Option

An option that expires unexercised.

Last Trading Day

Options cease trading at 3:00 P.M. Eastern Time on the third Friday of the expiration month.

Leg

A method of establishing a two-sided position involving a large amount of risk. The trader first executes one side of the position hoping to execute the other side at a later time and a better price. The risk materializes from the fact that a better price may never be available, and a worse price must eventually be accepted.

Liquidation

The voluntary or involuntary closing out of security positions.

Load Spread Option

The terms for allocating, or "spreading," the annual sales charge, or load, over a period of some years. For example, during the first four years of the contract, up to 20 percent of any year's contributions can be credited against the sales charge, but the total allocations for the four years may not exceed 64% of any annual contribution.

Local

In futures trading, a floor broker who buys and sells for his or her own account, seeking quick profits. A local may also execute orders for others.

Margin

The amount of money or securities that an investor must deposit with a broker to secure a loan from the broker. Brokers may lend money to investors for use in trading securities. To procure such a loan, an investor must deposit cash with the broker. (The amount is prescribed by the Federal Reserve System in Regulation T.) The cash represents the equity, or margin, in the investor's account.

In futures, the amount of money deposited with the broker to protect both the seller and the buyer against default. To establish a position in commodities, a client must deposit cash with the broker; the amount, or *rate of margin*, depends on exchange regulations and other factors. If a price change causes a contract to lose dollar value, the broker must require additional cash for the price of variation; this is *variation margin*. If the client cannot meet the requirement, the broker may liquidate the contract, using the cash necessary to offset the losses.

Margin Call

A demand on the customer to deposit money or securities with the broker when a purchase is made or when the customer's equity in a margin account declines below a minimum standard set by an exchange or the firm.

Margin (General) Account

An account in which a customer uses credit from a broker/dealer to take security positions.

See Margin

Margin Requirement

See Margin Call; Minimum Maintenance Margin.

Mark to the Market

As the market value of a borrowed security fluctuates, the lender may demand more in cash collateral for a rise in value or the borrower may demand a partial refund of collateral for a decline. The written notice for either demand is a "mark" to the market.

Minimum Maintenance Margin

The minimum equity customers must have in their accounts as defined by various Federal Reserve regulations and New York Stock Exchange rules. For example, 25% of long market value must equal equity.

Model

A formula used to price an option as a function of certain variables such as stock price, striking price, time to expiration, volatility, dividends to be paid, and the current risk-free interest rate.

Naked Option

An option that is written without any corresponding security or option position as protection in the seller's account.

Narrowing the Spread

The action taken by a broker/dealer to narrow the spread between bids and offers, by bidding higher or offering lower than the previous bid or offer. Also called closing the market.

Neutral

A term used to describe an opinion that is neither bearish nor bullish. Neutral option strategies perform best if there is little or no net change in the price of the underlying stock.

See Bearish; Bullish

Normal Market

In futures trading, a market with adequate supply. In this type of market, the price of a commodity for future delivery should be equal to the present cash price plus the amount of carrying charges needed to carry the commodity to the delivery date.

OCC

See Options Clearing Corporation

Opening

The price at which a security or commodity starts trading.

Open Interest

The total number of outstanding option or commodity contracts issued by the responsible clearing corporations.

Open Outcry

On a commodity exchange, the shouting out of orders to trade. A trader shouts a selling price and a buyer shouts a purchase price. When the two are the same, the contract is recorded.

Option

A contract wherein one party (the option writer) grants another party (buyer) the right to demand that the writer perform a certain act.

See Call Option; Listed (Stock) Option; Put Option

Option Class

All call options or all put options (not both) having the same underlying security.

Option Clearing Corporation (OCC)

A corporation owned jointly by all the exchanges trading listed options. On the basis of compared trades submitted by various exchanges, the OCC issues the option to the buyer and holds the writer to his or her obligation. The OCC is therefore the issuer of all listed options, and the holder must exercise against the OCC, not the original writer. The OCC maintains a system for collecting and remitting funds in settlement of option trades, and it holds collateral deposited by option writers to guarantee their performance.

Option Premium

The fee paid by a purchaser of an option to entice someone to give him or her the right of exercise any time within a specified period. Premium is composed of intrinsic value and time premium.

See Net Premium

Option Pricing Curve

The graph of the projected prices of an option at given points in time, reflecting the amounts of time value premium in the option for various stock prices.

See Delta; Hedge Ratio; Model

Option Series

All options (either puts or calls) having the same type of underlying security, strike price, and expiration date.

Option Spreading

A system of strategies calling for the simultaneous purchase and sale of options of the same class in order to establish hedged positions.

Option Type

The type of option as defined in the Options Clearing Corporation prospectus; calls are one type of option and puts are another.

Option Writer

The seller of a securities option who receives an immediate fee for providing a purchaser with the right to demand performance in a securities transaction. The writer incurs an obligation to sell stock (call writer) or to purchase stock (put writer).

Out of the Money

A term used to describe an option that has no intrinsic value. An option is out of the money if the striking price is unprofitable in comparison with the current market value of the underlying stock.

Overwriting

The act of a call writer who writes a call based on the notion that the underlying security is overpriced and will have to drop in price. If it doesn't, the call writer will suffer a loss.

Plus Tick

A transaction on a stock exchange at a price higher than the price of the last transaction. Also known as an uptick.

Plus-Tick Rule

A SEC rule stating that a short sale of a round lot has to be made at a price that was an advance over the last different regular-way sale of that security.

Position Limit

The maximum number of put or call contracts placed on the same side of the market being held by any one account or group related accounts. Short puts and long calls are placed on the same side of the market; short calls and long puts are also placed together.

Premium

The total price of an option, equal to the intrinsic value plus the time value premium. To determine the total dollar premium for a single index option, the quoted premium must be multiplied by the applicable index multiplier.

Price Spread

See Vertical Spread

Protected Strategy

A position having limited risk, such as a short sale or a protected straddle write.

See Combination; Straddle Option

Put Option

A privilege giving its holder the right to demand acceptance of his or her delivery of 100 shares of stock at a fixed price any time within a specified lifetime. Sometimes referred to as a seller's option.

Qualified Stock Option

An option granted to an employee by a corporation, entitling the employee to purchase capital stock at a special price, usually lower than its market value.

Ratio Calendar Combination

A strategy that uses a simultaneous position of a ratio calendar spread using calls combined with a similar position using puts. The striking price of the calls is greater than the striking price of the puts.

Ratio Calendar Spread

A spread in which near-term options are sold and longer-term options (either puts or calls) are bought, but the short-term contracts outnumber the long-term ones.

Ratio Spread

A ratio consisting of buying a certain amount of options and selling a larger number of out-of-the-money options. This strategy can be used with both puts and calls.

Ratio Strategy

A strategy involving unequal numbers of long and short securities, generally with a preponderance of short options over either long options or long stock.

Ratio Write

The process of buying stock and then selling a preponderance of calls against that stock. This is often constructed by shorting stock and selling puts.

Registered Options Principal (ROP)

An individual who has been approved by an options exchange to supervise the conduct of customers' accounts in which there are listed options transactions.

Registered Options Representative

A broker/dealer employee who has passed the examinations required before soliciting options trading orders.

Reverse Arbitrage

A riskless arbitrage involving the sale of the stock short, the writing of a put, and the purchase of a call with the options all having the same terms.

See Conversion Arbitrage

Reverse Conversion

A term used to describe the creation of a put option from a call option by means of taking a short position in the underlying equity.

Reverse Hedge (Synthetic Straddle)

A strategy using the sale of the underlying stock short and the purchase of calls on more shares than are sold short. It is now considered an outmoded strategy for stocks with listed puts trading.

See Straddle Option; Ratio Write

Reverse Strategy

Any strategy that is the opposite of any better known strategy. A ratio spread, for example, is a process of purchasing calls at a low strike and then selling more calls at a higher strike. A reverse ratio spread (or backspread) is the exact opposite: selling the calls at the low strike and then purchasing more calls at the higher strike.

See Reverse Hedge; Ratio Write

Risk Arbitrage

A purchase and short sale of potentially equal securities at prices that may realize a profit.

See Bona Fide Arbitrage

Roll Down

Closing out options at one strike price while simultaneously opening other options at a lower strike price.

Roll Forward

Closing out options at a near-term expiration date and then opening options at a longer-term expiration date.

Rolling

Any follow-up action taken by the strategist to close options currently in the position and to open other options with different terms, but on the same underlying stock.

See Roll Down; Roll Forward; Roll Up

Roll Up

Closing out options at a lower strike and then opening options at a higher strike.

ROP

See Registered Options Principal

Secondhand Option

See Special Option

Securities Industry Association (SIA)

An association devoted to instructing member employees and to lobbying for the members' interests.

See Long

To sell securities that one holds, that is, that one has a "long" position in.

Sell Short

See Short Sale

Series

A term referring to all option contracts having the same striking price, expiration date, and unit of trading on the same underlying stock.

Short Leg

The short option in a spread.

Short Sale

The sale of a security that is not owned at the time of the trade, necessitating its purchase some time in the future to "cover" the sale, or "close" the position. A short sale is made with the expectation that the stock value will decline, so that the sale will be eventually covered at a price lower than the original sale, thus realizing a profit. Before the sale is covered, the broker/dealer borrows stock (for which collateral is put up) to deliver on the settlement date.

Specialist

A member of the NYSE with two essential functions: First, to maintain an orderly market, insofar as reasonably practicable, in the stocks in which he or she is registered as a specialist. To do this, the specialist must buy and sell for his or her own account and risk, to a reasonable degree, when there is a temporary disparity between supply and demand. To equalize trends, the specialist must buy or sell counter to the direction of the market. Second, the specialist acts as a broker's broker, executing orders when another broker cannot afford the time. At all times the specialist must put the customer's interest before his own. All specialists are registered with the NYSE as regular, substitute, associate, or temporary.

Special (Secondhand) Option

This is an over-the-counter option with some remaining lifetime that is offered for resale by a put and call broker or dealer in a secondary market transaction.

Speculation

The employment of funds in high-risk transactions for relatively large and immediate gains in which the safety of principal or current income is of secondary importance.

Spread

The simultaneous purchase and sale of the same class of options.

Spread Option

In the OTC market, one put and one call option carrying the same expiration date but different strike prices. The call is written with a strike price above that current value of the underlying stock, while the put is written with a strike price below that value.

The simultaneous purchase and sale of listed options of the same class.

Spread Order

An order to execute the simultaneous purchase and sale of options of the same class for either a net debit or a net credit without regard to the prices of the individual options. Spread orders may be limit orders, not held orders, or orders with discretion, but they cannot be stop orders. The spread order may be either a debit or credit.

Spread Position

See Spread Option

Spread Strategy

Any option position on the same underlying security encompassing long and short options of the same type.

Straddle Option

One put and one call option on the same underlying security carrying the same striking price and expiration date.

Strap Option

In the OTC market one put and two call options on the same underlying security carrying the same striking price and expiration date. The total premium for this quantity transaction is generally cheaper than if the options were purchased separately. This is an old term, not generally used.

Strategy

A plan of selecting positions and executing transactions for the purpose of achieving the stated investment objectives.

Strike (Striking, Exercise) Price

The price at which an option may be exercised. That is, when the underlying stock reaches the strike price, an option holder may require the writer to perform the transaction as agreed upon in the original privilege.

Striking Price Interval

A distance measured between striking prices on an underlying security. With some exceptions, the interval is normally 5 points for stocks selling up to $50 per share, 10 points for stocks between $50 and $200 per share, and 20 points for any stock thereafter.

Strip Call

Redeeming municipal bonds by calling some of each maturity.

Strip Option

In the OTC market, one call and two put options on the same underlying security carrying the same striking price and expiration date. The total premium for this quantity transaction is generally cheaper than if the options were purchased separately. This is an old term, not generally used.

Strip Order

An order to buy serial bonds in successive maturities.

Synthetic Straddle

See Reverse Hedge

Synthetic Put

An unlisted security offered by some brokerage firms. The broker sells stock short and buys a call, giving the customer a "synthetic" put. Also known as a converted put.

Take a Position

To hold stocks or bonds, in either a long or short position.

To purchase securities as a long-term investment.

Take Delivery

In commodities trading, the taking of physical delivery of a commodity under a futures or spot market contract.

In securities, accepting a receipt of stock or bond certificates after they have been purchased or transferred between accounts.

Tick

A transaction on the stock exchange.

See Minus Tick; Plus Tick; Zero-Minus Tick; Zero-Plus Tick

Time Spread

The term is used interchangeably with calendar spread.

Time Value

See Extrinsic Value

Time Value Premium

The amount by which an option's total premium exceeds its intrinsic value.

Treasury Bill/Option Strategy

A method of investment where an investor uses approximately 90% of his or her funds in risk-free, interest-bearing assets, such as Treasury bills, while buying options with the remainder of the assets.

Triple Witching Hour

See Witching Hour

Type

A put is one type of option; a call is the other.

Uncovered Option

See Naked Option

Uncovering an Option

The act of selling a position (or covering a short position) that had been used in conjunction with a covered option, thereby leaving the option uncovered.

Up and Out Option

A block of at least ten put options with the same strike price and expiration date carrying a provision for immediate cancellation of the exercise privilege if the underlying stock rises by a predetermined, agreed-upon amount in the marketplace.

Up Delta

See Delta

Uptick

See Plus-Tick

Variable Ratio Hedging

A system of taking long and/or short positions in different securities and/or options for the purpose of creating a hedged position using other than a one-for-one relationship between the positions.

Variable Ratio Write

In options writing, a strategy in which an investor owns 100 shares of the underlying security and writes two call options against it with each option having a different striking price.

Volatility

A measurement of the price movement of a security during a specific period.

Volume

The number of bonds or shares traded during specific periods, such as daily, weekly, or monthly.

Witching Hour

Program trading, usually conducted by major Wall Street firms for their own trading accounts, involves the purchase or sale of huge blocks of stocks, set off against large positions in the options and futures markets in order to profit from changes in their relationships to each other. Such trading, which did not exist before 1982, has created last-minute chaos on the New York Stock Exchange on ''triple-witching-hour'' days when the options and futures contracts expire all at once.

''Triple witching'' occurs four times a year, on the third Friday of the last month of each quarter.

Writer

See Option Writer

Bibliography

BOOKS

Bookstaber, R. M. *Option Pricing and Strategies in Investing*. Reading, Mass.: Addison-Wesley Publishing Company, 1981.

Brenner, M., ed. *Option Pricing Theory and Applications*. Lexington, Mass.: D. C. Heath and Company, 1983.

Cox, J. C., and M. Rubenstein. *Option Markets*. Englewood Cliffs, N.J.: Prentice Hall, 1985.

Jarrow, A., and A. Rudd. *Option Pricing*. Homewood, Ill.: Dow Jones–Irwin, 1983.

McMillian, L. *Options as a Strategic Investment*. New York: New York Institute of Finance, 1980.

Ritchken, P. *Options Theory, Strategy, Applications*. Glenview, Ill.: Scott, Foresman and Company, 1987.

ARTICLES

Black, F. "The Pricing of Commodity Contracts." *Journal of Financial Economics,* January–March, 1976.

Black, F., and M. Scholes. "The Pricing of Options and Corporate Liabilities," *Journal of Political Economy,* May–June, 1973.

Hauser, R. J., and D. Neff. "Pricing Options on Agricultural Futures: Departures from Traditional Theory," *The Journal of Futures Markets,* Vol. 5, no. 4 (1985), 539–577.

Wolf, A. "Options of Futures: Pricing and the Effect of an Anticipated Price Change," *The Journal of Futures Markets,* Vol. 4, no. 4 (1984), 491–512.

Futures Contracts

To trade futures, you need to learn a new language and a handful of key concepts. (As we will see, the same is true of options.) At the heart of the futures arena is the concept of forward pricing, and it is with this concept that we begin.

FORWARD PRICING

Before there were futures contracts, there were forward contracts, which had their beginnings in agriculture. The ages-old concern of farmers is that their crop will not be worth what they expect it to be when it is harvested some months in the future. A bountiful harvest would mean large supplies and low prices. If, for example, a farmer who in March calculates that each bushel of corn must bring at least 90 cents when it is harvested in June. From his knowledge of the market, he knows that large corporate consumers of corn—breakfast food companies, processors who sell corn-based products—need to be assured a flow of this commodity. They are willing to guarantee corn producers a price if they are guaranteed a future supply. When the corn farmer and the corn consumer agree on a fixed price for delivery of a certain amount of corn in June, that price is a *forward price*, and that agreement is a *forward contract*.

The forward contract was an important antecedent to the futures contract because it contained all the elements needed for ultimately standardizing the futures contract:

- Quantity
- Quality
- Date of delivery
- Place for delivery
- Terms of payment

The forward contract is also important because it demonstrated that risk could be shared by mutual agreement of two parties. The farmer faced only the risks associated with production, such as blight or catastrophic weather. The user relieved the producer of market risk, in most cases because its cost/pricing structure was worked out well in advance and the forward price guaranteed the cost side. Thus both parties to the contract hedged their risk.

But what happened if either party wanted to get out of the contract? Suppose, for example, that sometime after signing the forward contract, it becomes clear that June corn will be bumper crop; the weather is perfect and nothing threatens the harvest. The breakfast food company foresees a bottoming of corn prices due to the abundant supply, with prices already dropping below the 90-cent level, which they now locked into. The profit margin would certainly look much better if somehow the corn could be purchased at the bottomed-out price levels. The company could ask the farmer to release them from their obligation, but the farmer would be foolish to do so, except on the condition that he receive a penalty that would make up the difference between the forward price and the anticipated market price—and make the release academic for the company.

What to do? Assuming that this forward contract is transferable, the company can seek out another party who for whatever reasons feels that the prices for corn in June will remain high, perhaps on the basis of anticipated demand that the breakfast food company does not recognize.

Perhaps a businessperson outside the area is aware of the need for a large supply of corn, and is convinced that prices will rise. This third party agrees to take ownership of the contract from the food company at 80 cents per bushel, the current market price of corn. (The company is paying 10 cents a bushel to get out of the contract, with the expectation that prices will go even lower.) Thus the businessperson enters the arena as a third party—a speculator. He neither produces nor uses the commodity in question; it could be corn, soybeans, gold, or anything else. His only aim is to earn a profit on the transaction, not to make or take delivery. To earn that profit, he is willing to assume the market risk.

In this case let's assume that prices start to rise. Sometime before the harvest in June, corn prices escalate to 95 cents a bushel. The speculator sells the contract to a start-up corn processing firm, to whom the businessman had already guaranteed the supply. The price is 5 cents a bushel, the difference between the market price (which the processor would have to pay) and the forward price (which the processor will have to pay the farmer).

Come June, the bumper crop is harvested. The farmer, by delivering the June corn to the food processor for 90 cents a bushel, makes a profit on the crop. The speculator, by buying and selling the contract, earns a profit on the transaction. The food processor avoids having to pay even higher prices for its raw materials. And the breakfast food company realizes its mistake.

THE STANDARDIZED FUTURES CONTRACT

Forward contracts were fine as far as they went. But they were not very liquid. They were negotiated business agreements, not trading instruments. Transferability had to be negotiated as a clause in the agreement, and finding buyers or sellers could be difficult. As a result, the market for forward contracts was not very *liquid*, that is, agreements could not be readily and easily traded.

The futures contract grew out of the need for greater liquidity. Today, exchange-traded *futures contracts* are standardized legal agreements that oblige the seller to make delivery, and the buyer to take delivery, of a uniform quantity and quality of the underlying commodity at a specified time (the expiration date). The terms of these agreements are for the most part fixed. (See Figure D-1.) Each contract can therefore be bought and sold in moments without negotiation and, because of the facilities provided by the exchanges, without having to seek out contra parties. Thus the role of the exchange is to provide a centralized, liquid marketplace where standardized contracts can be traded freely. With the appearance of the uniform agreement and central exchange, the futures contract became a trading instrument.

FIGURE D-1
Specifications of a standard contract for corn

Commodity	Corn
Exchange	Chicago Board of Trade (CBT)
Size of contract	5,000 bushels
Delivery months	March, May, July, September, December
Prices quoted in	Cents per bushel
Minimum fluctuation*	$.0025 per bushel ($.0025/bu)
Dollar value of minimum tick**	$12.50
Daily trading limit***	$.10/bu

   * Prices cannot change from one trade to the next in less than this amount, and they must trade at prices that are multiples of this amount.

   ** When the price of a bushel moves the minimum fluctuation (or "tick"), the value of the contract changes by $12.50 ($.0025 per bushel times 5,000 bushels).

   *** The price of a contract may not change more than $.10/bushel ($500 per contract) in a trading day.

In decades since the founding of the Chicago Board of Trade in 1848, futures exchanges and contracts have proliferated. Today the underlying interests of futures contracts extend well beyond corn and other agricultural commodities, to mining and livestock products, and even to financial instruments, such as securities, currencies, and indexes. Futures exchanges are now located throughout the world, and trading among them is global and nonstop. Almost anything is fair game for listing on a futures exchange.

THE ROLE OF THE CLEARING HOUSE

Every United States futures exchange is associated with an organization known as a *clearing house*, whose role is to act as a contra for every transaction and thereby enhance liquidity. Suppose, for example, someone in Chicago wishes to buy a pork belly contract; he is said to be going *long*. Another party is looking to sell a pork belly contract; she is going *short*. Each party places an appropriate order with his or her brokerage house, which has the order executed on the Chicago Board of Trade. On the floor of the exchange, one broker executes the sell order and another handles the buy order.

Throughout the trading day on an exchange, there cannot be a sale (a short) without an offsetting purchase (a long). If a broker has a sell order and there are no buyers, or if a broker has a buy order and there are no sellers, the order goes unexecuted. So, during a trading session, all the shorts must equal all the longs, and the dollar value of all the sales must equal that of the purchases. All the transactions in a trading day have to net out to zero.

This is the principle on which the clearing house operates. As orders are executed, the exchange turns the execution reports over to its clearing house, which is not concerned with who entered the orders. It knows only that broker A executed the sale, and broker B the purchase. One offsets the other. If during the day, broker A executed ten trades with broker B—a mixture of purchases and sales—the clearing house simply calculates one net figure for what one broker owes the other. It then has that amount transferred from one broker's account to the other's. And it does the same for all the transactions in a day and for all the brokers on the exchange.

In this capacity, the clearing house serves several purposes:

- It substitutes itself as the opposite party, the contra, to every trade. Without this function, the back offices of brokerage firms and exchanges would be clogged to a standstill within days. With them, the settlement paperwork and transfer of funds are kept current daily, and trading standardized futures contracts is as liquid as dealing in stocks, bonds, or any other listed security.

- It also guarantees the performance of the market participants. Settlements are made from broker to broker, enabling the market to function efficiently. The member firms of the exchange are left with the responsibility of ensuring the performance of their clients.

- It facilitates delivery of the contracts, as we will see later in this chapter.

TRADING PROCEDURES

Listing a Contract

Stocks and bonds come into being when a corporation seeks to raise capital for its operations. A futures contract, however, is "born" when the exchange decides that there is enough interest in it. Listing farm and mining product contracts on an exchange, with their long history of interest, does no take much thought. But an exchange will devote much research and study before listing a contract on, say, a stock index or currency. Does the contract serve a purpose for hedgers and speculators alike? Are the proposed terms of the contract appropriate for the underlying commodity? Assuming the exchange officials are satisfied that the contract will be widely traded, the contract is presented to the regulatory agency for futures, the Commodity Futures Trading Commission (CFTC). With this approval, the contract can be offered for trading.

The Life of a Contract

Futures contracts can be traded only during certain periods, as designated by the exchanges. Corn contracts, as an example of a farm product contract, may start trading more than a year before their expiration dates. In July of 19X1, trading was going on in the following contract months:

- July 19X1
- September 19X1
- December 19X1
- March 19X2
- May 19X2
- July 19X2
- September 19X2

As a contract expires, a new contract is added. In August of 19X1, when the July 19X1 contracts have expired, the December 19X2 contract will start trading. When the September 19X1 contract expires, the March 19X3 will become available, and so on.

The Wasting Asset Feature. Purchasers of stocks and bonds ordinarily need to be concerned with only two things: the direction of price changes (up or down) and the extent of price change (enough to offset commissions and other expenses, then go on to create a profit). Unless they are paying interest on a margin account or a short sale, time is not a factor. They can wait for the price to move in the expected direction, and they can wait for it to move far enough to make the investment a successful one.

Not so with futures. A futures contract month has a beginning, lifetime, and end, which all take place in a fairly predictable pattern. When the contract first "comes on board" (that is, first starts trading), activity is generally low, but it builds during the last two or three months before expiration. Then, as the expiration date nears, trading again drops off until the contract expires. (See Figure D-2.)

Because of this life cycle, a futures contract is considered a *wasting asset*. For the futures trader (someone who is not interested in making or taking delivery), the contract's value ultimately declines as expiration nears, and it becomes worthless at expiration unless it is

FIGURE D-2
A typical "life cycle" of a futures contract

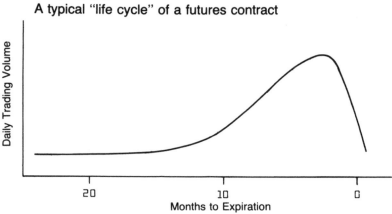

Source: Robert E. Fink and Robert B. Feduniak, *Futures Trading: Concepts and Strategies* (New York: New York Institute of Finance, 1988), p. 48.

traded away or the position otherwise liquidated. This aspect of futures trading adds a third dimension to trading futures—time. Prices must move in the direction desired, they must move enough to create a profit, *and* they must do so before the clock runs out on the contract.

Opening and Closing Transactions

In futures trading, a transaction must be identified as either "opening" or "closing" a position.

An *open position* results from the initial purchase or sale of a contract. The seller's position is open because it is considered short—the seller has sold a commodity that he does not own. The purchaser's position is long, even though the buyer does not yet have the commodity, because the contract obliges him to take delivery sometime in the future.

A *closing transaction* is one that offsets a position, which may be done in one of two ways: offset or delivery. Of the two methods, offset is by far the more frequent one. Only 2% or so of all positions are closed by delivery.

Offsetting (or Liquidating) Transaction. To close, or offset, a short position, a seller buys a comparable contract; this is a closing *purchase* transaction. A long closes a position by selling a comparable contract (a closing *sale* transaction).

Delivering or Receiving the Commodity. A short closes a position by delivering the commodity, a buyer by taking delivery.

While the rules for delivery vary from one exchange to another, several broad procedures apply. Most commodity-based futures contracts expire in the second half of their delivery month, and delivery may take place two to three weeks prior to the expiration date. March corn contracts, for example, expire about a week before the last day of March, and this last week in March comprises the *last trading days* for the contract. Delivery may take place any time during the last trading days.

Delivery takes place at the option of the seller (the short). Any time after the *first notice day* (the first day of the delivery period), the seller issues a *delivery notice* to the clearing house, through a member firm of the exchange. The clearing house distributes the notices among the holders of contracts (the longs). For commodity-based contracts, physical delivery then takes place. For contracts on financial instruments, the long is given a document indicating that the security or other type of asset has been transferred to an exchange-approved bank.

The underlying interest for index futures contracts is not ''deliverable'' in the ordinary sense; it is neither a commodity nor a financial instrument. In these cases, settlement is made in cash. The long receives the cash value of the contract according to an exchange-created formula. It might, for example, be the amount arrived at by multiplying the point value of the index by an assigned dollar value per point.

MARGIN

To ensure having the funds needed to cover their positions in the market, exchange member firms keep margin on deposit with the clearing house. The margin in futures trading, however, is different from margin in the stock and bond markets. Whereas at least 50% of the purchase value of a stock or bond has to be deposited with the broker, margin for a futures trade is typically less than 10%. (Of course, it varies according to exchange requirements.) Also, while buying securities on margin is optional, all futures transactions are done on margin.

The reason for these differences has to do with the purpose of margin. In securities trading, the margin amount goes toward the purchase of the asset; the rest is put up by the broker. In futures, the margin is a *performance bond*; it assures performance on the part of participants. No loans and no interest payments are involved. For this reason, margin is often referred to as ''earnest money.''

Two kinds of margin are involved in futures trading: initial and maintenance margin.

Initial Margin

Sometimes called ''original margin,'' this amount (typically about 10%) is deposited with the exchange whenever a position is opened. As in securities markets, the brokerage firms usually require a higher percentage that the exchange requires of its members. For example, if the exchange requirement is 10%, a member firm might require 12% of its clients. If a brokerage firm's client wishes to purchase a contract for British pounds, whose market price is $98,125.00, he would have to deposit $11,775.00 with the broker (12% of $98,125.00). The member firm, in turn would have to deposit $9,812.50 with the exchange (10% of the purchase price).

Original margin may be deposited as cash, which generally takes the form of margin certificates issued by exchange-approved banks. But it can also be posted in the form of stock in the clearing house, federal interest-bearing instruments, letters of credit from approved commercial banks, or any combination of these four forms.

Maintenance Margin

Also called "variation" margin, additional funds may have to be posted with the broker depending on the market value of the contract. When the value declines, more margin—as calculated by the clearing house—must be deposited. Generally, as a simplifying measure, the clearing house calculates variation margin as one figure for all transactions in a given contract. For example, if a member firm is long 20 crude oil contracts and short 15 of them, the maintenance margin is calculated as if the firm were only long 5 contracts.

QUOTATIONS

Figure D-3 shows futures contracts quotations from *The Wall Street Journal*, whose format is representative of the listings in the financial news. Contracts are grouped according to their underlying interests: Commodities are one group, indexes another, and so on. Within each group, the contracts are listed in categories, such as "Grains and Oilseeds" and "Livestock and Meat" in the "Commodities" group, or "T-bonds" and "Long Gilt" in the "Interest Rate Instruments" group. Note that there may be more than one contract for an underlying interest, if more than one exchange lists it.

The heading for each contract contains the following information:

FIGURE D-3
"Interest Rate Instruments" futures quotations

INTEREST RATE INSTRUMENTS

OPTIONS

Friday, September 30, 1988

For Notes and Bonds, decimals in closing prices represent 32nds; 1.01 means 1 1/32. For Bills, decimals in closing prices represent basis points; $25 per .01.

Chicago Board Options Exchange

U.S. TREASURY BOND—$100,000 principal value

Underlying Issue	Strike Price	Calls—Last			Puts—Last		
		Oct	Nov	Dec	Oct	Nov	Dec
8⅞% (ybm) due 8/2017	98	....	....	....	....	....	2.04
9⅛% (ybl) due 5/2018	101	....	1.19	....	....	....	....

Total call vol. 2   Call open int. 4,293
Total put vol. 10   Put open int. 2,244

5-YEAR U.S. TREASURY NOTE—$100,000 principal value
Total call vol. 0   Call open int. 50
Total put vol. 0   Put open int. 0

3 p.m. prices of underlying issues supplied by The Chicago Corp.: T-Bonds 12% 125.26; 8⅞% 98.17; 9⅛% 101.17. T-Notes 9¾% 100.16; 9% 101.18.

FUTURES

TREASURY BONDS (CBT)—$100,000; pts. 32nds of 100%

	Open	High	Low	Settle	Chg	Yield Settle	Chg	Open Interest
Dec	87-29	88-31	87-27	88-24	+ 32	9.244	−.122	347,279
Mr89	87-14	88-15	87-11	88-08	+ 32	9.305	−.123	71,902
June	87-00	87-31	86-30	87-24	+ 31	9.366	−.121	37,772
Sept	86-14	87-11	86-14	87-09	+ 31	9.424	−.122	10,867
Dec	86-00	87-02	86-00	86-27	+ 32	9.479	−.127	5,784
Mr90	85-18	86-13	85-18	86-13	+ 32	9.534	−.128	1,307

Est vol 400,000; vol Thur 234,029; op int 475,091, −10,229.

TREASURY BONDS (MCE)—$50,000; pts. 32nds of 100%

	Open	High	Low	Settle	Chg	Yield Settle	Chg	Open Interest
Dec	87-30	88-31	87-20	88-22	+ 26	9.252	−.099	6,340

Est vol 6,700; vol Thur 5,858; open int 6,401, −274.

T—BONDS (LIFFE) U.S. $100,000; pts of 100%

	Open	High	Low	Settle	Chg			Open Interest
Dec	87-29	88-11	87-25	88-10	+ 0-26	89-06	83-12	9,649

Est vol Fri 7,246; vol 7,185; open int 9,649, −151.

TREASURY NOTES (CBT)—$100,000; pts. 32nds of 100%

	Open	High	Low	Settle	Chg	Yield Settle	Chg	Open Interest
Dec	93-22	94-15	93-18	94-09	+ 25	8.874	−.125	83,028
Mr89	93-11	94-02	93-08	93-30	+ 25	8.929	−.126	4,888
June	....	....	....	93-19	+ 25	8.984	−.126	146

Est vol 20,000; vol Thur 13,021; open int 88,130, −7,481.

5 YR TREAS NOTES (CBT) $100,000; pts. 32 of 100%

	Open	High	Low	Settle	Chg	Yield Settle	Chg	Open Interest
Dec	96-27	97-115	96-27	97-09	+ 15.5	8.68	−.13	12,987
Mr89	96-19	97-02	96-19	97-00	+ 15.5	8.75	−.13	2,367

Est vol 5,300; vol Thur 2,556; open int 14,665, +232.

5 YR TREAS NOTES (FINEX) $100,000; pts. 32 of 100%

	Open	High	Low	Settle	Chg	Yield Settle	Chg	Open Interest
Dec	96-255	97-085	96-23	97-04	+ 14.5	8.72	−.13	9,679
Mr89	96-16	96-305	96-155	96-265	+ 14.5	8.79	−.13	3,123

Est vol 5,000; vol Thur 3,926; open int 13,605, +342.

→ **TREASURY BILLS (IMM)—$1 mil.; pts. of 100%**

	Open	High	Low	Settle	Chg	Discount Settle	Chg	Open Interest
Dec	92.59	92.68	92.57	92.66	+ .08	7.34	−.08	16,276
Mr89	92.62	92.71	92.60	92.68	+ .08	7.32	−.08	3,264
June	92.47	92.60	92.47	92.58	+ .11	7.42	−.11	885
Sept	92.29	92.42	92.29	92.41	+ .12	7.59	−.12	251
Dec	92.17	92.27	92.16	92.24	+ .11	7.76	−.11	192

Est vol 5,822; vol Thur 3,975; open int 20,879, −74.

EURODOLLAR (IMM)—$1 million; pts of 100%

	Open	High	Low	Settle	Chg	Yield Settle	Chg	Open Interest
Dec	91.19	91.28	91.15	91.22	+ .05	8.78	−.05	175,995
Mr89	91.27	91.37	91.24	91.33	+ .08	8.67	−.08	114,665
June	91.10	91.25	91.08	91.19	+ .10	8.81	−.10	43,806
Sept	90.92	91.06	90.89	91.02	+ .13	8.98	−.13	26,624
Dec	90.74	90.89	90.72	90.85	+ .14	9.15	−.14	18,825
Mr90	90.74	90.91	90.73	90.87	+ .15	9.13	−.15	18,876
June	90.68	90.84	90.66	90.80	+ .15	9.20	−.15	18,008
Sept	90.61	90.77	90.59	90.73	+ .15	9.27	−.15	13,814
Dec	90.55	90.69	90.55	90.65	+ .15	9.35	−.15	12,404
Mr91	90.54	90.68	90.53	90.64	+ .15	9.36	−.15	7,848
June	90.49	90.63	90.48	90.58	+ .14	9.42	−.14	13,332
Sept	90.44	90.59	90.44	90.54	+ .14	9.46	−.14	3,662

Est vol 132,521; vol Thur 90,345; open int 467,859, −20.

EURODOLLAR (LIFFE)—$1 million; pts of 100%

	Open	High	Low	Settle	Change	Lifetime High Low		Open Interest
Dec	91.19	91.21	91.16	91.20	+ .05	92.93 89.90	17,881
Mr89	91.29	91.30	91.25	91.30	+ .06	92.33 90.68	7,327
June	91.12	91.14	91.08	91.14	+ .06	92.10 90.54	2,879
Sept	90.93	90.93	90.93	90.97	+ .10	91.15 90.08	649

	Dec			90.79 +	.10	90.65	90.29	197

Est vol 3,395; vol Thurs 5,639; open int 29,005, +1,211.

STERLING (LIFFE)—£500,000; pts of 100%

	Open	High	Low	Settle	Chg			Open Interest
Dec	88.24	88.33	88.23	88.28	−.04	91.45	87.54	26,107
Mr89	88.97	88.04	88.94	88.01	+.01	90.94	88.07	9,474
June	89.20	89.24	89.18	89.21	−.01	90.66	88.35	2,511
Sept	89.27	89.32	89.27	89.30	−.03	90.47	88.61	1,002
Dec	89.38	89.38	89.31	89.31	−.02	90.22	88.61	654
Mr90	89.32	89.32	89.32	89.32	−.02	89.98	88.63	316
June	....	....	....	89.33	−.02	89.08	88.65	129

Est vol 14,030; vol Thurs 14,806; open int 40,193, +1,014.

LONG GILT (LIFFE)—£50,000; 32nds of 100%

	Open	High	Low	Settle	Chg			Open Interest
Dec	95-16	95-22	95-12	95-19	+ 0-02	95-31	93-04	23,591

Est vol 10,248; vol Thurs 18,062; open int 23,609, −51.

—OTHER INTEREST RATE FUTURES—

Settlement prices of selected contracts. Volume and open intrest of all contract months.

Treasury Bills (MCE) $500,000; 100.00 yield
Dec 92-66 +8; Est. vol. 20; Open int. 90
Treasury Notes (MCE) $50,000; pts. 32nds of 100%
Dec 94-10 +24; Est. vol. 0; Open int. 68

FUTURES OPTIONS

T-BONDS (CBT) $100,000; points and 64ths of 100%

Strike Price	Calls—Last			Puts—Last		
	Dec-c	Mar-c	Jun-c	Dec-p	Mar-p	Jun-p
84	4-63	5-10	....	0-17	1-04	1-45
86	3-18	3-50	4-04	0-37	1-40	2-22
88	1-58	2-38	3-03	1-10	2-22	3-12
90	0-60	1-47	2-12	2-10	3-26	....
92	0-26	1-06	1-38	3-40	4-48	....
94	0-12	0-45	1-10	5-25	....	....

Est. vol. 70,000, Thur vol. 28,666 calls, 19,383 puts
Open interest Thur; 242,634 calls, 273,858 puts

T-NOTES (CBT) $100,000; points and 64ths of 100%

Strike Price	Calls—Last			Puts—Last		
	Dec-c	Mar-c	Jun-c	Dec-p	Mar-p	Jun-p
92	2-38	....	....	0-24	1-00	....
93	1-53	2-18	....	0-35	1-21	....
94	1-14	1-47	....	0-59	1-50	....
95	0-47	1-18	....	1-28	2-21	....
96	0-26	0-61	....	2-07	3-00	....
97	0-15	0-45	....	2-59	....	....

Est. vol. 3,500, Thur vol. 668, 448 puts
Open interest Thur; 23,639 calls, 25,156 puts

TREASURY BILLS (IMM) $1 million; pts. of 100%

Strike Price	Calls—Settle			Puts—Settle		
	Dec-c	Mar-c	Jun-c	Dec-p	Mar-p	Jun-p
9225	0.47	0.61	....	0.07	0.19	....
9250	0.30	0.45	....	0.14	0.28	....
9275	0.16	0.32	....	0.25	0.39	....
9300	0.07	0.21	....	0.41	....	....
9325	0.03	....	....	0.61	....	....
9350	0.01	....	....	....	....	....

Est. vol. 0, Thur vol. 0 calls, 14 puts

EURODOLLAR (CME) $ million; pts. of 100%

Strike Price	Calls—Settle			Puts—Settle		
	Dec-c	Mar-c	Jun-c	Dec-p	Mar-p	Jun-p
9075	0.96	0.76	0.79	0.10	0.20	0.37
9100	0.39	0.58	0.64	0.18	0.29	0.45
9125	0.24	0.44	0.51	0.27	0.36	0.56
9150	0.14	0.32	0.39	0.41	0.48	0.69
9175	0.07	0.22	0.30	0.59	0.62	0.82
9200	0.04	0.15	0.23	0.80	0.79	0.98

Est. vol. 8,781, Thur vol. 4,514 calls, 5,965 puts
Open interest Thur; 55,225 calls, 73,974 puts

EURODOLLAR (LIFFE) $1 million; pts. of 100%

Strike Price	Calls—Settle			Puts—Settle		
	Dec-c	Mar-c	Jun-c	Dec-p	Mar-p	Jun-p
9075	0.56	0.76	0.81	0.11	0.21	0.22
9100	0.38	0.59	0.66	0.18	0.29	0.52
9125	0.25	0.45	0.52	0.30	0.40	0.63
9150	0.15	0.32	0.41	0.45	0.52	0.77
9175	0.08	0.22	0.31	0.63	0.67	0.92
9200	0.04	0.14	0.22	0.84	1.08	1.29

Actual Vol. Fri, 0 Calls, 0 Puts.
Open Interest Thurs 2,997, Calls, 3,967 Puts.

LONG GILT (LIFFE)—b£250,000; 32nds of 100%

Strike Price	Calls—Settle			Puts—Settle		
	Dec-c	Mar-c	Jun-c	Dec-p	Mar-p	Jun-p
92	3.44	4.25	....	0.06	0.19	....
94	1.58	2.53	....	0.20	0.47	....
96	0.46	1.40	....	1.08	1.34	....
98	0.12	0.52	....	2.38	2.46	....
100	0.04	0.23	....	4.30	4.17	....
102	0.01	0.09	....	6.27	6.03	....

Actual Vol. Fri, 1,403 Calls, 745 Puts.
Open Interest Thurs 22,026, Calls, 22,981 Puts.

Source: The Wall Street Journal (October 3, 1988). This issue is the first in the revised format for listings and contains a clear explanation of the rationale behind the change.

Information	*Example*
Name of contract:	Treasury bills
Exchange:	(IMM)—International Monetary Market at Chicago Mercantile Exchange
Contract size:	$1 million
Unit of quotation:	pts. of 100%

It is important to note that the contract size, in the case of Treasury bills and many contracts whose underlying interests are financial instruments, is *not* the market value of the contract. That value must be computed from the size of the contract, the unit of quotation, and the quoted unit price. For example, in Figure D-3, March 89 T bill contracts closed at 92.68, or 92.68% of the face value of the T bill, also the size of the contract. That's $926,800.00 (92.68% of $1,000,000.00). (The discount $73,200.00 (7.32% of $1,000,000.00.)

In commodity futures contracts, the calculation is the same but not as self-evident. As shown in Figure D-4, copper-standard futures contract is quoted in terms of cents per pound and the contract size is 25,000 pounds. For the October contract, a settling price of "116.60" translates to a market value of $29,150.00: 116.6 cents, or $1.166, times 25,000 pounds of copper.

Each line provides the following information to the prior day's trading:

1. *Month of expiration:* These are listed in chronological order, starting with the "near" months. Let's look at the December Treasury Bill contract in Figure D-3 (left-hand column, under "Futures").

2. *Opening price (open):* This contract opened trading at 92.59, or $925,900.00 ($1,000,000.00 times .9259). The fact that prices are quoted to two decimal places reflects the minimum unit of fluctuation; prices may change in hundredths of percentage points. Each hundredth would have a dollar value of $10,000.00 (contract value of $1,000,000.00 times .001).

   In the case of the copper-standard contract (see Figure D-4 again), each unit of quotation is a tenth of a cent. This is clear from how the contract is quoted: The price of 116.6 and all the other

FIGURE D-4
Commodities futures prices

COMMODITIES FUTURES PRICES

Friday, September 30, 1988.
Open Interest Reflects Previous Trading Day.

	Open	High	Low	Settle	Change	Lifetime High	Low	Open Interest

—GRAINS AND OILSEEDS—

CORN (CBT) 5,000 bu.; cents per bu.
Dec	286¼	289¾	285¼	285¾	− ¾	370	184	146,489
Mr89	291½	294¼	290¼	291	− ½	370	193½	48,007
May	294¼	295½	292¼	293¼	....	369	207½	18,709
July	290½	292	289½	291¼	+ 1	360	233	14,798
Sept	270	272	270	271½	+ 2	317¾	245	3,280
Dec	257½	259½	256¾	258¾	+ 2	295	234	9,825

Est vol n.a.; vol Thur 49,318; open int 241,116, +2,097.

OATS (CBT) 5,000 bu.; cents per bu.
Dec	241½	246	241½	241½	− ½	389½	162	4,162
Mr89	246	250	245¾	246¼	+ ¼	367¾	161	1,743
May	248½	250½	247	247¼	− 1¼	340	187	512
July	227	227	223¾	223¾	− 2¼	277	221	522

Est vol n.a.; vol Thur 977; open int 6,950, +94.

SOYBEANS (CBT) 5,000 bu.; cents per bu.
Nov	810	818	806½	812	+ 5	1045	499½	60,940
Ja89	819	828	817½	823½	+ 5½	1034	553	23,262
Mar	826	834½	824½	829¾	+ 4¼	1023	579	14,132
May	825	832	824	826¾	+ 1¾	1003	647	6,288
July	818	823	816	819½	+ 3¼	986	685	7,304
Aug	805	809	804	808	+ 4	951	725	1,109
Sept	750	755	749	751	+ 2	835	701	1,277
Nov	720	721	717	720	− 2	793	663	5,417

Est vol n.a.; vol Thur 36,480; open int 119,647, −253.

Nov	126.30	126.70	126.30	126.50	+ .70	133.10	78.50	3,272
Dec	128.50	129.30	128.40	129.00	+ .60	135.70	78.90	18,042
Mr89	135.10	136.00	135.10	135.80	+ .70	142.00	105.00	3,606
May	139.30	139.60	139.20	139.20	+ .10	148.50	125.50	1,737
July	....	....	....	142.10	+ .50	147.00	135.40	1,251

Est vol 3,880; vol Thurs 2,557; open int 34,145, −174.

FLAXSEED (WPG) 20 metric tons; Can. $ per ton
Oct	430.00	433.00	429.00	433.00	+ 2.00	482.00	237.20	726
Dec	437.50	440.00	436.50	437.10	− .90	482.00	242.10	4,185
Mr89	447.00	447.00	445.90	446.50	+ .90	485.00	266.00	1,665
May	449.00	450.50	448.50	450.00	+ 1.50	490.00	410.00	1,244
July	....	....	450.00	− 1.00	492.00	448.00		200

Est vol 810; vol Thurs 1,679; open int 8,025, −31.

RAPESEED (WPG) 20 metric tons; Can. $ per ton
Nov	368.50	371.20	368.30	370.00	+ .60	482.00	261.00	11,452
Ja89	374.50	377.80	374.50	376.50	+ .50	486.70	291.00	9,525
Mar	379.50	382.80	379.50	381.50	+ 1.00	489.50	300.70	3,522
June	390.00	390.20	388.30	389.50	+ 1.00	490.00	380.00	987
Nov	384.50	386.00	384.50	385.50	+ 3.50	482.00	261.80	1,096

Est vol 1,820; vol Thurs 4,279; open int 26,646, +552.

WHEAT (WPG) 20 metric tons; Can. $ per ton
Oct	162.50	165.00	162.50	164.80	+ 2.30	167.00	85.50	1,708
Nov	163.70	165.40	163.70	165.20	+ 1.70	166.90	94.40	1,267
Dec	161.90	164.00	161.90	164.00	+ 2.50	167.00	94.00	5,392
Mr89	161.50	163.80	161.50	163.80	+ 2.50	170.50	103.50	5,495
May	....	....	161.70	+ 2.20	168.50	135.50		2,051
July	160.00	160.30	160.00	160.30	+ 1.80	166.50	144.30	533

Est vol 1,520; vol Thurs 1,022; open int 16,446, −267.

RYE (WPG) 20 metric tons; Can. $ per ton
Oct	142.00	145.20	140.80	144.80	− .20	193.00	105.50	516
Dec	148.00	150.20	145.80	149.50	+ .70	194.50	140.00	1,698
Mr89	151.30	156.00	151.30	156.00	+ 2.00	178.00	149.90	1,160

Est vol 970; vol Thurs 484; open int 3,472, +111.

—LIVESTOCK & MEAT—

CATTLE—FEEDER (CME) 44,000 lbs.; cents per lb.
Oct	81.60	82.75	81.50	82.45	+ 1.05	82.85	69.70	4,169
Nov	82.65	83.75	82.55	83.47	+ 1.05	83.85	70.25	4,853
Ja89	83.65	84.45	83.50	84.02	+ .50	84.45	74.00	4,181
Mar	82.45	83.15	82.40	82.97	+ .50	83.60	74.00	3,052
Apr	81.65	82.20	81.65	82.10	+ .40	82.45	74.40	867
May	80.40	80.80	80.40	80.70	+ .30	80.80	60.00	420
Aug	79.75	79.75	79.75	79.75	+ .25	79.50	78.50	135

Est vol 3,656; vol Thur 1,164; open int 18,431, +57.

CATTLE—LIVE (CME) 40,000 lbs.; cents per lb.
Oct	71.20	71.92	71.15	71.75	+ .65	73.47	58.65	14,572
Dec	73.25	74.05	73.12	73.77	+ .65	74.05	60.25	26,594
Fb89	73.60	74.05	73.50	73.55	− .05	74.62	65.10	18,758
Apr	74.85	75.30	74.75	74.80	− .05	75.75	67.20	7,953
June	73.25	74.22	73.70	73.77	− .07	75.20	68.75	3,307
Aug	71.50	71.70	71.35	71.35	....	73.20	69.70	1,432
Oct	70.80	71.00	70.70	70.70	....	74.00	69.50	510

Est vol 19,143; vol Thur 11,328; open int 73,131, −140.

HOGS (CME) 30,000 lbs.; cents per lb.
Oct	39.60	40.40	39.55	39.60	+ .12	46.40	37.40	3,765
Dec	42.80	43.75	42.80	43.02	+ .22	48.50	38.30	12,269
Fb89	45.85	46.85	45.85	46.40	+ .65	52.00	41.80	5,765
Apr	45.02	45.95	45.02	45.82	+ .90	51.65	40.60	4,116
June	49.00	49.40	48.85	49.10	+ .07	56.25	42.50	1,235
July	49.15	49.95	49.15	49.85	+ .50	56.00	47.07	823

Est vol 10,617; vol Thur 6,763; open int 28,127, −1,288.

PORK BELLIES (CME) 40,000 lbs.; cents per lb.
Feb	50.25	52.32	50.12	52.32	+ 2.00	67.00	46.40	7,871
Mar	50.95	52.77	50.70	52.67	+ 1.90	66.35	46.75	2,748
May	52.40	54.50	52.40	54.40	+ 1.75	65.50	48.50	2,164
July	53.20	55.07	53.00	54.92	+ 1.85	64.50	49.35	1,894
Aug	52.00	53.25	51.90	52.42	+ 1.17	58.25	47.00	203

Est vol 5,086; vol Thur 3,841; open int 14,880, −414.

ORANGE JUICE (CTN)—15,000 lbs.; cents per lb.
Nov	179.45	180.40	179.45	180.25	+ 1.55	185.50	132.00	3,847
Ja89	169.90	171.00	169.50	171.00	+ 2.20	179.05	132.00	3,464
Mar	166.75	168.15	166.75	167.75	+ 1.60	174.40	152.90	1,562
May	165.90	167.25	165.90	167.25	+ 2.75	173.50	149.00	411

Est vol 1,500; vol Thurs 461; open int 9,344, −85.

—METALS & PETROLEUM—

COPPER-STANDARD (CMX)—25,000 lbs.; cents per lb.
Oct	118.50	118.70	116.20	116.60	− .75	118.70	108.00	559
Dec	110.30	110.50	108.70	109.60	+ .15	110.50	64.70	26,814
Mr89	100.25	100.25	98.00	99.15	− .60	100.50	66.50	6,389
May	94.60	94.60	94.60	95.20	− .75	97.00	73.15	964
July	94.30	94.30	93.50	92.60	− .85	94.50	76.00	565
Sept	....	....	....	90.80	− .65	92.00	76.00	343
Dec	88.85	88.85	88.85	89.15	− .60	90.50	77.45	492

Est vol 6,000; vol Thur 6,298; open int 36,172, +230.

GOLD (CMX)—100 troy oz.; $ per troy oz.
Oct	398.20	398.20	391.80	394.40	− 2.40	533.50	391.80	4,061
Dec	402.50	403.20	396.80	399.20	− 2.40	546.00	395.50	84,637
Fb89	408.20	408.20	402.00	404.30	− 2.50	549.50	401.00	11,611
Apr	411.90	411.90	407.80	409.40	− 2.60	550.00	407.00	8,392
June	417.00	417.00	412.00	414.60	− 2.70	570.00	412.00	16,003
Aug	....	....	420.00	− 2.90	575.00	420.50		7,204
Oct	....	....	425.50	− 3.00	575.50	423.00		8,290
Dec	430.30	431.00	430.00	431.00	− 3.10	514.50	428.00	8,898
Fb90	....	....	436.60	− 3.20	516.00	439.70		4,081
Apr	....	....	442.20	− 3.30	525.80	443.00		3,016
June	....	....	448.10	− 3.40	497.00	448.30		1,236

Est vol 36,000; vol Thur 28,777; open int 157,429, −1,268.

EXCHANGE ABBREVIATIONS
(for commodity futures and futures options)

CBT-Chicago Board of Trade; CME-Chicago Mercantile Exchange; CMX-Commodity Exchange, New York; CRCE-Chicago Rice & Cotton Exchange; CTN-New York Cotton Exchange; CSCE-Coffee, Sugar & Cocoa Exchange, New York; IPEL-International Petroleum Exchange of London; KC-Kansas City Board of Trade; MCE-MidAmerica Commodity Exchange; MPLS-Minneapolis Grain Exchange; NYM-New York Mercantile Exchange; PBOT-Philadelphia Board of Trade; WPG-Winnipeg Commodity Exchange.

Source: The Wall Street Journal (October 3, 1988).

quotations were down to one decimal place. Cattle—live contracts are quoted in hundredths of a cent; note the two decimal places in those listings.

3. *High:* It traded at a day's high of 92.68.

4. *Low:* The day's low was 92.57.

5. *Settle:* The contract closed trading at 92.66.

6. *Change:* A plus sign indicates that yesterday's close was higher than the close the day before; a minus sign means it was lower. Given that the quotations in Figure D-3 are for Friday, then the December Treasury Bill contract was up .08 ("+.08") from Thursday. So Thursday's closing (settle) price was 92.58 (Friday's close of 92.66 less .08). If the change is negative, you would *add* the difference to get the prior day's close.

7. *Discount—settle and change:* These two columns, peculiar to T-bill futures quotations, show the discount at closing and the percentage of change. Note that the discount is the complement of the closing price and that the two of them add to 100 (.9266 plus .734). Note also that the percentage of change for the discount is the same as that for the price.

   In other types of contracts, these two columns may contain different information. For other types of interest rate contracts— Treasury bonds, gilts, etc.—they show the settle and change in yield. In commodities, the lifetime high and low prices are listed.

8. *Open interest:* This last column contains the number of open positions in the contract, including both longs and shorts, at the close of trading. For the December T-bill contract, there are 16,276 long and/or short positions. Note how open interest decreases as the contract months get "farther out."

9. *Volume:* Below the lists is a line relating to the volume of trading, in this case 5,822 for *all* the T-bill contracts (not just December). Volume is the total number of transactions, whether the open or close positions, for the day. It is "estimated" because most newspapers are printed before all of the day's transactions are tallied; the exact number is usually not available until well after the paper is on press.

Other information may also be present. For the T-bill contracts, you can also learn the volume (3,975), open interest (20,879), and change in open interest in relation to the preceding day, Thursday (-74). Other types of futures contract listings will always have open interest for the day but may have different additional information.

One last point about volume and open interest. During the course of a session, volume can only increase as long as there is trading going on. Each transaction—whether an opening or closing one—adds to total volume. Open interest, however, may rise and decline during the day because it reflects a net figure, the number of positions. If, for example, most of a heavy trading volume consists of closing positions, open interest could be reduced theoretically to zero, while volume mounts.

NORMAL AND INVERTED MARKETS

Note, in Figure D-4, that the prices of the "near" months are *generally* lower than those for the months "farther out." (There are exceptions. October Cotton contracts are selling at a higher price than all other months, perhaps because of a scarcity of supply or some other aberration.) When the near months' prices are lower than those of the other contracts, the market is said to be *normal*. It is also called a "carrying charge market" because the higher prices reflect the higher cost of "carrying" the contracts. Holding contracts entails paying for insurance, warehousing, and the cost of money—all carrying charges. The longer a contract has to be held, the higher these charges will be.

With the appropriate information on hand, carrying charges can be calculated. For example, corn is produced only once a year, but it is warehoused for the rest of the year. Let's say that it costs 8.3 cents per bushel per month to carry corn:

Type of Charge	Cost (cents/bushel)
Storage	6
Interest	2
Insurance	.30
Total	8.30

The full carrying charges from November to March are 33.2 cents (4 months times 8.3 cents per month). (March is not included because the corn will be delivered that month; delivery is always assumed to take place at the earliest possible time.) Theoretically, then, the difference in prices from one month to the next should be 8.3 cents, more or less.

In a normal market, therefore, the most that the farther-out contract can sell over the nearer one is the amount of the carrying charges. If the price included more than this difference, arbitrageurs would sell the distant month short and take delivery with the nearer, cheaper month, thus taking a profit whether the farther-out month's price went up or down.

In an *inverted market*, sometimes known as a "discount" market, the distant months sell at a discount over the near months. In Figure D-4, the market for Copper-Standard is inverted, with October contracts selling above all others. The inverted market implies that the copper is in short supply. Buyers are driving the prices up to a level above the carrying cost differential. Whereas in a normal market the price differences from month to month are limited to the carry charge amounts, the price differences in an inverted market are not limited in any way; they can be as great as supply and demand conditions warrant.

LIMITS

Futures exchanges impose three types of limits on trading: position limits, reportable positions, and trading limits.

Position Limits

According to exchange regulations, a trader is permitted to have a position in only so many of a given contract; that is the contracts *position limit*. This limit, which may be ten or more times the size of the reportable limit, varies from broker to broker depending on his individual capitalization level. All exchange limits have to be approved by the Commodity Futures Trading Commission.

Reportable Positions

The *reportable limit* is the number of contracts at which a broker must report his overall position to the exchange and the CFTC. In the United States, the usual limit, as set by the CFTC, is 25 contracts. Anyone holding more than 25 long or short positions in any contract is said to be a "large trader."

Like position limits, reportable limits apply only to traders, not to hedgers, whose needs necessitate their holding sizable positions.

Trading Limits

A *trading limit,* which is set by the exchange, is the maximum that a contract may move in price for a trading session. For a T-bond contract traded on the Chicago Board of Trade, for example, the daily trading limit is 64/32nds. Once prices hit the limit, the market is said to be "limit up" (or "bid limit," if prices have risen) or "limit down" (if they have dropped). To prevent a market "stampede," no one may execute transactions beyond the limit.

But that does not mean trading ceases. Transactions may occur at the limit-up or -down level, as long as there are willing buyers and sellers. Sooner or later, market participants on either the buy or sell side will withdraw. For instance, in a limit-up situation trading may continue as long as there are sellers. After a while, sellers are likely to leave the market, thinking there is the potential for greater price advances—and tomorrow is another day.

Index